Recovering the Lost Legacy

Moral Guidance for Today's Christians

Jean Risley

WESTBOW®
PRESS
A DIVISION OF THOMAS NELSON
& ZONDERVAN

Revised Standard Version of the Bible, copyright 1952 [2nd edition, 1971] by the Division of Christian Education of the National Council of the Churches of Christ in the United States of America. Used by permission. All rights reserved.

Scripture quotations taken from the New American Standard Bible®, Copyright © 1960, 1962, 1963, 1968, 1971, 1972, 1973, 1975, 1977, 1995 by The Lockman Foundation. Used by permission. (www.Lockman.org)

WestBow Press books may be ordered through booksellers or by contacting:

WestBow Press
A Division of Thomas Nelson & Zondervan
1663 Liberty Drive
Bloomington, IN 47403
www.westbowpress.com
1 (866) 928-1240

Because of the dynamic nature of the Internet, any web addresses or links contained in this book may have changed since publication and may no longer be valid. The views expressed in this work are solely those of the author and do not necessarily reflect the views of the publisher, and the publisher hereby disclaims any responsibility for them.

Cover art © Barbara Applegate from a painting of Pemaquid Point Lighthouse, Bristol, Maine, used by permission.

ISBN: 978-1-4908-4665-1 (sc)
ISBN: 978-1-4908-4667-5 (hc)
ISBN: 978-1-4908-4666-8 (e)

Library of Congress Control Number: 2014913725

Print information available on the last page.

WestBow Press rev. date: 3/31/2015

to those faithful Jews
who, despite many centuries of injustice,
are still willing to share their wisdom
with the followers of Jesus

The law of the Lord is perfect, reviving the soul; the decrees of the Lord are sure, making wise the simple; the precepts of the Lord are right, rejoicing the heart; the commandment of the Lord is clear, enlightening the eyes; the fear of the Lord is pure, enduring forever; the ordinances of the Lord are true and righteous altogether. More to be desired are they than gold, even much fine gold; sweeter also than honey, and drippings of the honeycomb. Moreover by them is your servant warned; in keeping them there is great reward. (Psalm 19:7-11)

Only conduct yourselves in a manner worthy of the gospel of Christ, so that whether I come and see you or remain absent, I will hear of you that you are standing firm in one spirit, with one mind striving together for the faith of the gospel; (Phil 1:27)

Contents

Preface

This book is for committed Christians, especially pastors and active church members who want to follow the moral teaching of Scripture despite the contrary pressures in modern society.

Evangelical Christian leaders—pastors, seminarians, church leaders, and teachers—need to give their people clear moral guidance grounded in Scripture. These people believe in the authority of Scripture to guide daily life, and they are under attack by those who minimize or discredit biblical statements about moral behavior. As preachers and teachers, they desperately need clear explanations of what the Bible requires in order to respond to current conflicts over moral issues.

I am convinced that Jesus, Paul and their associates should be understood as Jews, not as inventors of a new way of thinking, but as people who grew up and lived within Jewish tradition and culture. Many Jewish and Christian scholars in recent years have pioneered this approach, and I am grateful to Joseph Klausner; Krister Stendahl; W. D. Davies; David Novak; David Flusser and his students Brad Young and Steven Notley; Jacob Neusner and his student Gary Porton; E. P. Sanders; Richard Bauckham; Markus Bockmuehl; John Hesselink, even more than his two famous mentors; Frank Theilman; Jonathan Klawans; Alan Segal; and Dennis Hollinger. Their writings encouraged me to look into the New Testament from a perspective that was grounded in Jewish rather than western Christian tradition, in order to see the issues around morality and law framed in a different way.

Jesus and his immediate followers were Palestinian Jews, not Greeks, Romans, or even Hellenistic Diaspora Jews. Paul, although born outside of Palestine, spent a part of his formation and education within the culture of Israel. Even when modern scholarship takes their Jewish backgrounds into account, western scholars, thinking in a western way, often miss the implications of the style of thought that comes out of this formative environment. Modern Jewish scholars are sometimes able to see the implications of New Testament writings more clearly, because they are approaching these writings as Jews who are familiar with the thought of early Jewish sages. As a result, the insights of Jewish New Testament scholars not only provide cultural nuances to clarify specific points, but they also resonate with the thinking of the New Testament speakers in a way that gives a window into their thought processes.

This work assumes that the gospels represent the teachings of Jesus from the memories of those who knew him about as accurately as one can expect of witnesses reporting from different perspectives.[1] The letters generally accepted to be Paul's own, including the letters to the Galatians, Philippians, Romans, Corinthians, Thessalonians, and Philemon, are assumed to be genuine and reliable. The Book of Acts is also assumed to be genuine and to be reliable as a source of information about the early church. Luke's perspective shades his selection of material and the form of his presentation, but with this caveat Luke's writings can be trusted to reflect relatively accurately the events and personalities he portrays.

For the opportunity to explore these ideas, I am deeply grateful to the interfaith programs at Andover Newton Theological School, and particularly the collaboration with Hebrew College, which made it possible for Christian and Jewish students to study together with a professor from each school. This opportunity to study and listen with students and teachers who saw the long familiar Scriptures in such a different light was life changing.

I am also grateful to the Jesuits of the Campion Center in Weston, MA, and particularly Father Lawrence Corcoran, S. J., for their willingness to include this Presbyterian in the formative process of the Ignatian Spiritual Exercises. Father Corcoran said at the beginning of the Exercises that "When you begin this process, there are four gospels. When you finish there will be five—with the one that you believe happened." My understanding of the person of Jesus was built on the foundation of those weeks of prayer.

The third pillar on which these thoughts stand is the pilgrimage "In the Footsteps of Saint Paul" led by Father Timothy Joyce, O. S. B., of the Glastonbury Abbey in Hingham, MA. It was standing on the stones of the agora in Corinth that I finally had to come to terms with the reality of the person of Paul. Worshipping in the places the apostles lived and worked forged a link that led me to try to understand their perspectives, and to see our modern church through the eyes of their struggles.

Thanks also go to my advisor Mark Heim of Andover Newton Theological School for his insight and willingness to explore the nuances of interfaith interaction, to John Jefferson Davis of Gordon-Conwell Theological Seminary for his understanding of Reformation thought, to Robert Pazmiño for his work in helping me capture these ideas, to Diana Yount who as librarian was able to make the most obscure resources appear, and to all the family and friends who had to put up with listening to each insight as it emerged. This work could not have been done without a community of support or without my husband Curt who would remind me that one did sometimes have to take breaks for meals.

PART I

The Legacy of Law in the Old Testament

The purpose of this book is to show that the legacy of moral law in the Mosaic covenant was not rejected in the New Testament church and that it continues to apply in the present day. The study follows the moral provisions of law from their origins in the Hebrew Bible, as seen through the teachings of Jesus, expressed in the letters of Paul and the life of the early church, and available to be used in the church in the present. This study recovers what was lost— Jewish moral law as it applied to Gentile Christians in the first century.

The story of our lost legacy begins with the beginnings of the people of Israel. At the time of the Exodus, the people were a group of tribal families defined by their common heritage as descendants of Abraham. Under the leadership of Moses, they left Egypt to found a new nation in a territory that God had promised to Abraham and his descendants. During their travels in the wilderness, their identity as a people was formed by an agreement between God and the people, the Mosaic covenant.

The covenant included promises and commitments made by both God and the people. God called all the people to righteous living and defined what this meant both for the people of Israel and for those living with them. God also specified what it would mean to be a chosen

1

people, a people set apart for a particular relationship with God. This included very specific rules that define and preserve an ethnic identity, rules about worship, food, marriage, and daily life. Righteousness was for all, and these additional directions for the people of Israel created and preserved their identity as a people.

Most of those who traveled with Moses considered themselves descendants of Abraham, although some others came out of Egypt and were traveling with the group. The covenant was made with the entire community, descendants of Abraham and those others as well. Provisions were made for the fellow travelers in the covenant, specifically indicating which provisions of the covenant applied to the Israelites and which of those provisions also applied to the others, the "aliens" living among them.

If we want to understand what righteousness meant for Jews and non-Jews living in the time of Jesus, we need to discover the roots of that understanding in the Old Testament. This legacy provided the foundation for the understanding of righteousness, sin, repentance, and salvation that is the heart of the gospel message.

1

Why Should We Care
about Ancient Laws?

For years now, Christians have been arguing about sex (and other kinds of sin). The fight usually involves whether or not a particular activity is allowed for those living by the standards in the Bible. People argue about which parts of the Bible can be used as an authority to guide modern life. One pastor friend of mine asked, "How can we tell which commands in the Old Testament we still need to obey? After all, I have more than one kind of fiber in my shirt, and no one seems to have a problem with that."

This question haunted me, and I brought it to a class I was taking with Christian students from Andover Newton Theological School and Jewish students from Hebrew College. I asked a rabbinic student in the class, "How can we tell which laws we need to obey?" His response was something I had never heard.

"You only have seven laws," he said, "but we Jews have six hundred and thirteen."[2] I had heard of the Ten Commandments, but I had never heard of seven laws before. So, when I got home and saw my local rabbi, I asked him.

"Hey, Joel, how many laws are there?"

"That's easy," he said. "We have six hundred and thirteen, but you've only got seven."[3]

This led me on a voyage of discovery into the sacred documents of Rabbinic Judaism—the Mishnah, the Tosefta, and the two Talmuds.[4]

Through them, I learned that, at the time of the separation of Judaism and Christianity, the Jewish authorities had a sound understanding of what it meant to be righteous before God, even if one was not a Jew.

This exploration, of course, led to many more questions. Was Paul aware of the difference between the requirements for righteousness among Jews and among Gentiles? Was the law for the children of Noah—as the law for non-Jews was called—part of the thinking in the apostolic council described in Acts 15? How do we decide what provisions are included in moral law? This work represents the results of a period of struggling with these and many other related questions.

What Is Good Behavior?

Do you think of yourself as a good person? Do you think of yourself as a pretty good person? Do you hope, over time, to grow into a better person? How is that working out for you? After all, many folks out there want to tell you what to do. The self-help shelves at the bookstore have dozens of books to choose from, and each one has a different action plan. How do we pick the best source of advice from many, knowing that this year's bestseller will be next year's old news?

We face hundreds of choices every day. The person we are, the person we are becoming, is the result of the choices we make. How do we know which choices will help us grow better? What criteria can we trust in our choosing? Finding guidance we can depend on is unexpectedly difficult in our chaotic, postmodern world.

To begin with, it is hard to find a source of advice that we can trust. Much advice is self-interested, from authors who want to sell books or leaders who want to add to their bands of followers. Businesses make fortunes appealing to our senses, creating desires that become needs, and telling us that we "deserve" to be enjoying the best of everything. Even friends invite us to enjoy their own favorite activities, such as alcohol, drugs, or sex, to convince themselves that "everybody" thinks those activities are okay.

We are bombarded by commercial messages selling all kinds of activities and products. Our culture encourages us to try everything, to dive into whatever feels good. As a result, we are led by our senses, lapping up experiences that feel good and devoting our efforts to obtaining more good feelings. The more we reach for good feelings, the more we are tossed around by one stimulating possibility after another. Jane Eyre, the prototypical heroine of the Victorian gothic novel, described her own situation:

> Laws and principles are not for the times when there is no temptation; they are for such moments as this, when body and soul rise in mutiny against their rigor; stringent are they; inviolate they shall be. If at my individual convenience I might break them, what would be their worth? They have a worth—so I have always believed; and if I cannot believe it now, it is because I am insane: with my veins running fire, and my heart beating faster than I can count its throbs. Preconceived opinions, foregone determinations, are all I have at this hour to stand by; there I plant my foot.[5]

Today's romance novel heroine does not struggle this way, and she would probably wonder why on earth Jane did not just give in and enjoy. This heroine leaps from relationship to relationship, with little ground, other than the moment's feelings, for deciding when to indulge and when to decline.

Each of us wants to be a good person, to grow into and to become a good person. We all face two choices at each decision point: do what we feel like at the moment, or do what we believe to be right. Sometimes these lead to the same action, but often they are in opposition. If we can find an action that will satisfy both needs, then we feel good about doing the right thing. However, if we choose with feelings alone, either going against what we know to be right or avoiding thinking about what we know to be right, our choices become as changeable as our feelings. When I shop, sometimes I remember the bills at home, and sometimes I buy new clothes anyway. I spend money when I am tired that would stay in my pocket if I were better rested. Choices based on feelings are unpredictable, and they lead to second-guessing and late-night backtracking into regrets.

Have you ever felt overwhelmed by the number of choices you need to make? Have you ever been lost in a maze of turbulent feelings, trying to decide what to do next? Do you long to know that the choices you make will match your hopes and ideals and not change with each new stimulation? The good news is that basing our choices on the direction in the Bible puts us on solid ground. The Bible's commands—God's plan for growing into goodness—do not change. We can look for dependable guidance where God has put it whenever we need help.

How Did We Lose Our Biblical Guidance?

The best source of direction for Christians is, of course, the Bible. The Bible is God's own story, recorded by real people who have their own perspectives and their own human limitations. It is easy to accuse the Bible of being inaccurate, inconsistent, irrelevant, or just plain out of date, because you can always find problematic passages. The Bible contains both good examples for us to emulate and bad examples for us to avoid. Some biblical figures, such as King David, provide both. Our challenge is to discover and understand those parts of the Bible that contain God's guidance for our own lives, and then to follow it.

This is not as easy as it sounds.

We are often confused when we turn to the Scripture for help. If we try, we can usually find a passage saying that what we want to do is not a problem. Even when we are sincerely struggling to discover what is right, we can find passages with seemingly contradictory directions. Why are we so often puzzled? What is our basis for knowing what righteousness really is and means?

Jesus and Paul seem to be very clear about what kinds of behavior are righteous and what kinds are sinful. For example, in the area of sexuality, Jesus is very clear that adultery is sinful, whether one is a Jew or a Samaritan. Paul has no trouble identifying sexual relationships within a family as sexual immorality, even in the Greek church in Corinth. Sexual immorality is defiling, whether one is Jewish or not, and righteousness is the goal for all people, Jews and all others. How do we know what it means to be righteous?

From our perspective, the apostles and the evangelists of the early church may seem to be somehow "against" the Jews. We tend to forget that most of them were Jews, although they were Jews for whom the long-expected Messiah had come. The early followers of Jesus were called followers of "the way" (Acts 9:2; 18:25, 26; 19:23; 22:4; 24:14, 22), and this "way" was just another one of the many kinds of Judaism in the first century. This community, steeped in the values of its Jewish identity, understood that righteousness for all people was defined by God's commandments. This included moral law for all people and special requirements that defined the identity of the chosen people. A person who chose to remain a Jew was bound to obey the whole law, but a person who was not a Jew was not excused from the goal and hope of becoming a righteous Gentile.

The knowledge of what it meant to be righteous before God was a gift from the Jewish faith of the founders to the whole church. It was the goal toward which each person should strive. Righteousness, the behavior God asked of us, was given to us through the moral provisions of the law. It was a critical part of the gospel because it showed us our direction and guided the steps to take on the path of righteousness. It was the great legacy that Judaism gave to the Christian community. Somehow, somewhere, it was lost.

How did this happen? The separation of the church from the Jewish roots of faith only came after decades of evangelism across the Roman Empire and after large numbers of Gentiles became part of the churches. Initially, Christianity was considered just another form of Judaism, just another group of ethnic Jews.[6] The first Gentiles accepted into the movement were minority members of a largely Jewish community and were in the position of "resident aliens" among the people of Israel. The expectations in the Hebrew Bible for Gentiles among the people provided the basis for the integration of Gentiles into the communities that became the early church.

Once the majority of people in the church no longer had the common basis of Jewish law and customs, the memory of what it meant to be non-Jewish in a Jewish community was lost. During the second and third centuries, the relationship between Jews and Christians changed. They went from being brothers and sisters, siblings within the same family who had their squabbles, to being rival clans, each solidifying its distinct identity at the expense of the other. In the process, the knowledge of what it meant to be righteous before God, knowledge captured in the moral law, faded away.

Morality Is Not a Popular Topic

Our current culture has a great distaste for talking, or even thinking, about moral law. By moral law I mean the conduct expected of human beings when they are behaving properly. Law generally refers to a group of rules or guidelines for behavior, established by an authority that is able to enforce them.[7] In a Jewish or Christian context, God is the authority, and these guidelines are set down in Scripture. Moral law relates behavior to basic principles of right and wrong in order to identify things that should or should not be done.[8] These principles are expected to apply to all people as best they are understood in the context of the current local culture.

Our culture has abandoned the use of moral standards generally and shown a resistance to attempts to discuss them at all. Many behaviors that were not acceptable to recent generations have become common, redefining the boundaries of what is acceptable. Well-intentioned Christians look foolish arguing among themselves about moral principles and how they apply. Those who hold a particular set of moral principles are seen as judgmental, condemning those who do not conform to their particular set of rules. There is prejudice against Christians generally as people who cannot, because of their faith, engage in rational discussion of moral issues.[9]

Our secular culture has rejected the confident and optimistic rationality of the Enlightenment. It has moved to a more experiential approach based on the perspective of each individual. The postmodern way of thinking prefers the local to the global, the particular to the general, and the distinctive to the universal.[10] Explanations based on general principles and logical reasoning are seen to be inadequate to describe the richness and nuances of individual experience. No explanatory framework is widely accepted, and, as a result, the faith traditions and secularism itself are all seen as alternative positions with no underlying common ground.[11] A person's faith (or lack of it) has become a matter of private personal opinion. Society has fragmented into groups holding disparate and often contradictory worldviews, with no particular worldview seen as having greater credibility than any other.

We Still Need Guidance

The validity of moral law and its use as a standard and guide for Christians is not just a theological exercise. It is a critical part of the ongoing practice of faith in daily life. On a recent Sunday at a local church I was attending, several men shared the struggles in their lives during a worship service. The first was feeling uncertain and grateful for the support of the church, having just turned away from "burning up in sin" to embark on a new way of life. Another had come to the area to be reconciled to his mother and family a few years ago and, after this time of healing, had once again found work out west. Another was grateful that God had permitted him to survive serious injuries and given him a new chance to turn his life around. One shared a Scripture passage that had become a theme in his life:

> For we ourselves were once foolish, disobedient, led
> astray, slaves to various passions and pleasures, passing
> our days in malice and envy, despicable, hating one
> another. But when the goodness and loving kindness
> of God our Savior appeared, he saved us, not because
> of any works of righteousness that we had done, but
> according to his mercy, through the water of rebirth
> and renewal by the Holy Spirit. (Titus 3:3–5)

For those of us who have come to recognize the destructiveness of
sin, we find the standard by which it can be identified, the guide that
warns us away from it, and the strength to resist that comes from the
Holy Spirit to be lifesaving.

Within a Christian community, moral law is a guide to living a life
of faith. Even John Calvin recognized that perfection was a goal and
not a possibility:

> I insist not so strictly on evangelical perfection, as to
> refuse to acknowledge as a Christian any man who has
> not attained it. In this way all would be excluded from
> the Church. . . . Let us set this before our eye as the end
> at which we ought constantly to aim. Let it be regarded
> as the goal towards which we are to run.[12]

The need for a guide to moral behavior begins in earliest childhood
and continues through adulthood. Those who study the internal
mechanisms that control addiction have discovered that control
of impulsiveness, delaying gratification, and including long-term
considerations in decision making grow over time.[13] Even in adulthood,
establishing control over addictive behaviors requires encouragement,
advice, feedback, and consequences.[14] The presence of law as a standard
and guide is a benefit to those who are willing to use it.

This benefit is for all human beings and not uniquely for Christians
and Jews. This need for a road sign to be able to tell one direction from

others, to recognize the positive from the many kinds of negative, is valid for all people. Those Christians fortunate enough to recognize the value of the law are blessed by a gift of grace. Law is our signpost and companion on the path to righteousness.

Conflicts within Protestant denominations typically have to do with the application of moral law—what behavior is permissible and how standards of behavior are to be agreed on and used. Moral law within the Mosaic covenant provided the foundation for expectations of behavior among early believers. The Pharisaic, and later rabbinic, tradition of disputation (public debate among religious authorities) provided a process of interpretation to apply law to specific situations. By applying the moral law and the process of interpretation used in the first century to our present conflicts, we may be able to find common ground for discussion as well as a process for living together in the dynamic tension of our different perspectives.

Jews, Gentiles, and Christians

The Hebrew Bible describes the history of the people of Israel through a series of covenants—formal agreements between God and the people. The sequence begins with the original creation of human beings and then has a new beginning after the flood with the covenant agreement with Noah. The people of Israel are defined by the covenant with Abraham, and their role in relationship with God is described in the covenant with Moses at Mount Sinai and continued through the covenant with David.

The people of Israel were unique in their direct relationship with God, invited into this relationship by God's own choice. This voluntary action of God is identified as grace, because there was and is nothing that human beings can do to earn this divine favor. In this biblical view, all human beings are divided into two groups: the people of Israel who are the recipients of this divine kindness, and all other peoples, the Gentiles.

Our current cultural and religious climate is characterized by diversity on almost any measurable scale. Our pluralism goes beyond people of different races, nationalities, ethnic groups, and cultures living together and includes having contradictory worldviews, ideologies, and moral frameworks interspersed with each other.[15] Strangely enough, this intense diversity bears striking similarities with the first-century environment in which Christianity was formed. The early Roman Empire was also cosmopolitan and individualistic, with an unprecedented level of interaction between cultures. It was also a time when the effects of war, imperial rule, and human suffering threatened confidence in traditional beliefs.[16] Our current situation is very much like that faced by the people of the early church.

How Do We Know Which Commandments to Follow?

The principles Christians live by come from the teachings of Jesus, and those teachings were developed in the context of the first-century Judaism in which Jesus grew up. Judaism then was a lively and varied combination of ethnic identity and religious practice, with active differences of opinion among religious leaders and practicing groups. Jesus grew up in the Judaism of his time and used the Scriptures of his people in his thought. When large numbers of Gentiles entered the early churches, many of the assumptions that came from this Jewish background were forgotten.

This study recovers what was lost— Jewish moral law as it applied to Gentile Christians in the first century. The process includes uncovering the understanding of moral purity and law for Gentiles at that time and then finding these ideas in the writings and sayings of Jesus, Paul, and the early churches. The reasoning is that:

- The part of the Mosaic law that applied to Gentiles consists of moral (as opposed to ceremonial or ritual) provisions.
- Jesus did not reject the Mosaic law, but interpreted the priority of its provisions differently.

- Paul did not reject the Mosaic law, but accepted this reinterpretation.
- The first apostolic council ruled in Acts 15:20 and 29 that this moral law applied to Gentile Christians.
- The first and third uses of law described by John Calvin show how the law can work for current Christians.

The Mosaic law, offered as part of a covenant relationship between the chosen people and God, included provisions for non-Israelites who lived among the people. These provisions were accepted by the resident aliens present at the receiving of the law. They included prohibitions on idolatry, blasphemy, bloodshed, and sexual immorality, as well as the requirement that all receive equal justice and treatment under the law. Recent study of the difference between ritual and moral purity identifies these provisions as belonging to the moral, as opposed to ritual, law. The law for the children of Noah described in early rabbinic documents, applying to Israelites before the Mosaic covenant and to all other people, identify these same provisions as binding on the righteous among the Gentiles.

Neither Jesus nor Paul rejected or superseded the Mosaic law in their teaching. Jesus, in his messianic role of interpreter of the law, changed the relative priorities of specific provisions within the body of law and criticized those who claimed to, but did not, live by the law. The apostolic council in Acts 15, decided to prohibit exactly those behaviors already forbidden to Gentiles under the Mosaic covenant. Paul emphasized that obedience to the law was not the basis for salvation, but he continued to convey to his Gentile converts the importance of behavior conforming to the moral provisions of the law that were binding on non-Israelites.

Jesus' interpretation of the Mosaic law did not invalidate or change the content of the law, but he did modify its relative priorities in specific situations. In the early church, the provisions of the Mosaic law that applied to Jews continued to apply to Jewish Christians, and the provisions that applied to Gentiles continued to apply to Gentile Christians. This study will show how the provisions of the Mosaic law that apply to Gentiles—typically those of moral law—are still in force for present-day Gentile followers of Jesus. Acknowledging this moral law and finding ways to apply it in our churches will help us in our current conflicts over issues such as abortion, homosexuality, and warfare.

Questions for Reflection and Discussion

1. What are your standards for behavior? Where do they come from?
2. Have you ever been in conflict with a friend over different standards? How did it end?
3. Do your close friends and family share your values? When they do not, do they try to influence your choices? How do you respond?
4. How do you decide that one activity is "better" or "worse" than another? What factors do you include? How do you decide that one factor takes precedence over another?
5. Do you find it valuable to have a friend in faith to help you with your discernment?
6. What similarities and differences can you think of between our culture and the first-century Roman Empire?
7. What criticisms have you heard of the Bible? How do you respond to them?
8. Consider the life of King David (2 Samuel 5–16). When is he a good example? How do we relate to the times when he is a bad example?
9. How might Adam have written to us on the subject of temptation, deception, and will?
10. Consider the covenants with Noah (Genesis 9:1–17), Abram (Genesis 15:12–20, 17:1–14), Moses (Exodus 19:1–9), and David (1 Chronicles 17:1–15). How do you see God's relationship with the people growing and changing through these covenants?
11. What do you think is God's hope for human beings? How do the covenants reflect this hope?

2

How Does the Law of Moses Relate to Modern Christians?

The first step in discovering how the Old Testament law relates to present-day Christians is to look at the law itself. During the lifetime of Jesus, Jewish people were subject to two different kinds of law—civil law imposed by the Roman government and religious law centered on Scripture.

Because many different cultures were joined together under the Roman Empire, the Romans developed an interesting approach to law. There were two bodies of law in the empire: one for Roman citizens, known as the *ius civile*, and another for non-Roman citizens living under Roman rule, the *ius gentium*. As early as 242 BCE, there was a Roman official, known as the *praetor peregrinos*, who acted as judge in cases involving the law for non-citizens.[17] The people who lived in Palestine during the Roman occupation were subject to this part of the secular Roman law.

The people of Israel also had a religious law that was uniquely their own. The first five books of the Bible were known as the Pentateuch, the books of Moses, and sometimes as the books of the law. The distinction between "law" and "prophets" in Scripture is mentioned in several places in the New Testament, and the law included at least the five books of Moses. There are many different theories about how and when these books were written, but we do know that they were part of the Scriptures of the people of Israel during the first century.

Greek was the common international language in the first century CE, and a group of translators in Alexandria in Egypt translated the books of law into Greek in the third century BCE. There are variations among different versions of Scripture, especially between the Greek of this translation, the *Septuagint*, and available Hebrew texts. There are also variations among different versions of the Hebrew text.[18] In the first century, the written law was expressed in the Pentateuch and the text was largely stable, although it was subject to changing interpretation in specific areas.

The Roman division of law into one part that applied to everyone and another part that applied to citizens parallels the way the Mosaic law worked. Under Mosaic law, some provisions applied to all people while other provisions applied only to the people of Israel. In this chapter, we will look at the law to discover which provisions applied *specifically* to non-Jews living among the people. This describes the behavior that Jews would expect of their Gentile neighbors in a largely Jewish community. This is also the behavior that would have been expected of individual Gentile newcomers in dispersed Jewish communities such as the early church.

What Is Jewish Law?

What did law mean in first century Judaism? Jesus used the Greek word νομός (*nomos*) to refer to the law in Matthew 5:17. This is a general word used for something that is assigned—an expected practice, a custom, or a particular provision of law.

The word Torah itself can have as many as seven meanings. It can be

- A scroll containing divinely revealed words
- Divine revelation as a body of doctrine
- Something that is studied and taught
- A category, classification or body of rules
- Teaching at a particular level of authority

- Teaching that can be oral or written
- A source of salvation for the people of Israel

Different groups used different combinations of these definitions in the first century. Pharisees, for example, accepted the oral traditions as part of one whole oral and written Torah, while Sadducees did not. Although the whole Scripture consisted of law, prophets, and writings, the five books of Moses in the Pentateuch were the center of authority.

The law was not a set of arbitrary rules imposed on the people without reason. The Torah was understood to be a guide to living as people in relationship with God, a relationship initiated and defined by God. As such, it was the source of hope, security, abundance, and even life itself.

> You shall keep my statutes and my ordinances; by doing so one shall live: I am the LORD. (Lev 18:5)

> You must follow exactly the path that the LORD your God has commanded you, so that you may live, and that it may go well with you, and that you may live long in the land that you are to possess. (Deut 5:33)

The promises of security and prosperity in the land are linked to faithful compliance with the law.

> You shall observe my statutes and faithfully keep my ordinances, so that you may live on the land securely. The land will yield its fruit, and you will eat your fill and live on it securely. (Lev 25:18–19)

> If you follow my statutes and keep my commandments and observe them faithfully, I will give you your rains in their season, and the land shall yield its produce, and the trees of the field shall yield their fruit. Your threshing shall overtake the vintage, and the vintage

shall overtake the sowing; you shall eat your bread to the full, and live securely in your land. (Lev 26:3–5)

The promises of continuing blessings to future generations are also linked to continuing participation in the relationship with God through the law.

. . . so that you and your children and your children's children may fear the LORD your God all the days of your life, and keep all his decrees and his commandments that I am commanding you, so that your days may be long. (Deut 6:2)

Keep, then, this entire commandment that I am commanding you today, so that you may have strength to go in and occupy the land that you are crossing over to occupy, and so that you may live long in the land that the LORD swore to your ancestors to give them and to their descendants, a land flowing with milk and honey. (Deut 11:8–9)

The law is not phrased as a conditional ("if you do this, then I will give you this reward"), but as an enabling foundation ("live this way, and you will have these blessings").

Moses Presented the Law, and the People Accepted It

All of the people of Israel, as well as the Gentiles who were living among them, were gathered together as Moses proclaimed the covenant. He described the relationship agreement between God and the people:

You stand assembled today, all of you, before the LORD your God—the leaders of your tribes, your elders, and your officials, all the men of Israel, your children, your

women, and the *aliens* who are in your camp, both those
who cut your wood and those who draw your water
—to enter into the covenant of the LORD your God,
sworn by an oath, which the LORD your God is making
with you today; (Deut 29:10–12)

The covenant was reread every seventh year to all the people, Israelites
as well as non-Israelites living among them, to remind all of the law
under which they lived:

Assemble the people—men, women, and children, as
well as the *aliens* residing in your towns—so that they
may hear and learn to fear the LORD your God and to
observe diligently all the words of this law, (Deut 31:12)

All of the provisions of the law were given for the people of Israel,
while some provisions also applied to the aliens living among them.

The term for aliens in this and other places in the Pentateuch is גֵּר
(gēr) in Hebrew. This word can be translated as *alien, sojourner, foreigner,*
or *stranger.* It carries the implication of living in a place without being a
member of the local society or culture. This is typically a situation in
which foreigners do not own land and where any rights they may have
are only the ones granted by the culture around them. The Mosaic
covenant was enacted when the people had just come from an extended
period as aliens in Egypt, and the law expected that they would treat
the aliens in their midst better than they themselves had been treated.

The *alien* who resides with you shall be to you as the
citizen among you; you shall love the *alien* as yourself,
for you were aliens in the land of Egypt: I am the Lord
your God. (Lev 19:34)

Non-Jewish aliens—Gentiles—were provided for under the law, and
the law clearly stated which provisions applied to them.

What Happened to Law-Breakers?

The law included provisions for those who did not keep it perfectly but who did not intend to violate it. The fourth through seventh chapters of Leviticus address in detail the process for restitution in situations of sin and guilt. However, these chapters do not include resident aliens. The fifteenth chapter of Numbers does include aliens as well as Israelites when it specifies what can be done in the case of error and unintentional sin:

> An individual who sins unintentionally shall present a female goat a year old for a sin offering. And the priest shall make atonement before the LORD for the one who commits an error, when it is unintentional, to make atonement for the person, who then shall be forgiven. For both the native among the Israelites and the alien residing among them—you shall have the same law for anyone who acts in error. (Num 15:27–29)

Aliens and Israelites must both follow the same procedures, and they receive the same forgiveness for their mistakes.

Intentional sins are treated very differently from unintentional sins for both Israelites and aliens:

> But whoever acts high-handedly, whether a native or an *alien*, affronts the LORD, and shall be cut off from among the people. Because of having despised the word of the LORD and broken his commandment, such a person shall be utterly cut off and bear the guilt. (Num 15:30–31)

One who acts with a "high hand" has a hand (or finger) raised in defiance. The same verb is used in the Psalms to describe those who are rebellious:

> There we rejoiced in him, who rules by his might
> forever, whose eyes keep watch on the nations—let
> the rebellious not exalt themselves. (Ps 66:6–7)

The rabbis who explained Numbers 15:31 in the *Sifré to Numbers*, written between 200 and 600 CE, gave examples of what it meant to "despise the word of the LORD." This included refusing to learn Torah, ignoring Torah teachings, interpreting the Torah impudently, desecrating holy things, ignoring festivals, removing the marks of circumcision, and outright idolatry.[19] The verb translated here as "despised" is the same one used in the exchange between Jacob and Esau:

> Then Jacob gave Esau bread and lentil stew, and he
> ate and drank, and rose and went his way. Thus Esau
> despised his birthright. (Gen 25:34)

Rebellion, disrespect, and devaluing the law by either Israelite or alien are grounds for separation from the people and the land. For an alien, this means losing the privilege of living among the people.

Idolatry Is Forbidden

The first and greatest prohibition applying to both Israelites and aliens is the prohibition of idolatry. There is only one God, the God of Israel, and the people and their resident aliens must not give their offerings and sacrifices to anyone other than this one God.

> Anyone of the house of Israel or of the aliens who
> reside among them who offers a burnt offering or
> sacrifice, and does not bring it to the entrance of the
> tent of meeting, to sacrifice it to the LORD, shall be cut
> off from the people. (Lev 17:8–9)

No other god may be honored with a gift. People may only bring their gifts to the priests, so that the priests can make sure that the gifts are delivered in the proper way. Israelites and resident aliens are particularly forbidden to sacrifice children to the god Molech:

> Say further to the people of Israel: Any of the people of
> Israel, or of the aliens who reside in Israel, who give any
> of their offspring to Molech shall be put to death; the
> people of the land shall stone them to death. (Lev 20:2)

Gentile aliens, whatever their previous religious practices might have been, are forbidden to worship the gods of their original culture. Regardless of their previous ethnic or cultural affiliation, living in the territory of the God of Israel required that the Lord replace any other gods they had been worshipping.

Blasphemy Is Forbidden

Neither Israelites nor resident aliens may blaspheme the name of God:

> One who blasphemes the name of the LORD shall
> be put to death; the whole congregation shall stone
> the blasphemer. Aliens as well as citizens, when they
> blaspheme the Name, shall be put to death. (Lev 24:16)

The word translated as *blaspheme* here is נָקַב *(nāqab)*. It is only used in the sense of blasphemy or curse in this section of Leviticus, in Numbers (23:8, 25), in Proverbs (11:26; 24:24), and in Job (3:8; 5:3). Its more common definition is to pierce or bore a hole in something, and even the derivation of the word is the subject for some discussion.[20] If, as best it is understood, this refers to cursing God by name, it makes sense that this kind of insult should be forbidden to both Israelites and aliens.

Bloodshed Is Forbidden

The laws against murder and shedding blood apply to both the Israelite and the resident alien:

> Anyone who kills a human being shall be put to death. Anyone who kills an animal shall make restitution for it, life for life. Anyone who maims another shall suffer the same injury in return: fracture for fracture, eye for eye, tooth for tooth; the injury inflicted is the injury to be suffered. One who kills an animal shall make restitution for it; but one who kills a human being shall be put to death. You shall have one law for the alien and for the citizen: for I am the LORD your God. (Lev 24:17–22)

The word that is translated *kill* here is נָכָה *(nāḵā)*, a much more comprehensive word than the one translated *murder* in the ten commandments (רָצַח *(ratsach)* in Exodus 20:13. The word for murder involves taking life intentionally or unintentionally. This verb, based on the idea of striking a blow, carries implications of violence and other kinds of destruction as well. This provision forbids destruction by violence, and it is binding on aliens as well as Israelites.

Various Kinds of Sexual Immorality Are Forbidden

Both the Israelite and the resident alien must obey the laws against various forms of sexual immorality. These are usually referred to as "abomination."

> Do not defile yourselves in any of these ways [of sexual immorality listed above in Lev 18:6-23], for by all these practices the nations I am casting out before you have

---

Jean Risley

> defiled themselves. Thus the land became defiled; and I punished it for its iniquity, and the land vomited out its inhabitants. But you shall keep my statutes and my ordinances and commit none of these abominations, either the citizen or the alien who resides among you (Lev 18:24–26)

These activities are identified as sources of defilement—sources of pollution for the people who practice them and for the land on which they live. The list of prohibitions includes a man having sexual relations with women who are relatives in his family, with women connected to each other, with women during their menstrual periods, with other men, and even with animals (Lev 18:6–23). Aliens as well as Israelites are forbidden to indulge in any of the practices on the list.

Justice Must Be Provided for All People

Israelites and resident aliens are to be treated as equals under the law, and justice must be provided equally to both:

> [T]here shall be one law for the native and for the alien who resides among you. (Exod 12:49)

> As for the assembly, there shall be for both you and the resident alien a single statute, a perpetual statute throughout your generations; you and the alien shall be alike before the LORD. You and the alien who resides with you shall have the same law and the same ordinance. (Num 15:15–16)

> I charged your judges at that time: "Give the members of your community a fair hearing, and judge rightly between one person and another, whether citizen or resident alien." (Deut 1:16)

24

Even the need for a place of refuge to provide safety from a blood feud has been considered, and the alien is offered the same sanctuary as the Israelite.

> These six cities shall serve as refuge for the Israelites, for the resident or transient alien among them, so that anyone who kills a person without intent may flee there. (Num 35:15)

The importance of equal treatment under the law must not be forgotten by those who have been victimized themselves, even when they deal with those who have been their oppressors.

No One is Allowed to Eat Blood

At the end of the flood, when God established the covenant with Noah and his sons, God said to them:

> Every moving thing that lives shall be food for you; and just as I gave you the green plants, I give you everything. Only, you shall not eat flesh with its life, that is, its blood. (Gen 9:3–4)

Thus the Mosaic law also forbids consuming blood or meat containing the blood of life, and this applies to both Israelites and resident aliens:

> If anyone of the house of Israel or of the aliens who reside among them eats any blood, I will set my face against that person who eats blood, and will cut that person off from the people. . . . No person among you shall eat blood, nor shall any alien who resides among you eat blood. And anyone of the people of Israel, or of the *aliens* who reside among them, who hunts down

an animal or bird that may be eaten shall pour out its
blood and cover it with earth. (Lev 17:10, 12–13)

Because blood contains life, all people, Israelite and alien, are forbidden
to consume it.

Non-Jews Can Become Unable
to Participate in Worship

Ritual impurity means that a person may not enter the temple or
participate in Jewish rituals. There are two ways in which aliens may
become ritually impure and require a ritual process to become clean
again. First, any contact with a corpse can cause ritual impurity.

This shall be a perpetual statute for the Israelites and
for the alien residing among them. Those who touch
the dead body of any human being shall be unclean
seven days. They shall purify themselves with the water
on the third day and on the seventh day, and so be
clean; but if they do not purify themselves on the third
day and on the seventh day, they will not become clean.
All who touch a corpse, the body of a human being
who has died, and do not purify themselves, defile the
tabernacle of the LORD; such persons shall be cut off
from Israel. (Num 19:10–13)

Eating meat from an animal that has died of natural causes, instead
of being butchered, involves contact with its corpse and is therefore
a source of ritual impurity. Those who eat this meat, Israelite or
alien, must perform the ritual of washing to remove the impurity.
Eating the corpse of an animal will convey impurity to the one who
consumes it, and this impurity is removed by washing and waiting
until evening.

All persons, citizens or aliens, who eat what dies of
itself or what has been torn by wild animals, shall wash
their clothes, and bathe themselves in water, and be
unclean until the evening; then they shall be clean.
(Lev 17:15)

This kind of meat may be given to resident aliens or even sold to
foreigners, who would then be responsible for dealing with the impurity
if they recognize it or care about it.

You shall not eat anything that dies of itself; you may
give it to aliens residing in your towns for them to eat,
or you may sell it to a foreigner. (Deut 14:21)

Are Non-Jews Allowed to Participate in Worship, Sabbath, and Festivals?

What kinds of worship are explicitly permitted to the aliens who
are living among the people of Israel? Gifts to God from those who
are not members of the people of Israel are welcome and to be treated
in the same way as offerings from among the people.

An alien who lives with you, or who takes up permanent
residence among you, and wishes to offer an offering
by fire, a pleasing odor to the LORD, shall do as you do.
(Num 15:14)

The offerings of aliens should be of the same kind and quality as those
offered by Israelites.

Speak to Aaron and his sons and all the people of Israel
and say to them: When anyone of the house of Israel or of
the aliens residing in Israel presents an offering, whether

> in payment of a vow or as a freewill offering that is offered to the LORD as a burnt offering, to be acceptable in your behalf it shall be a male without blemish, of the cattle or the sheep or the goats. (Lev 22:18–19)

This worship and offerings of resident aliens are welcome before the Lord.

Resident aliens are also expected to respect the Sabbath and to rest on it.

> But the seventh day is a sabbath to the LORD your God; you shall not do any work—you, your son or your daughter, your male or female slave, your livestock, or the alien resident in your towns. (Exod 20:10)

> Six days you shall do your work, but on the seventh day you shall rest, so that your ox and your donkey may have relief, and your homeborn slave and the resident alien may be refreshed. (Exod 23:12)

Aliens are welcome to share in the festival of weeks and the festival of booths, and they are even permitted to keep the Passover according to the law.

> Rejoice during your festival [of weeks and festival of booths], you and your sons and your daughters, your male and female slaves, as well as the Levites, the strangers, the orphans, and the widows resident in your towns. (Deut 16:14)

> Any alien residing among you who wishes to keep the passover to the LORD shall do so according to the statute of the passover and according to its regulation; you shall have one statute for both the resident alien and the native. (Num 9:14)

Resident aliens must also respect the day of atonement:

> This shall be a statute to you forever: In the seventh month, on the tenth day of the month, you shall deny yourselves, and shall do no work, neither the citizen nor the alien who resides among you. For on this day atonement shall be made for you, to cleanse you; from all your sins you shall be clean before the LORD. (Lev 16:29–30)

The refreshment of Sabbath and the celebration of festivals are all available to the alien who lives among the people of Israel.

Law for Non-Jews Is Built into the Mosaic Covenant

The primary restrictions imposed on non-Jews by the law of Moses are prohibition of idolatry, blasphemy, bloodshed, and sexual immorality. Non-Jews are to be protected with equality under the law and treated with the same expectations as Israelites. Their offerings are acceptable to God, and they are welcome to share in the worship celebrations of the people. The two areas in which additional restrictions are placed on aliens are the prohibition against consuming blood and the requirement for ritual purification after touching a corpse or eating the body of an animal that has died naturally. These are the primary provisions of the Mosaic law that mention specifically applying to those who are not members of the people of Israel, but who are living among them. These are the provisions of the law required of a non-Jew under the Torah.

These requirements provide the context into which Gentiles must fit as they approach joining the people of Israel in the first century. Those interested in converting into Judaism would have been expected to abide by the whole law. Those who did not want to convert, continuing to be non-Jews in a Jewish community, would have been expected to follow the law for resident aliens. These provisions of Torah would have been understood by Jesus and by his early Jewish followers as the foundation of behavioral expectations for non-Jews.

Questions for Reflection and Discussion

1. Do you have positive or negative feelings when you think of law? Do you see law as a restrictive burden, an irritation to avoid, a useful tool for keeping people in line, or . . . ?
2. How effective do you think the threat of punishment is in motivating people to obey the law? What other motivations are there?
3. What kinds of punishments can work in a tribal culture like that of the Israelites in Moses' time?
4. Do you think that Israelites treated foreigners better or worse than others (e.g., the Egyptians) did at that time?
5. Compare Leviticus 19:17–18 with Leviticus 19:33–34. What similarities and differences do you see between the passages?
6. How do you relate to the idea of two levels of law, one for citizens and one for "others" living in a place? What advantages and disadvantages do you see?
7. Consider Exodus 20:1–17. Where do you notice the specific inclusion of foreigners? Do you think this explanation of "you" is true for all the commandments?
8. How did foreigners interact with the Israelites' religious life?
9. Where is idolatry found in our present culture?
10. Consider Deuteronomy 5:11. What is blasphemy? How is it manifested these days?
11. Consider the sexuality provisions in Leviticus 18:6–23. Which of them are considered acceptable in today's culture? Which things considered unacceptable these days are not on the list?

3

How Are Moral Law and Ritual Regulations Different?

If we want to understand the way the provisions of the Mosaic law operate, we need to look at the different kinds of provisions in the law. Some have to do with worship and with situations that might interfere with proper worship. Some provisions have to do with sin and with identifying unacceptable behavior in relationships with God and others. Some provisions have to do with the routines of daily life, such as eating or sexual activity. Provisions that have to do with worship are referred to as ritual regulations, while those having to do with sin are referred to as moral regulations. These categories are based on the kinds of restrictions in the law and on the prescribed remedies for violations. Here we will look at the way provisions within the law fit into these categories and how these categories relate to non-Jews.

Jewish scholar Jonathan Klawans developed a way to distinguish between ritual and moral requirements in the Mosaic law. He uses the word "purity" to describe satisfying these provisions and the word "impurity" to indicate violations. Klawans examined the various causes and characteristics of impurity in the Torah, and he described the two types of impurity he found.[21] He called them ritual impurity and moral impurity, and he described the characteristics of provisions that fall into each of the two groups.[22]

What Is Ritual Impurity?

Ritual impurity has to do with a person's relationship with holy things and holy places. It does not have anything to do with the person's moral status or position in the community. This kind of impurity only results in a person not being able to participate in religious activities or come into sacred places.[23] For example, for a woman after childbirth of a male child,

> Her time of blood purification shall be thirty-three days; she shall not touch any holy thing, or come into the sanctuary, until the days of her purification are completed. (Lev 12:4)

The causes of ritual impurity are natural and sometimes cannot be avoided, even when we carefully try to avoid them. Ritual impurity comes from direct or indirect contact with natural substances—childbirth (Lev 12:1–8), skin diseases (Lev 13:1—14:32), genital discharge (Lev 15:1–33), the body of an impure animal (Lev 11:1–47), or a human corpse (Num 19:10–22). Priests could even become ritually impure (unclean) while they were performing their responsibilities in worship.[24] For example,

> The one who burns the heifer shall wash his clothes in water and bathe his body in water; he shall remain unclean until evening. Then someone who is clean shall gather up the ashes of the heifer, and deposit them outside the camp in a clean place; and they shall be kept for the congregation of the Israelites for the water for cleansing. It is a purification offering. The one who gathers the ashes of the heifer shall wash his clothes and be unclean until evening. (Num 19:8–10)

Ritual impurity can be transmitted directly to other people by contact, and in this way ritually impure people can affect the status of those around them.[25] For example, when a person has a genital discharge, his bed and anything he sits on also become unclean. Any contact with that person's body, his bed, his saddle, other things he sits on, and even his saliva makes others unclean. Those who come into contact with a person who is unclean also need to go through purification. This kind of impurity is contagious and can be passed from person to person.

The good news is that this kind of impurity is both temporary and fixable. Each type of ritual impurity comes with its own prescription for purification. This prescription can include sacrifices, sprinkling, washing, bathing, and/or waiting for a specified time.[26] For example, those who are unclean through a genital discharge or contact with a person having one must wash their clothes, bathe in water, and wait until the evening (Lev 15:5–11).

This kind of impurity or uncleanness is not caused by sin. The primary way that this kind of impurity can lead to sin is if the affected person refuses to perform the required purification. If ordinary people or priests enter the sanctuary or touch holy things while they are in an unclean state, they defile the holy place or holy things. This defilement is not a result of impurity being contagious, but because their refusal to stay away from sacred places is sinful. This sin then puts them in a condition of moral impurity, which we will look at in the next section.[27]

What the different forms of ritual impurity have in common is that:

- They result from natural causes that are not generally avoidable.
- The impurity can be addressed and removed with specific actions.
- The impurity can be passed from person to person.
- It is not sinful to be in a condition of ritual impurity.

What Is Moral Impurity?

On the other hand, moral impurity is the result of committing sins which are described in the law as "defiling" or "abomination." Impurity that is morally defiling has its effect on the person who has committed the sin, on the land itself, and on the sanctuary of God.[28] The consequences of sin reach far beyond the individuals who have committed the sin.

The effect on the land of moral impurity created by sexual sins is described in Leviticus 18:

> Do not defile yourselves in any of these ways, for by all these practices the nations I am casting out before you have defiled themselves. Thus the land became defiled; and I punished it for its iniquity, and the land vomited out its inhabitants. But you shall keep my statutes and my ordinances and commit none of these abominations, either the citizen or the alien who resides among you (for the inhabitants of the land, who were before you, committed all of these abominations, and the land became defiled); otherwise the land will vomit you out for defiling it, as it vomited out the nation that was before you. (Lev 18:24–28)

Bloodshed also has the effect of polluting the land.

> You shall not pollute the land in which you live; for blood pollutes the land, and no expiation can be made for the land, for the blood that is shed in it, except by the blood of the one who shed it. You shall not defile the land in which you live, in which I also dwell; for I the LORD dwell among the Israelites. (Num 35:33–34)

Idolatry has the effect of defiling the sanctuary itself:

> Any of the people of Israel, or of the aliens who reside in Israel, who give any of their offspring to Molech shall be put to death; the people of the land shall stone them to death. I myself will set my face against them, and will

> cut them off from the people, because they have given
> of their offspring to Molech, defiling my sanctuary and
> profaning my holy name. (Lev 20:2–3)

The prophets Jeremiah and Ezekiel both talk about this defiling effect
of idolatry on the sanctuary.

> For the people of Judah have done evil in my sight, says
> the LORD; they have set their abominations in the house
> that is called by my name, defiling it. (Jer 7:30)

> Therefore, as I live, says the Lord GOD, surely, because
> you have defiled my sanctuary with all your detestable
> things and with all your abominations—therefore I will
> cut you down; my eye will not spare, and I will have no
> pity. (Ezek 5:11)

Those who have committed sins are not forbidden to enter the sanctuary,
however. In some cases, such as that of a woman suspected of adultery,
the suspected sinner is brought into the sanctuary for examination.

> If any man's wife goes astray and is unfaithful to him,
> if a man has had intercourse with her but it is hidden
> from her husband, so that she is undetected though she
> has defiled herself, and there is no witness against her
> since she was not caught in the act; . . . the priest shall
> bring her near, and set her before the LORD; (Num 5:16)

Moral impurity does pollute the sanctuary, but the pollution is a result
of the sin itself and not of contact with the one who committed the sin.

Each kind of moral defilement created by sin applies to both
Israelites and to non-Jews living with them. Indulging in sinful
activities, described as defiling or abominations, causes the impurity.
The impurity is not contagious. A person who has committed idolatry,

murder, or sexual sin cannot pass the contagion of guilt along to another person. In the case of sexual sin, the guilt is shared with the other participants in the sin, but not contagious by physical contact. There is also no simple prescription for removing this kind of impurity. The effects of moral impurity last until the sinful situation is resolved.

Resolving a situation of moral impurity follows one of two tracks. For those who are rebellious and refuse to acknowledge their sin, some form of punishment follows. For those who continue to resist, pollution of the land and sanctuary leads to poisoning the relationship between the sinner and God. On the other track, for those who repent of their sin, their repentance and atonement provide restoration of their relationship with God.[29]

The people of Nineveh showed a proper response to Jonah's warning.

> When God saw what they did, how they turned from their evil ways, God changed his mind about the calamity that he had said he would bring upon them; and he did not do it. (Jon 3:10)

The situation in Israel before the exile showed the same sort of sinful behavior, but the warnings of the prophets did not bring the people to repentance. In that case, God, as a righteous judge, responded to moral corruption with punishment, affliction, political downfall, and exile. The goal and outcome of the punishment, however, were always repentance and salvation.[30]

The consequences of sin are punishment and separation from the land, but the goal of punishment is repentance. The point of punishment is to bring the sinner to repentance and to use atonement to restore a condition of moral purity. The ultimate goal of the process is a commitment to preserve moral purity by avoiding sin in the first place.

What Is the Difference between Ritual and Moral Impurity?

There are several important differences between ritual impurity and moral impurity. While ritual impurity is usually not sinful, moral impurity is the result of serious sin. While ritual impurity is contagious— one can "catch" ritual impurity from a person who is ritually impure— moral impurity does not pass from the person who committed a sin to others. While ritual impurity is temporary until a purification ritual, moral impurity has a long-lasting effect on the sinner and ultimately on the land as well. Moral impurity cannot be removed by ritual cleansing, but requires a process of punishment, repentance, and atonement. Causes of ritual impurity are ordinary and natural, while more forceful terms such as "abomination" and "pollution" are used for sources of moral impurity.

The following summarizes the differences between the two types of impurity:

cause of the impurity:

> Ritual: contact with bodily flows, corpses, etc.
> Moral: idolatry, sexual sin, bloodshed

effect of the impurity:

> Ritual: separation from worship and sanctuary
> Moral: pollution of sinners, land, sanctuary

contagiousness of the impurity:

> Ritual: contagious
> Moral: not contagious

duration of the impurity:

> Ritual: temporary
> Moral: long-lasting or permanent

resolution of the impurity:

> Ritual: bathing, washing, waiting
> Moral: repentance and atonement, punishment and exile

relation of the impurity to sin:

> Ritual: not inherently sinful, but can cause sin by refusal
> to stay away from sanctuary or holy things
> Moral: caused by sin

Where Do Food Regulations Fit In?

Dietary laws, along with circumcision and Sabbath observance, provided a way to distinguish Jewish identity and prevent assimilation into surrounding cultures.[31] Where do the dietary laws of Leviticus 11 and Deuteronomy 14 fit into the two kinds of impurity? In fact, they do not appear to fit into either category.

There are purity issues related to contact with specific kinds of dead animals and with the bodies of animals that have died on their own without being slaughtered. However, the kind of impurity contracted in these cases is a result of contact with the dead body rather than with eating the meat.[32]

> By these you shall become unclean; whoever touches
> the carcass of any of them shall be unclean until the
> evening, and whoever carries any part of the carcass of
> any of them shall wash his clothes and be unclean until
> the evening. (Lev 11:24–25)

Although the dietary regulations appear just before the ritual purity provisions in Leviticus, there are significant differences between them. Eating forbidden foods does not create a contagious condition that can be passed on to others. There is no provision for a process that can reverse the effect of having eaten forbidden foods. In some cases, foods such as birds and fish are simply forbidden without being described as defiling.[33]

Some authorities group dietary laws in the category of moral defilement, since they are linked with holiness and since consuming the forbidden items has a harmful effect on the one who does it.

> You shall not make yourselves detestable with any creature that swarms; you shall not defile yourselves with them, and so become unclean. For I am the LORD your God; sanctify yourselves therefore, and be holy, for I am holy. (Lev 11:43–46)

While dietary laws are included in the factors that may lead to exile (Lev 20:22), they are not identified as defiling the sanctuary.

Although dietary laws have some similarities with each kind of impurity, Klawans suggests that they should be seen on their own terms as a separate system.[34] Dietary laws are kept separate from the laws of ritual purity in the rabbinic writings in the *Mishnah*, appearing in the section on Holy Things rather than the section on Purities. There are no dietary restrictions for non-Jews other than the restriction that has to do with contact with corpses. As a result, dietary laws themselves are not clearly identified as relating to either ritual or moral purity.

How Was Purity Understood in the First Century?

Now that we have seen the basis for the two kinds of purity and impurity in the law, we can determine how these ideas were understood in first century Judaism. What was the timing of awareness of the distinction between ritual and moral impurity?

Documents from Jewish communities outside Palestine and from the Dead Sea Scrolls of the Qumran community show different perspectives. Philo, who wrote from the Diaspora in Egypt, was an idealist philosopher. He saw ritual impurity as an analogy for the way that sin can defile the soul.[35] The Letter of Aristeas,[36] also from the Diaspora, describes dietary restrictions as a mechanism for keeping Jews separate from the Gentile environment with its the morally defiling practices.[37] In the Qumran community ritual and moral impurity were intermingled. Sin was considered ritually defiling, and repentance from sin also required ritual purification.[38] However, it is unlikely that any of these perspectives would have had an influence on the early Christian community in Jerusalem or during the first expansion outside of Palestine.

The most promising source of information about ideas in Palestine just before the destruction of the temple is the material preserved in the *Mishnah*, the *Tosefta*, the *Talmuds*, and the early rabbinic commentaries on Scripture. These sacred rabbinic texts contain a great deal of material about ways to live with issues of ritual impurity. According to Klawans, this literature clearly shows separation of ritual impurity and sin. The occasions and effects of sin are carefully distinguished from those of ritual impurity, and the processes for ritual purification and atonement are also kept carefully separate. Klawans concludes that "In contrast to the sectarians at Qumran, the Tannaim[39] chose to interpret Scripture in such a way as to keep ritual impurity and sin as distinct from each other as possible."[40] The general characteristics of ritual impurity in the Pentateuch—unavoidability, temporary contagion, and lack of sinfulness—also characterize ritual impurity in the early rabbinic (Tannaitic) writings.

Moral impurity is discussed less frequently in the rabbinic sources—not at all in the *Mishnah* and only a few times in the *Tosefta*. Mentions usually relate to specific passages from Scripture, and interpretation is usually quite literal. The consequences of sin are still pollution of the person, the land, and the sanctuary. The departure of the divine presence, the *Shekhinah*, from the land in response to sin ultimately leads to the exile of the people. *Mishnah* tractate Abot says, "Exile comes into the world because of those who worship idols, because of fornication, and because of bloodshed."[41] As in the Pentateuch, idolatry, bloodshed, and sexual sins are seen as morally defiling, but these writings also include arrogance, deceit, and blasphemy. In these materials, violations of the food laws are not considered a source of moral defilement.[42]

Klawans concludes that ". . . since the idea of moral impurity is found in the Hebrew Bible, in Jewish literature of the second temple period, and in Tannaitic sources, it does seem likely that many first century Jews, Pharisees included, also accepted the idea."[43]

How Did the Early Rabbis Understand Righteousness for Non-Jews?

What do the rabbis say about how the Mosaic law relates to Gentiles? What is the hope for the righteous among the Gentiles? A discussion among rabbis in the *Tosefta* shows that this was an important question.

> 13.2 A. Another matter:
> B. *Root*—this refers to the soul.
> C. And *branch*—this refers to the body.
> D. And the children of the wicked among the heathen will not live [in the world to come] nor be judged.
> E. R. Eliezer says, "None of the gentiles has a portion in the world to come,
> F. "as it is said, The wicked shall return to Sheol, all the gentiles who forget God (Ps. 9:17)."
> G. "*The wicked shall return to Sheol*—these are the wicked Israelites."
> H. [Supply: "*And all the gentiles who forget God*—these are the nations."]
> I. Said to him R. Joshua, "If it had been written, '*The wicked shall return to Sheol, all the gentiles*', and then

41

said nothing further, I should have maintained as you do.

J. Now that it is in fact written, *All the gentiles who forget God*, it indicates that there are also righteous people among the nations of the world, who do have a portion in the world to come."[44]

The Pharisees believed in the immortality of the soul and in a place for the righteous in the world to come. But what would happen to the righteous among the Gentiles? After much thought and careful consideration, a position emerged: the righteous among the Gentiles would also have a place in the world to come. The experiences and discussions during the time before the destruction of the second temple brought the rabbis to the place Isaiah had prophesied, where Gentiles will also be present in the end of days, worshipping the God of Israel.

How Can Non-Jews Be Righteous before God?

The rabbinic writers refer to Gentiles as the children of Noah, a category that also includes all Jews who lived before the Mosaic covenant. The laws for the children of Noah first appear in the *Tosefta*, which is a supplement to the rabbinic writings in the *Mishnah*. They are then discussed at some length in several places in the *Babylonian Talmud*.

The early rabbinic writings were collected and edited into the *Mishnah* around 200 CE. The *Tosefta* was collected at the same time and completed around 220 CE. The *Talmuds*, appearing around 600 CE, contain discussion and commentary based on the earlier rabbinic writings. Each section of the *Babylonian Talmud* is a commentary on the corresponding section of the *Mishnah*, and the *Mishnah* has the same structure of sections and chapters as the *Talmud*. The *Talmud* usually includes additional information and comments from the *Tosefta* with the corresponding section of the *Mishnah*.

Although the *Talmud* normally follows and comments on the *Mishnah* in order, the laws for the children of Noah are not mentioned in the *Mishnah* at all. The first discussion of laws for the children of Noah is in the *Tosefta*, and it is not found in the section on law, the tractate Sanhedrin. In the *Tosefta*, these laws appear in Abodah Zarah, the chapter that deals with pagans and with relationships between Jews and Gentiles. Even stranger, the portion of the text about the laws for the children of Noah is simply stuck on at the end of Abodah Zarah. It seems almost as if the editor had the material and knew that it belonged somewhere, but could not find quite the right place to put it. Centuries later, when there was an opportunity to arrange things into their proper places, the editors of the *Talmud* were able to move this material to the section dealing with other forms of law where it belonged.

The provisions of the law for the children of Noah in the *Tosefta* are found in Abodah Zarah 8.4–8.8. As usual in rabbinic materials, the text is presented as a conversation. In this case, some of the participants are anonymous while others are named specifically.

> 8.4 A. Concerning seven religious requirements were the children of Noah admonished:
>
> B. setting up courts of justice, idolatry, blasphemy [cursing the Name of God], fornication, bloodshed, and thievery.
>
> C. *Concerning setting up courts of justice*—how so?
>
> D. Just as Israelites are commanded to call into session in their towns courts of justice.
>
> E. *Concerning idolatry and blasphemy*—how so? . . .
>
> F. *Concerning fornication*—how so?
>
> G. "On account of any form of prohibited sexual relationship on account of which an Israelite court inflicts the death-penalty, the children of Noah are subject to warning," the words of R. Meir.

H. And sages say, "There are many prohibited relationships, on account of which an Israelite court does not inflict the death-penalty and the children of Noah are [not] warned. In regard to these forbidden relationships the nations are judged in accord with the laws governing the nations.

I. "And you have only the prohibitions of sexual relations with a betrothed maiden alone."

8.5 A. *For bloodshed*—how so?

B. A gentile [who kills] a gentile and a gentile who kills an Israelite are liable. An Israelite [who kills] a gentile is exempt.

C. *Concerning thievery?*

D. [If] one has stolen, or robbed, and so too in the case of finding a beautiful captive [woman] and in similar cases:

E. a gentile in regard to a gentile, or a gentile in regard to an Israelite—it is prohibited. And an Israelite in regard to a gentile—it is permitted.

8.6 A. *Concerning a limb cut from a living beast*—how so?

B. A dangling limb on a beast, [which] is not [so connected] as to bring about healing,

C. is forbidden for use by the children of Noah, and, it goes without saying, for Israelites.

D. But if there is [in the connecting flesh] sufficient [blood supply] bring about healing,

E. it is permitted to Israelites, and, it goes without saying, to the children of Noah.

F. [If] one took a bird which is not of the volume of an olive's bulk and ate it—

G. Rabbi declares exempt.

H. And R. Eleazar b. R. Simeon declares liable.

I. Said R. Eleazar b. R. Simeon, "Now if on account of a limb from a bird [which is alive] one is liable, for the whole [bird] should not one be liable?"

J. [If] one strangled it and ate it, he is exempt.

K. R. Hananiah b. Gamaliel says, "Also on account of blood deriving from a living beast,"

L. R. Hidqa says, "Also on account of castration."

M. R. Simeon says, "Also on account of witchcraft."

N. R. Yosé says, "On account of whatever is stated in the pericope regarding the children of Noah are they subject to warning,

O. "as it is said, *There shall not be found among you any one who burn his son or his daughter as an offering, any one who practices divination, soothsayer, or an augur, or a sorcerer, or a charmer, or a medium, or a wizard or a necromancer* (Deut. 18:10–11).

8.7 A. "Is it possible, then, that Scripture has imposed a punishment without imparting a prior warning?

B. "But it provides a warning and afterward imparts the punishment.

C. "This teaches that he has warned them first and then punished them."

8.8 A. R. Eleazar says, "Also as to 'mixed seeds'" it is permitted for child of Noah to sow seeds [which are mixed species] or to wear garment which are of mixed species [wool and linen].

B. "It is prohibited to breed a hybrid beast or to graft trees."[45]

The first six requirements—just courts and prohibitions on idolatry, blasphemy, fornication, bloodshed, and thievery—are similar in moral content and scope, while the last, having to do with food, is clearly more challenging. As part of the covenant with Noah, God said,

> Every moving thing that lives shall be food for you; and
> just as I gave you the green plants, I give you everything.
> Only, you shall not eat flesh with its life, that is, its
> blood. For your own lifeblood I will surely require a
> reckoning: from every animal I will require it and from
> human beings, each one for the blood of another, I will
> require a reckoning for human life. (Gen 9:3–5)

The rabbis typically struggle to understand exactly how one lives out the requirements of Torah, and their consideration of this section is no exception.

Was Non-Jewish Righteousness Discussed in the First Century?

The *Tosefta* was edited and completed after 200 CE, and this is at least a century and a half after Jesus and Paul were active in ministry. However, the *Tosefta* was compiled from earlier oral traditions, and some of those traditions were preserved from the period before the lives of Jesus and Paul. How can we tell whether the ideas in the laws for the children of Noah were in circulation during the time of Jesus' or Paul's life and ministry?

Identifying the different layers of the oral tradition within the *Mishnah* and the *Tosefta* is not easy. The good news is that the editors of the *Mishnah* and *Tosefta* as well as of the *Talmuds* probably accurately preserved the opinions of specific sages. The bad news is that they used the sayings to create conversations that could never have occurred during the rabbis' lifetimes. Jacob Neusner was the first to use literary criticism, developed for New Testament work, to study rabbinic writings. He and his student Gary Porton separated the layers by dating the words of specific speakers based on the times they lived.

Neusner describes the standard forms for statements of law in the writings. The material about the laws for the children of Noah uses the second variation of the standard form, where the named participants are in dispute or dialog with an anonymous statement of law.[46] In principle, an anonymous statement must be at least as old as the sages who comment on it. In this case, most of the conversation in AZ 8.4, 8.5, the beginning of 8.6, and 8.7 is completely anonymous, except for comment from R. Meier. The list in 8.4 A–B must not be later than the commentary on it in 8.4 C–F, 8.5, or 8.6 A–E. The principles in 8.6 F–O must not be earlier than the material they are supplementing. Thus we can make a time sequence that puts some lines of the passage either before or at the same time as others.

> 8.4 A–B (the list) must come before or at the same time as
> 8.4 C–F, 8.5, and 8.6 A–E, which must come before
> or at the same time as
> 8.6 F–O (which includes Rabbi, R. Eleazar b. R. Simeon, R. Hananiah b. Gamaliel, R. Hidqa, R. Simeon, R. Yosé)

Gary Porton has identified the time periods in which particular rabbis were active, and his list includes some of those who are mentioned in this "conversation."[47]

- Rabbi Hananiah ben Gamaliel active 70–135 CE
- Rabbi Hidqa active 70–135 CE
- Rabbi Meir active 135–160 CE
- Rabbi Simeon active 135–160 CE
- Rabbi Yosé active 135–160 CE
- Rabbi (Judah the Patriarch) active 160–220 CE
- Rabbi Eleazar ben Rabbi Simeon active 160–220 CE

Rabbi Hananiah ben Gamaliel and Rabbi Hidqa were both active in the period immediately following the destruction of the temple in 70 CE and before the revolt of Bar Kochba in 132–136 CE. Therefore the items identified in the list as applying to the children of Noah could not have been formulated later than that time. It is possible and reasonable that the anonymous conversation in the first part of the passage was in circulation before the destruction of the temple. If so, it would have been available to Jesus and to Paul during the time of their formation and ministry.

This dating is not commonly accepted among scholars. David Novak puts the time slightly later, in the period after the destruction of the temple. He bases this on the absence of earlier evidence for the laws and on the demarcation between Jews and Gentiles when conversion was no longer widespread.[48] I argue that it was exactly at a time when potential conversion was an active and even frequent process that the qualifications for potential converts would have been of interest. Markus Bockmuehl, who links these laws to the *ius gentium* of Roman civil law, also places their origins after the destruction of the temple. He argues that the comments of R. Meir put the date in the first half of the second century.[49] I argue that the discussions that lead to the conceptions of standards for Gentiles would have originated slightly earlier, when contact with Gentiles in a wide variety of relationships and circumstances were more likely.

Rabbinic Judaism's expectations for the righteous among the Gentiles grew out of the open and factionalized environment before the destruction of the temple. The range of interactions and relationships with Gentiles, from accommodating to the hostile, made Gentiles a topic for conversation and dispute. Jews participated in interactions with Gentiles at all levels of society during this period, and guidance for these interactions was needed. This guidance could be found in the Torah, and Scripture study would have revealed the basic expectations for Gentiles found in the Mosaic law. These expectations were later specified and clarified in rabbinic writings.

What Did the Early Rabbis Require of Non-Jews?

The various mentions of the laws for the children of Noah later in the Talmud show three capital offenses: fornication, bloodshed, and blasphemy or idolatry.[50] Bockmuehl points out that

The Noachide laws form the basic ethical foundation for both Jews and Gentiles: the extensive discussion in tractate *Sanhedrin* concludes that "there is nothing permitted to Jews that is forbidden to Gentiles."[51]

A similar perspective in a rabbinic decision is reported in the *Talmud* tractate Sanhedrin 74b, that on pain of death one may commit any transgression in the Torah, with the exception of idolatry, fornication, and bloodshed. One must rather die, as did the sons of 2 Maccabees 7:20–23, rather than commit any of these offenses.

The following is comparison of the provisions of the laws for the children of Noah with the Ten Commandments:

> You shall have no other gods before me. You shall not make for yourself an idol (Exod 20:3-4) – idolatry is prohibited

> You shall not make wrongful use of the name of the LORD your God (Exod 20:7) – blasphemy is prohibited

> Remember the sabbath day, and keep it holy. (Exod 20:8) – (no equivalent)

> Honor your father and your mother, so that your days may be long in the land that the LORD your God is giving you. (Exod 20:12) – (no equivalent)

> You shall not murder. (Ex 20:13) – bloodshed is prohibited

> You shall not commit adultery. (Ex 20:14) – fornication is prohibited

> You shall not steal. (Ex 20:15) – thievery is prohibited

> You shall not bear false witness against your neighbor.
> (Exod 20:16) – justice is required

> You shall not covet your neighbor's house; you shall
> not covet your neighbor's wife, or male or female slave,
> or ox, or donkey, or anything that belongs to your
> neighbor. (Exod 20:17) – (no equivalent)

The commandment to Noah that no person among you shall eat blood, nor shall any alien who resides among you eat blood (Lev 17:12) is equivalent to the requirement not eat the limb torn from a live animal, that flesh with the life of it, the blood in it, shall not be eaten.

The commandments about the Sabbath, honor to parents, and covetousness have no equivalents in the laws for all people. The equivalent to the restriction on eating the limb of a living animal is found within the dietary laws in Leviticus. With these exceptions, the prohibitions have very similar parallels in the commandments.

Moral Purity Is for All People

There is a clear distinction between the two different kinds of provisions within the law and the two different kinds of impurity caused by infractions of them. This distinction was evident in the writings that came out of early Judaism after the first century. The causes of moral impurity—idolatry, bloodshed, and sexual sins—are issues that, as we saw in the last chapter, were particularly identified in the Torah as applying to non-Jews. Richard Bauckham lists some of the many Scripture references that deal with the impurity caused by sin (Lev 16:30; Isa 1:16; 6:5; Jer 33:8; Ezek 36:33; Hos 5:3; 6:10; Ps 51:2, 7, 11; Prov 20:9; Eccl 7:20; Sir 21:28; 51:5; Jub 22:14; 34:19; Pss Sol 9:6; 18:5; 2 Bar 21:19; 39:6; 50:38; 60:2; 2 Enoch 10:4). He then observes that these sins usually fall into the categories of idolatry, sexual immorality (including incest as defined in Leviticus), and murder (shedding innocent blood).[52]

Ritual impurity, on the other hand, has to do with natural events that temporarily bar an Israelite from access to the sanctuary and from contact with others in the community. Ritual impurity is a concern for Jews rather than for Gentiles because it affects worship life and relationships in the family and the immediate community. Wherever there is a conflict between ritual and moral purity, the ritual yields to the moral.[53]

Sin and its resulting moral impurity are kept carefully distinct from failure to observe the provisions of the ritual law. Gentiles are capable of directing their own behavior and responsible for their sins, but they are not bound by the requirements and practices of ritual purification. In addition, compliance with dietary laws is not required for Gentiles, and those regulations have to do with neither ritual nor moral purity and impurity. The importance of the distinction between ritual and moral purity and the relevance of moral but not ritual purity for Gentiles will become evident in the teaching of Jesus and in the expectations of the New Testament churches.

If this understanding of the expectations for the children of Noah was available to the leaders of the early church, they would have known that the prohibitions of idolatry, blasphemy, fornication, and bloodshed would apply to all righteous Gentiles. In fact, idolatry, bloodshed, and fornication became the main points of prohibition for non-Jewish Christians in the ruling of the Jerusalem conference.

Questions for Reflection and Discussion

1. How are "purity" and "cleanness" misleading terms when talking about doing what the law asks? Can you think of better words?
2. Consider Leviticus 12. If you were the mother of a new baby, would you understand what you needed to do about your impurity?

3. Consider 2 Maccabees 6 and 7. How do these chapters show the seriousness of ritual purity requirements? How do the first-century Romans compare in this respect with the Greek rulers the Maccabees confronted two centuries earlier?

4. What are the consequences of moral failures, and how can they be addressed?

5. Make a list of the things you think a good person would do and not do. How does this list compare with the Ten Commandments and the seven laws for the children of Noah?

6. Consider the rabbis' conversation about the place of Gentiles in the world to come. What are the advantages of this kind of reasoning? What are the disadvantages?

7. Do you think Paul was aware of the conversation about the conditions for righteous Gentiles? Does his writing show signs of those conditions?

PART II

The Living Law of the New Testament

Jesus was born into interesting times. The Roman Empire with its military efficiency, bureaucracy, and communications exposed many relatively isolated cultures to a wider, cosmopolitan world. Israel had experienced a period of relative independence, and rebellion against outside rule, based in religious and ethnic identity, was everywhere. The faith centered in the second temple was lively, with great teachers, evangelism, conversion, puritan reform, new monastic communities, and new ideas all around.

Jesus was born and raised as a Jew, studied the Scriptures of his people, and engaged in the ongoing conversations of his time. As we read his words and about the events of his life, we read with patterns of thought and cultural assumptions of a multicultural and rationalistic society. In order to understand the teachings of Jesus and his followers, it is necessary, as much as possible, to immerse ourselves in the ways of thinking as well as the language and culture of the time.

The distinction between Jew and non-Jew was important to many aspects of life in the first century, and the struggle to bring both together in one community was visible in the early church. Within two centuries there was a sharp and hostile separation between "Jews "and largely non-Jewish "Christians". As a result, many of the Jewish assumptions about righteousness and law were lost to the church.

We can see the legacy of moral law, particularly as it related to Gentiles, throughout the New Testament. Jesus affirmed the complete law of Moses, and he taught that internal moral purity should not be lost in compliance with external details. Paul and the apostles expected righteousness to be the goal for all new believers, whether they were Jews or not.

Righteousness for all people was part of the understanding of the leaders who gathered for the Jerusalem council, and their decision reflects the same requirements for non-Jews as the Mosaic law. When later translation changed the decree from a moral to a food-related issue, the church abandoned its best explicit call to righteousness for all people. The connection was lost, and with it one of our greatest assets.

4

How Did Jesus Relate
to Jewish Law?

We have seen how to identify the moral provisions of the Mosaic law and how to identify the provisions that applied to non-Jews. Now it is time to look at the relationship that Jesus had with the law. People often assume that Jesus was somehow against the law because he often argued with scribes and Pharisees. Nothing could be further from the truth. In those days it was normal for teachers to argue among themselves about how the law worked in different situations. The questions that the authorities on law brought to Jesus are the same things they discussed in conversation with each other. These interactions show that Jesus was treated like a respected colleague in their conversations, not that he was an outsider or an enemy.

What Jesus said about the law was consistent with the Mosaic covenant and its view of righteousness and moral purity. In his explicit statements, Jesus openly supported the provisions of law in the covenant. He also criticized those he believed were living by the letter of the law while violating its spirit. Jesus attacked hypocrisy along with others of his time, but he did not attack the law recorded in the books of Moses. He took issue with the oral tradition of interpretation and application of the law, and he emphasized that internal conformity with the intent of the law was as important as external action. Jesus did not criticize the law itself, but he did attack those who claimed to live by it but did not.

Jesus built on the foundation of the Jewish culture into which he was born. He accepted its Scripture, its common wisdom, and the many ways that relationship with God was lived out. His teaching was not directed to creating a new religion or a new way of life. Instead, he interpreted the provisions of the Mosaic covenant to bring human practices closer to the will of God.

Non-Jewish Christians lost access to Jewish culture when Christianity and Judaism grew apart after the first century. As a result, later followers of Jesus assumed that some teachings that came out of his cultural background were his original insights. Jewish scholar Jacob Neusner describes this assimilation of ideas from his own Jewish perspective:

> Among the earliest writers in Jewish Christianity, Jesus finds ample representation not only as King-Messiah, but as prophet, perfect priest, and sacrificial victim, and always as sage or rabbi (which is why most of the sublime ethical sayings attributed to him in fact are commonplaces in other versions of Judaism.)[54]

Jewish scholar David Flusser shows more appreciation for Jesus' work of interpretation. Brad Young, a student of Flusser, tells of a conversation that happened one evening at Flusser's house in Jerusalem:

> In a Sunday evening seminar that met at Prof. Flusser's home, a religious Jewish student seemed offended by the esteem Prof. Flusser gave to the teachings of Jesus. The student remarked that he could write a gospel based on the Talmud. Prof. Flusser answered, "Yes. You could do that now, but only after Jesus, in his wisdom, had already done it for you."[55]

It is much easier to see how elements from the *Talmud* could be combined into a gospel after one has seen the way Jesus actually arranged them. As Flusser points out, "From ancient Jewish writings we could easily construct a whole gospel without using a single word that originated with Jesus. This could only be done, however, because we do in fact possess the gospels."[56] Jesus' achievement was in interpreting and prioritizing the material that he received, not in creating it out of whole cloth, independent of his faith or his culture.

In the Reformed tradition, John Calvin argued against misinterpreting the Mosaic law to reflect only external actions and not internal conviction: "This error . . . proceeds on the supposition that Christ added to the Law, whereas he only restored it to its integrity by maintaining and purifying it when obscured by falsehood."[57] For Calvin and the Reformed tradition, Jesus is one who restored the law to its original focus and purpose, not one who added to it or changed it.

One example shows how Jesus incorporated material available to him. The prominent teacher Antigonos of Sokho lived around 175 BCE, and the *Mishnah* reports his words, which include:

> Antigonos of Sokho received [the Torah] from Simeon the Righteous. He would say, (1) "Do not be like servants who serve the master on condition of receiving a reward, (2) but [be] like servants who serve the master not on condition of receiving a reward. (3) And let the fear of Heaven be upon you."[58]

Jesus used this idea of not being motivated by a reward in his teachings about making a show of piety (Matt 6:1), giving alms (Matt 6:2–4), fasting (Matt 6:16–18), and loving enemies (Matt 5:43–48, Luke 6:27–28, 32–36). Jesus did not invent the idea of not being motivated by a reward, but he used that idea in several different situations.

Much of the material Jesus used in his teaching was generally available in his culture during his lifetime. His principles were consistent with common wisdom and proverbs seen in literature inside and outside of the Scriptures.[59] The unique contribution Jesus made to understanding the law had two aspects: (1) he refocused priorities within the law and its application, and (2) the spread of his teaching made it possible for the principles in Jewish law to reach a wider audience in the Gentile world.

How Do We Know that Jesus Respected the Law?

According to his own words, Jesus did not come to eliminate the Mosaic law, but to live within the culture and expectations defined by it. It is the Scripture, after all, that gave his mission its meaning. In the opening section of the Sermon on the Mount, he says, "Do not think that I have come to abolish the law or the prophets; I have come not to abolish but to fulfill" (Matt 5:17).

Matthew emphasized fulfillment of prophecy as he related the events in Jesus' life. The Greek words translated here as "abolish" and "fulfill" have matching Hebrew words that refer to interpretation of Scripture. The Greek word καταλύω *(kataluō)* is equivalent to the Hebrew word אָבַד *(abad)*, which can include the idea of canceling Torah by misinterpreting it. The Greek word πληρόω *(plēroō)* is equivalent to the Hebrew word קוּם *(qum)*, which has a primary meaning of arise or stand. In Aramaic, the primary meaning to fulfill can also include confirm, ratify, or establish.[60] When Jesus began his sermon, he implied he would be strengthening and not undermining the law.

The sermon goes on to emphasize the importance of the Mosaic commandments.

> Therefore, whoever breaks one of the least of these commandments, and teaches others to do the same, will be called least in the kingdom of heaven; but whoever does them and teaches them will be called great in the kingdom of heaven. For I tell you, unless your righteousness exceeds that of the scribes and

Pharisees, you will never enter the kingdom of heaven.
(Matt 5:19–20)

Jesus set a standard of obedience to law for every person that should
be at least as high as that of those who devoted a lifetime to studying
the law. This is hardly a repudiation of the Mosaic law.[61]

Jesus often referred to the authority of the law in his responses to
questions. Luke reports that, when Jesus healed a man with leprosy, he
told the man to follow the procedure specified in the law. He said, "Go
and show yourself to the priest and make an offering for your cleansing,
just as Moses commanded" (Luke 5:14). When a ruler asked Jesus what
he should do, Jesus replied, "You know the commandments." He then
listed a sampling of the ten (Luke 18:18–20). When a lawyer approached
him with the same question, Jesus asked, "What is written in the Law?
How does it read to you?" He was satisfied when the lawyer replied
with the commandments to love God and neighbor (Luke 10:25–28).
Jesus even gave the devil himself quotations from the law (Deut 8:3;
Deut 6:13; Deut 6:16) in reply to his temptations.

Jesus spoke about the Mosaic law when he said, "truly I tell you,
until heaven and earth pass away, not one letter, not one stroke of a
letter, will pass from the law until all is accomplished" (Matt 5:18).
Jesus spoke, not just for the main points of the law, or for a selection
of the provisions of the law but for the whole thing. The law must be
kept complete and whole; even the smallest part must not be lost. This
reference to "one stroke of a letter" in the law also appears in Luke's
gospel:

> The law and the prophets were in effect until John
> came; since then the good news of the kingdom of
> God is proclaimed, and everyone tries to enter it by
> force. But it is easier for heaven and earth to pass away,
> than for one stroke of a letter in the law to be dropped.
> (Luke 16:16–17)

In a story from an early rabbinic commentary (Leviticus Rabbah 19.2), a book of law objects to dropping the tiny letter yod י from the word יַרְבֶּה *(yarbeth)*, which means to multiply or increase in number. Deuteronomy 17:16-17 says that a king must not "acquire many horses for himself" or "acquire many wives for himself." Rabbi Simeon ben Yochai taught that the book of Deuteronomy protested to the Holy One that King Solomon had acquired many wives and horses by ignoring this letter. The Holy One replied, "not even a single yod that is in you shall ever be cancelled."[62] When Jesus said that no letter could be dropped from the law, he was thinking like a rabbi. When Jesus talked about preserving every stroke of every letter in the law, he was speaking out of the traditions of his people in his respect for the whole law.

Did Jesus Teach about Purity?

Jesus addressed purity and defilement explicitly in one incident that appears in both the gospels of Matthew and Mark. This is one of his most important teachings about the law, and he used the word "defilement" in it. Pharisees and scribes attacked Jesus because his disciples did not wash their hands before eating as required by the oral law. In his response, Jesus made a policy statement:

> He called the crowd again and said to them, "Listen to me, all of you, and understand: there is nothing outside a person that by going in can defile, but the things that come out are what defile." (Mark 7:14–15)

To the disciples he gave this additional explanation:

> It is what comes out of a person that defiles. For it is from within, from the human heart, that evil intentions come: fornication, theft, murder, adultery, avarice, wickedness, deceit, licentiousness, envy, slander, pride,

folly. All these evil things come from within, and they defile a person. (Mark 7:20–23)

Matthew's gospel has a slightly different version of these sources of defilement.

But what comes out of the mouth proceeds from the heart, and this is what defiles. For out of the heart come evil intentions, murder, adultery, fornication, theft, false witness, slander. (Matt 15:18–19)

What these two lists have in common is that they include sources of impurity from the moral provisions and not the ritual provisions of the Mosaic law. For Jesus, the moral defilement of sin was far more important than ritual defilement coming from unwashed hands.

This story also makes a distinction between the written provisions of the Mosaic law and the oral traditions. The requirement for washing hands was part of the oral tradition but not part of the written law. The original question from the Pharisees and the scribes was "Why do your disciples not live according to the tradition of the elders, but eat with defiled hands?" (Mark 7:5) The violation was not one of written law but of oral tradition. Jesus' initial response was:

Isaiah prophesied rightly about you hypocrites, as it is written, "This people honors me with their lips, but their hearts are far from me; in vain do they worship me, teaching human precepts as doctrines." You abandon the commandment of God and hold to human tradition. (Mark 7:6–8)

Jesus emphasized the priority of the written law over oral traditions, and it is important to notice that he did not criticize or oppose the written law itself.

What was Jesus' position on ritual purity? We have the teaching of Jesus on a few particular topics such as divorce, making oaths, and Sabbath practices, but we have no mention of his actions in response to the ordinary sources of ritual impurity. Jesus must have encountered ordinary ritual impurity as he traveled, but we do not hear about his violating the procedures for dealing with it. He did not teach that the regulations about these ordinary sources of impurity were eliminated. Silence in this area means that whatever practice Jesus followed was not interesting to those around him and not surprising enough to merit their attention. Thus it is most likely that Jesus complied with the customary practice of the time.[63]

How Does Jesus Distinguish between Ritual and Moral Purity?

There is strong disagreement among scholars about how much Jesus distinguished between moral and ritual provisions in the law. John Meier, for example, wrote about the historical Jesus. He says that

> Hostile opposition between the "cultic," "ritual," or "purely legal" elements of the Mosaic law on the one hand and the "truly moral" or "ethical" elements on the other would have been alien to the mind-set of the ordinary Palestinian Jew of Jesus' day. . . . [A]ncient Jews saw no opposition between a type of behavior that was "purely ritual" (and hence to be considered of little value) and a type of behavior that was "purely moral" (and hence to be valued highly in the eyes of God).[64]

Meier presumes that a distinction between moral and ritual purity implies opposition between the two. He does not see that Jesus could make statements about the relative importance of two different approved aspects of doing God's will. It is possible to make distinction between "good" and "better" without forcing one of the choices to be considered "bad."

As an interpreter, Jesus affirmed the different priorities of oral tradition and written provisions of the purity code. He elevated written law to precedence over oral tradition. When he criticized those who used a minor regulation (making an offering) to get out of a major commandment (honoring parents) (Mark 7:9–13), he demonstrated the precedence of moral over ritual law. He compared an infraction of a less important kind (eating procedures) with impurity of a more significant kind (sin).

Jesus established the primary importance of moral purity by saying that what comes out of a person defiles and that evil intentions from the heart are the source of defilement.[65] The personal defilement of moral impurity is critically important. It is more important than tradition and more important than social conventions. Moral purity is alignment with the commandments of God, and it must not be set aside for human desires, preferences, traditions or wishful thinking. For Jesus, moral purity is a result of obedience to God's commandments as found in the moral law.

How and when did people come to assume that Jesus' comments about purity related to dietary laws? The comment "Thus he declared all foods clean" (Mark 7:19) most likely came out of a later Gentile Christian confusion about ritual purity and dietary laws. A papyrus with parallels to the gospel of Matthew,[66] probably written in the late second century, shows a similar misunderstanding. P. Oxyrhynchus 840 tells about a high priest claiming that "the Savior" and his disciples have not passed through ritual purification. Although the fragment shows some understanding of temple purification practices,[67] its attitude toward the water of the purification process does not match Jesus' verbal style and attitude toward purification.[68] By the time of the papyrus, understanding of second temple Jewish purity practices had been lost in the polarization between the early church and the Jewish community.

What Did Jesus Teach about Following the Law?

Jesus strongly criticized those not living in conformity with the law. These attacks did not focus on recognized "sinners" such as prostitutes, drunks, tax collectors, and other highly visible violators but were aimed at those who claimed to be living by the law but were doing it inadequately or halfheartedly. Jesus made strong statements to and about those who do not admit their failure to follow the law. The issue is not whether one should or should not follow the law; one is expected to follow it. What draws Jesus' anger is the pretense that someone is following the law while not actually doing it.

Jesus tells a parable about the two sons of a vineyard owner, neither of whom feels like obeying their father, to show different ways of responding to the commandments of the law.

> A man had two sons; he went to the first and said, "Son, go and work in the vineyard today." He answered, "I will not"; but later he changed his mind and went. The father went to the second and said the same; and he answered, "I go, sir"; but he did not go. Which of the two did the will of his father? (Matt 21:28–31)

Jesus tells this parable in the temple, and it is aimed at chief priests and elders. According to Matthew, the chief priests and Pharisees realize that the parable is told in order to criticize them directly.

Shortly afterward, Jesus spoke to his disciples and supporters: "The scribes and the Pharisees sit on Moses' seat; therefore, do whatever they teach you and follow it; but do not do as they do, for they do not practice what they teach." (Matt 23:1–3) Jesus' complaint is not about the law of Moses that the Pharisees teach, but about the fact that they do not follow that law themselves. Jesus emphasized that his followers must heed the law that the scribes and Pharisees teach, even though he criticized the behavior of those who teach it.

Matthew 23 and Luke 11 both contain a series of criticisms from Jesus to his opponents, although other similar criticisms are scattered throughout the gospels. Matthew identified the opponents as scribes and Pharisees, while Luke added lawyers as well. In some situations, chief priests, elders, and other members of the temple establishment were included. These criticisms fall into four general categories:

- Apparent compliance with the law is for show to impress a human audience.
- Compliance with law is an external action not matched by commitment of the heart.
- Trivial provisions are followed while the more important provisions are not.
- Teachers not conforming to law themselves are leading others astray.

The issue in all of these criticisms is not the authority of the law itself, but the lack of real conformity in those who claim the authority to lead.

Jesus criticized his opponents for their love of show, for the way they enjoyed the reactions of others to their appearance of holiness. He accused them of doing everything to be seen by others (Matt 23:5), of liking to be greeted with respect in the marketplace (Matt 23:7; Luke 11:43), of liking to be addressed as rabbi (Matt 23:7), of liking to have the best seats in the synagogues (Matt 23:6; Luke 11:43), and of enjoying the place of honor at banquets (Matt 23:6). Jesus tells his parable about choosing seats at a feast after watching guests of a Pharisee leader carefully choose their places at the table (Luke 14:7–11). Obedience to law, like good works and prayer (Matt 6:1–6), should not be for the applause of bystanders, but to do that which is directly pleasing to God.

Jesus, in common with others in later Judaism, emphasized the importance of conformity with law from the inside out. The intent behind an action is as important, or even more important, than the action itself. As Jesus said to one group of Pharisees, "You are those who justify yourselves in the sight of men, but God knows your hearts;

for that which is highly esteemed among men is detestable in the sight of God." (Luke 16:14–15)

In his discussion of washing hands (Matt 15:1–20; Mark 7:1–13), Jesus quoted Isaiah to say that the observances of the scribes and Pharisees are with words and not from the heart: "these people draw near with their mouths and honor me with their lips, while their hearts are far from me." (Isa 29:13) What is within matters, whether or not it is visible to others. "So you also on the outside look righteous to others, but inside you are full of hypocrisy and lawlessness." (Matt 23:28) Jesus focused on the irony of careful attention to washing cups and plates (see Mark 7:3–4), while the heart is full of hypocrisy and lawlessness (Matt 23:28) or greed and wickedness (Luke 11:39). God sees what is in the heart, and what is in the heart matters.

Jesus attacked those who emphasized less important parts of the law while violating critical ones. In his words, "You strain out a gnat but swallow a camel! (Matt 23:24)" It is not acceptable to ignore minor regulations because they are less important than major ones. Jesus is quite clear that all matter, and that one may not choose to practice some while ignoring others (Matt 23:23; Luke 11:42). However, important commands such as justice, mercy and faith (Matt 23:23) or justice and the love of God (Luke 11:39) cannot be ignored because one has been careful to tithe the produce from the herb garden. The commandment to honor father and mother cannot be set aside by making an additional donation to the temple (Mark 7:9–13). Jesus supported the whole law, and no one may pick and choose which provisions to honor or ignore. Each person needs to make sure that the most important parts of the law are given attention first, before those that are less critical.

Finally, Jesus criticized the leaders for the effect that their lack of true conformance with divine law is having on those around them. Jesus said, "you are like unmarked graves, and people walk over them without realizing it." (Luke 11:44) In these words, the leaders were compared with a hidden source of contagion, a place from which hidden impurity spreads to those who pass by without their noticing it. As Matthew records it, Jesus said, "you are like whitewashed tombs, which on the outside look beautiful, but inside they are full of the bones of the dead and of all kinds of filth." (Matt 23:27) All the effort on external image only covers inward impurity. The effort spent in nurturing converts is wasted.

The repeated theme is that the leaders are blind guides, leading the people in wrong directions because of their own darkness. Without the core commitment to God which is the center of the law, public practice degenerates into a hypocrisy which only pretends to focus on God. In the end, as Jesus explained to his disciples, pretense is pointless and all will be made clear. "Beware of the yeast of the Pharisees, that is, their hypocrisy. Nothing is covered up that will not be uncovered, and nothing secret that will not become known." (Luke 12:1–2)

Why would Jesus see these criticisms of the religious leaders of his day as part of his ministry? Malachi, in his prophecy against a corrupt priesthood, said of the coming Messiah,

> he is like a refiner's fire and like fullers' soap; he will sit as a refiner and purifier of silver, and he will purify the descendants of Levi and refine them like gold and silver, until they present offerings to the LORD in righteousness. (Mal 3:2–3)

This important part of Jesus' ministry was directed to the religious leaders of his day, challenging their complacency and holding a mirror to their hypocrisy and misplaced priorities. In his advocacy for the law, Jesus confronted those whose public role was to teach it, challenging them to live by what they taught.

Was Jesus the Messianic Interpreter of the Law?

Modern Christians are used to hearing that Jesus was the expected Messiah who was heir of David. We rarely hear about the other messiahs who were also expected in the first century. It turns out, looking at the literature of the time, that there can be as many as four messianic roles: the king of the house of David, the priest of the house of Aaron, the war leader of the house of Joseph, and the prophet representing Elijah. In the first century, many speculated about the Messiah or messiahs. Most scholars agree that there was an unreconciled diversity of opinion between groups and even within single groups.[69] Probably the one element that all agree on is that the Messiah or messiahs would be paragons of righteousness. They are exemplary in their respect for God and their conformance with the Torah.

The heir of David is the best known of the messianic figures. He will have an eternal kingdom, which he will rule with justice and righteousness. He will have many virtues—wisdom, understanding, counsel and might, knowledge, sanctification, fear of the Lord, truth, and uprightness.[70] Where there is a priestly messiah of the house of Aaron, he is also described as perfect in righteousness. He is the Interpreter of the Law, the one through whom the words of the Lord will be revealed. Sometimes he is also mentioned as the one who will judge the earth. He is represented by a star and called the Sun of Righteousness who walks with the children of mortals in gentleness. He and the heir of David are the ones through whom the Lord can be seen as living examples of righteousness. Some ancient sources expect these two roles to be filled by one single person.

Just as the kingly messiah must be a descendant of David, the priestly messiah must be a descendant of Aaron. Jesus is often referred to as a descendant of David, but could he be a descendant of Aaron as well? According to Jesus ben Sirach, descent in the Davidic line works differently from the descent of the children of Aaron. Descent in David's line is only from father to son, while descent from Aaron passes through all children, male and female. Jesus can only be an heir to David through his father, Joseph, but he could be an heir to Aaron through his mother's family.

What do we know about Mary's family? Mary is a blood relative, συγγενίς (*syngenis*), of Elizabeth, wife of the priest Zechariah (Luke 1:36). Elizabeth herself is described as a daughter of Aaron (Luke

1:5), carrying the inheritance of the children of Aaron. As her blood relative, Mary can also be expected to be a daughter of the house of Aaron. Jesus received from his mother the right of descent that would make him eligible to be the priestly messiah, the Messiah of Aaron.

Looking at the work of interpretation Jesus did with the law, it is likely that this priestly role of Interpreter of the Law was a conscious part of his ministry. Why did Jesus' interpretation lead to different conclusions from those of the rabbis? Brad Young considers the way the same law that influenced Jesus also informed the rabbis and how that same material could lead to different conclusions.

> First and foremost, the Gospels and the rabbis are connected to each other through a common Jewish heritage. The real question is to discover the rich sources that formed a foundation, or database, for both the Gospels and the rabbinic literature. Jesus used this database in different ways than the rabbis did. The powerful originality of Jesus is discovered in the incredible combinations of teachings he puts together.[71]

How Did Jesus Interpret Scripture?

Jesus was clear that his role was not to change the content of the law in any way (Matt 5:17–18). He wanted the priorities among the provisions of the law to match the intent behind the law in order to achieve righteousness from the heart outward. One may not disobey the law at will, but one must make sure that the most important aspects of the law are given attention first, before those that are less critical.

In the rabbinic writings, the wisdom of the fathers in Abot in the *Mishnah* describes four patterns of thought for those who come to learn from the sages—the sponge, funnel, strainer, and sifter.

> There are four traits among those who sit before the
> sages: a sponge, a funnel, a strainer, and a sifter. A
> sponge—because he sponges everything up; a funnel—
> because he takes in on one side and lets out on the
> other; a strainer—for he lets out the wine and keeps
> in the lees; and a sifter—for he lets out the flour and
> keeps in the finest flour.[72]

A sifter is one who separates the coarse particles from the fine flour,
picking and choosing from all that is acceptable to find the particles
that are the best. Jesus saw himself as a sifter and described his ideal
teacher of the law: "Therefore every scribe who has been trained for
the kingdom of heaven is like the master of a household who brings
out of his treasure what is new and what is old." (Matt 13:52) This
expert teacher, like Jesus himself, is one who chooses from among
many possibilities and brings out of the treasure the most precious
parts, both old and new.

Jesus and his followers, like the Pharisees with whom they
interacted, were grounded in Scripture. The differences between the
directions in their teachings had to do with the way the elements of
the Scripture were prioritized and used in practice. Pharisees and the
rabbis of the *Mishnah*, for example, paid attention to parts of Leviticus
and Numbers, while Jesus and his followers paid attention to other
parts of Scripture that the Pharisees ignored. From the neutral base
of Scripture, we can trace the similarities and differences between the
interpretations Jesus proposed and those that were accepted in his
environment at the time.

How "Jewish" Were Jesus' Teachings?

David Flusser notes that within the Synoptic gospels Jesus is shown
as a faithful and law-observant Jew.[73] As a result, it should not be
surprising that many of his teachings were consistent with popular

positions. For example, while Jesus disagreed with the Pharisees about the authority of the oral traditions, he agreed with them about resurrection of the dead.

His emphasis on care for those in need was consistent not only with the Hebrew Bible but also with the expectations of his contemporaries. When Jesus said, "Give to everyone who begs from you, and do not refuse anyone who wants to borrow from you" (Matt 5:42) he was echoing the ideas of his predecessor Jesus ben Sirach:

> Do not reject a suppliant in distress, or turn your face away from the poor. Do not avert your eye from the needy, and give no one reason to curse you; for if in bitterness of soul some should curse you, their Creator will hear their prayer. (Sir 4:4–6)

The teaching of Jesus on forgiveness, requiring forgiving others first, also echoes ben Sirach: "Forgive your neighbor the wrong he has done, and then your sins will be pardoned when you pray." (Sir 28:2) Jesus concludes his instruction on prayer in the Sermon on the Mount with very similar words: "For if you forgive others their trespasses, your heavenly Father will also forgive you; but if you do not forgive others, neither will your Father forgive your trespasses." (Matt 6:14–15)

Similarly, resolving conflicts with others was also a contemporary concern. Making peace with others who have been hurt was a requirement for forgiveness on the Day of Atonement.

> This exegesis did R. Eleazar b. Azariah state: "*From all your sins shall you be clean before the Lord* (Lev. 16:30)— for transgressions between man and the Omnipresent does the Day of Atonement atone. For transgressions between man and his fellow, the Day of Atonement atones, only if the man will regain the good will of his friend."[74]

71

Jesus shared this requirement as well:

> So when you are offering your gift at the altar, if you
> remember that your brother or sister has something
> against you, leave your gift there before the altar and
> go; first be reconciled to your brother or sister, and then
> come and offer your gift. (Matt 5:23–24)

The teaching of Jesus about judging others is also very similar to the teaching of the great rabbi Hillel who lived in the generation before him. Hillel said, "Do not walk out on the community. And do not have confidence in yourself until the day you die. And do not judge your fellow until you are in his place. And do not say anything which cannot be heard, for in the end it will be heard."[75] Jesus expressed his prohibition of judgment even more strongly:

> Do not judge, so that you may not be judged. For with the
> judgment you make you will be judged, and the measure
> you give will be the measure you get. (Matt 7:1–2)

Jesus was selecting and reflecting ideas that were already present in his environment, but in these situations bringing them to attention and emphasizing their importance.

In some cases where the teachings of Jesus were similar to positions of those around him, he added different emphases. For example, Jesus' teaching on humility goes beyond that taught by other rabbis,[76] who put limits on the blame for those who act "presumptuously."[77] Ithamar Gruenwald describes the way Jesus made a change in the understanding of maiming. When the rabbis dealt with the verse "An eye for an eye and a tooth for a tooth," they were concerned with judicial implications. Jesus, on the other hand, was primarily concerned with a moral issue.[78] The rabbis did not make a point of the issue Jesus raised because their concern was with how to implement the law, while his concern was with the moral issues involved in revenge.

Jesus and his followers visited the temple often and accepted the authority of the temple leadership. This was not true for some other groups at the time, such as the Qumran community which rejected the temple establishment.[79] Jesus taught in the temple and visited it in festival seasons (Luke 19:47; John 18:19–20). After his departure, Jesus' followers continued to meet and worship there (Luke 24:52–53; Acts 2:46).

There are many possible explanations for Jesus' behavior during the incident of the "cleansing" of the temple (Matt 21:12–17; Mark 11:15–19; Luke 19:45–48; John 2:13–25). In using the quotation from Isaiah, Jesus affirms the place of non-Jews in the temple.[80]

> And the foreigners who join themselves to the LORD, . . . these I will bring to my holy mountain, and make them joyful in my house of prayer; their burnt offerings and their sacrifices will be accepted on my altar; for my house shall be called a house of prayer for all peoples. (Isa 56:6–7)

In saying "you have made it a den of robbers" (Matt 21:13; Mark 11:17; Luke 19:46), Jesus may have been protesting against corruption and greed in the temple, against the temple tax, against the coin used, against trading in the temple, against taking advantage of poor pilgrims, or against the temple's placing a financial burden on the poor. Regardless of the specific cause, Jesus was defending the temple itself and trying to restore it to the standard in the vision God gave to Isaiah.

The use of purity regulations was changing during Jesus' lifetime. Food regulations, which had only been required during festival times, were becoming a regular daily practice in ordinary homes. Jesus criticized the Pharisees, who were advocates of increasing purity requirements in daily life, saying "They tie up heavy burdens, hard to bear, and lay them on the shoulders of others; but they themselves are unwilling to lift a finger to move them." (Matt 23:4) Jesus may have been opposed to the increase in requirements for food preparation during ordinary times, without being opposed to the ritual purity regulations and processes in general.

Where Did the Priority of Love Come From?

Probably the best place to see Jesus' change of focus regarding the law is in the question about the most important commandment. When Jesus is asked for the greatest commandment, he answers by quoting the verses from Deuteronomy 6:4–5 as they appear in Greek in the *Septuagint*:

> The first is, "Hear, O Israel: the Lord our God, the Lord is one; you shall love the Lord your God with all your heart, and with all your soul, and with all your mind, and with all your strength." (Mark 12:29–30)

This first part of his response was one with which most Jews, including his opponents, would have agreed. Then Jesus raised a second issue:

> The second is this, "You shall love your neighbor as yourself." There is no other commandment greater than these. (Mark 12:31)

All could agree on the first commandment, but where did Jesus find his choice for second?

It comes from the middle of a list of Levitical laws for ritual and moral holiness, after the laws forbidding partiality and unjust judgments and before the laws against interbreeding animals and sowing a field with mixed seed. The law that said one must love one's neighbor was always there (Lev 20:18), but Jesus shined a light on it and raised it to a level of attention and importance that it had not had before. This is a work of interpretation, of relative prioritization, and not an act of elimination or disrespect to the remainder of the law.

The technique that Jesus used to link the two verses (Deut 6:5; Lev 20:18) was common in rabbinic interpretation at the time. The two phrases have a similar structure, and they begin with the same word/phrase "and you shall love" (וְאָהַבְתָּ *'āhabtā*).[81] For Jesus, already particularly conscious of the role of love, this use of love, אָהַב *(ahab)*, would cause the similarity between the verses to leap off the page and bring the second commandment to high priority in his attention along with the first.

Jesus brought the law of love to prominence, but he also extended the requirement to love beyond love of one's neighbor. In the parable of the Samaritan (Luke 10:25–37), Jesus defines a neighbor as one who acts out of love—one who shows mercy—rather than as one who shares any other characteristics of culture, religion, or proximity. Jesus interprets the command to love as expanding far beyond contemporary practices.

> You have heard that it was said, "You shall love your neighbor and hate your enemy." But I say to you, Love your enemies and pray for those who persecute you, so that you may be children of your Father in heaven; for he makes his sun rise on the evil and on the good, and sends rain on the righteous and on the unrighteous. (Matt 5:43–45)

This sense of God's blessing on the undeserving as well as the deserving also appears in the *Mekhilta of Rabbi Ishmael* in the commentary on Exodus 15:2. This rabbinic commentary edited by the first half of the second century on the victory of Jehoshaphat in 2 Chronicles 20:21 talks about the rejoicing—or rather the lack of it—before the Lord over the deaths of the wicked: "But it is as though there were no rejoicing before him in the heights on account of the annihilations of the wicked."[82] God's mercy, according to the *Mekhilta*, extends to all, and not only the righteous:

> "I will sing to the Lord," who is merciful: "The Lord, the Lord, God, merciful and gracious (Exod 34:6); "For the Lord your God is a merciful God" (Deut 4:31);

> "The Lord is good to all, and his tender mercies are
> over all his works" (Ps 145:9).[83]

Flusser explains that this mindset was an active part of Jewish thought
of the Greek and Roman period. Because people were no longer easily
separated into the good and the wicked, some had discovered that God
showed love and mercy to all.[84] For the rabbis, imitating God's actions,
being merciful as God is merciful, is a demonstration of our respect.[85]
Jesus extended this to say that we are to love the way God loves—freely,
unconditionally, without consideration of reward or return—simply
because it is God's way.

> But love your enemies, do good, and lend, expecting
> nothing in return. Your reward will be great, and you
> will be children of the Most High; for he is kind to the
> ungrateful and the wicked. Be merciful, just as your
> Father is merciful. (Luke 6:35–36)

Jesus emphasized and magnified the importance of love for all,
particularly for enemies, on this basis. His interpretation broadened
the use of current teachings about love and mercy and led to his truly
revolutionary application of love in situations of hostility, opposition,
and hatred.

Jesus did not suggest that the law of love should become a substitute
for the whole law itself. Jesus saw these two commandments as the
greatest among many, not as the only portion of the law to consider.
This focus on love within the law led to stronger teaching about
relationships with others.

Was the Golden Rule Unique to Jesus?

Treating others as we would like to be treated is an extension of
the concept of love for all others. It would be hard to say who first

invented the Golden Rule, but Jesus demonstrated the importance in the law of treating others the way one would want to be treated. "In everything do to others as you would have them do to you; for this is the law and the prophets." (Matt 7:12) The great Pharisee sage Hillel, who lived a generation before Jesus, made a similar comment about the importance of the Golden Rule to a student who wanted to learn the whole law quickly.

> A certain gentile once came to Hillel and said, "I'm ready to become a Jew, but only if you can teach me the whole Torah while I stand on one foot." Hillel answered him, "What is hateful to you, don't do to your fellowman; that is the whole Torah, and the rest . . . is just a commentary. Go then and learn it!"[86]

For Jesus, the law to love others grew out of the parts of the law that specified the duty to love all people, Jew and non-Jew.[87]

> You shall not take vengeance or bear a grudge against any of your people, but you shall love your neighbor as yourself: I am the LORD. (וְאָהַבְתָּ לְרֵעֲךָ כָּמוֹךָ) (Lev 19:18)

> The alien who resides with you shall be to you as the citizen among you; you shall love the alien as yourself, for you were aliens in the land of Egypt: I am the LORD your God (כְּאֶזְרָח מִכֶּם יִהְיֶה לָכֶם הַגֵּר | הַגֵּר אִתְּכֶם וְאָהַבְתָּ לוֹ כָּמוֹךָ) (Lev 19:34)

Jesus stressed the importance of love and equal treatment for all kinds of neighbors in conformity with the law in the Torah.

How Did Jesus Advocate for the Disadvantaged?

For Jesus, care for those in need went far beyond providing for their physical needs through acts of charity required by law. He advocated full inclusion for all people, including children, in the gospel message. Jewish scholar Alan Segal points out that Jesus' audience included a wide range of people who had an urgent interest in what he had to say. They included social outcasts such as prostitutes and tax collectors, as well as ordinary people with low self-esteem (Matt 19:30; Mark 10:31; Luke 13:30).[88] All people—regardless of their wealth or lack of it, their social acceptability, their physical condition, or their age, gender, and ethnicity—were offered equal access to acceptability before God through repentance and forgiveness. Segal observes that the message that all are equal before God was also typical of the end-times prophecy of different sects at the time.[89]

Repentance and forgiveness form a single point of entry for everyone into the gospel. Jesus' gospel always began with a call to repentance. No one, from the self-righteously religious to the publicly sinful, received a free pass from the requirement to turn away from the sinful behaviors of his or her previous life. Jesus' invitation welcomed all, often to the surprise of the disciples, his other followers, and even his opponents.

As Jesus explained to his host at dinner, after a parable about the similarity between forgiveness and canceling debts of various sizes, "Therefore, I tell you, her sins, which were many, have been forgiven; hence she has shown great love. But the one to whom little is forgiven, loves little." (Luke 7:47) Women, children, outcasts, criminals, foreigners, and even those with skin diseases were offered the same opportunity and equal treatment in both judgment and forgiveness. Equal justice for all, in the sense of law equally applied and mercy equally offered, was a hallmark of the gospel.

What Did Jesus Teach about Marriage and Divorce?

One of the most interesting and problematic discrepancies between the teachings of Jesus and the Mosaic law is the teaching on marriage and divorce. In modern times, the focus is typically on the statements about divorce.

> They said, "Moses allowed a man to write a certificate of dismissal and to divorce her." But Jesus said to them, "Because of your hardness of heart he wrote this commandment for you. But from the beginning of creation, 'God made them male and female.' 'For this reason a man shall leave his father and mother and be joined to his wife, and the two shall become one flesh.' So they are no longer two, but one flesh. Therefore what God has joined together, let no one separate." (Mark 10:4–9)

Jesus acknowledged that the Mosaic law allowed divorce, and he provided an explanation for it. Human hardness of heart permits a separation for one who is suffering from being bound to an unloving spouse. In a mutually loving context, one where the kingdom of God is in control, this option for safety would no longer be needed.[90] Lutz Doering, comparing this passage from Mark with the Damascus covenant from Qumran, believes that the divorce provision in Deuteronomy 24:1 is an emergency ruling no longer needed.[91] Jesus does not question the need for the provisions for divorce in a destructive marriage relationship, but he puts responsibility for the disruption of the relationship on the one who causes the separation.

Jesus does not abandon the Scripture in questioning the provision for divorce. Instead, he goes back to a prior level of authority.[92] Jesus is clear that the foundation of marriage is not within the Mosaic law, but it is established at the very beginning of creation to apply to all human beings:

Have you not read that the one who made them at the beginning 'made them male and female,' and said, 'For this reason a man shall leave his father and mother and be joined to his wife, and the two shall become one flesh'? So they are no longer two, but one flesh. Therefore what God has joined together, let no one separate. (Matt 19:4–6)

In the Damascus covenant found at Qumran, marriage issues are addressed also by appeal to creation.[93] The joining of a man and a woman reflects God's intent at creation for a complementary pair to become a single unit.

Why Should We Care about Small Infractions?

Jesus was clear that small violations of the law were to be taken very seriously because smaller offenses, if not dealt with, would lead to similar major offenses. The rabbinic commentators in *Sifré to Deuteronomy* also shared this concern.

If, however, a person who is the enemy of another lies in wait for him and sets upon him . . . (Deut. 19:11–13). On this basis, sages have ruled: If a person has violated a minor religious requirement, in the end such a person will violate a major religious requirement. If one has violated the rule, "You will love your neighbor as yourself" (Lev. 19:18), in the end that person will violate the rule, "you shall not take vengeance nor bear any grudge" (Lev. 19:18), "You shall not hate your brother" (Lev. 19:17), and "That your brother may live with you" (Lev. 25:26), ending up shedding blood.[94]

The *Sifré to Numbers* says, "In the beginning sin is like a silken thread, but in the end it is like a cart rope."[95]

> Rabbi says, "He who does a single religious duty for its own sake need not rejoice on account of that single religious duty alone, for in the end it will bring to pass successful performance of many more religious duties. And he who does a single transgression should not worry about that transgression alone, for in the end it will make a great many transgressions come to pass, for doing one religious duty makes possible the doing of many more, and doing one transgression brings about the doing of many more."[96]

Small offenses lead to larger ones, and single offenses lead to many more.

From the time of the Maccabees, all violations of law were to be taken seriously because small violations could lead to a lack of respect for the law itself.

> We, O Antiochus, who have been persuaded to govern our lives by the divine law, think that there is no compulsion more powerful than our obedience to the law. Therefore we consider that we should not transgress it in any respect. . . . Therefore do not suppose that it would be a petty sin if we were to eat defiling food; to transgress the law in matters either small or great is of equal seriousness, for in either case the law is equally despised. (4 Macc 5:16–17, 19–21)

Jesus agrees that all the commandments matter, those seen as critical as well as only minor ones.

> Therefore, whoever breaks one of the least of these commandments, and teaches others to do the same, will

> be called least in the kingdom of heaven; but whoever
> does them and teaches them will be called great in the
> kingdom of heaven. (Matt 5:19)

The word *least* (ἐλάχιστος *elachistos*) here implies small or light, as opposed to the more important or weighty commandments.[97] In his condemnation of hypocrites, Jesus said that they "have neglected the weightier matters of the law: justice and mercy and faith. It is these [they] ought to have practiced without neglecting the others." (Matt 23:23) Focusing on the more important commandments does not mean that the others can be neglected. Jesus is clear that all commandments matter, not just "important" ones. This implies a stricter application of law for his followers rather than a more lenient one.

Jesus specifically addresses three areas in which small offenses lead to larger ones: anger leading to murder, lust leading to adultery, and false oaths.

> You have heard that it was said to those of ancient
> times, "You shall not murder"; and "whoever murders
> shall be liable to judgment." But I say to you that if you
> are angry with a brother or sister, you will be liable to
> judgment; (Matt 5:21–22)

> You have heard that it was said, "You shall not commit
> adultery." But I say to you that everyone who looks at a
> woman with lust has already committed adultery with
> her in his heart. (Matt 5:27–28)

> Again, you have heard that it was said to those of
> ancient times, "You shall not swear falsely, but carry
> out the vows you have made to the Lord." But I say to
> you, Do not swear at all. (Matt 5:33–34)

In these three examples, presented in parallel constructions in the Sermon on the Mount, Jesus makes it clear that the weighty commandments—murder, adultery, and a false oath in the name of God—each have their precursors. Jesus forbids the smaller sins which lead to the larger: dwelling on anger which leads to violent action, indulging in lustful fantasies which lead to forbidden sexuality, and any use of an oath in addition to a simple statement of commitment.

Did Jesus Live by the Law?

Jesus positioned himself as a strong advocate for the Mosaic law. He explicitly stated his purpose to uphold rather than undermine or supersede the law. He reinforced the understanding that defilement—moral impurity—was the product of evil intentions that come from the heart, while he emphasized the critical nature of moral purity. He supported the primacy of the written Torah over the practices of oral tradition. He repeatedly criticized those who claimed to live according to the law, but whose conformance was incomplete or inadequate. His solid support for the written law became the basis for his interpretation of the relative priorities of the provisions within the law.

Jesus accepted the provisions of the law as they stood for observant Jews. He often focused on the moral implications of law, while his contemporaries tended to focus on judicial implications—ways to conform to the law through specific actions. Jesus was emphatic about the importance of following the whole law and not simply selecting those parts that one considered to be more important.[98]

With this sense of the priorities within the law, behavior is seen primarily through its impact on relationships—our relationships with God and with each other. What was permitted and encouraged is still encouraged. What was forbidden is still forbidden, but behavior is defined in terms that include broader implications for relationships. We cannot make a decision based on physical actions taken, such as picking or picking up grain. We need to include broader considerations, including human needs, conflicting considerations, selection of principles to be engaged, and, above all, impact on relationships.

Jesus did not reject the law or even rearrange it. He did expand the territory in which it applied, moving from simple external action into the territory of the mind, heart, and soul.

Questions for Reflection and Discussion

1. Have you had the feeling that Jesus rejected or was somehow "against" the law?

2. Consider Matthew 4:1–11, Deuteronomy 8:3; 6:13; and 6:16. How does Jesus use the law to respond to his own temptations?

3. Consider Luke 18:18–21. Why do you think Jesus made the choice to quote the law rather than reply in his own words?

4. Consider Luke11:43–44. With what you understand about ritual impurity, why is an unmarked grave particularly dangerous to those who touch it?

5. Consider Matthew 15:3–9. What priority is Jesus advocating?

6. Consider Matthew 23:23. Does the focus Jesus brings to some aspects of the law mean that one can bypass others?

7. Consider Mark 7:14–23. What does Jesus mean by "defilement" in his list of evils that come out of the human heart?

8. Consider Matthew 5:43–48 and Leviticus 19:17–18 and 33–34. How is Jesus reflecting what is already present in the law?

9. Why did Jesus come to different conclusions from the scribes and Pharisees using the same Scripture?

5

How Did Jesus and His Followers Include Non-Jews?

Do you believe that Jesus intended his message exclusively for Jews, or that he meant it to be for both Jews and Gentiles? There is a misconception, based on a conversation that Jesus had with a Syrophoenecian woman in Mark 7:24–30, that Jesus only intended to reach out to the people of Israel. This misconception is far from the truth.

Jesus taught mixed crowds of Jews and non-Jews in the international environment of the Roman province of Palestine. Gentiles as well as Jews received in his gospel message. Jesus interacted with Gentiles and healed them. One Gentile woman whom he met at a well in Samaria was the first to go and spread the message from Jesus to her neighbors. Jesus spoke about the saving faith that he found in Gentiles. The messianic age described by the prophets had included a welcome for all nations, and the mission to the Gentiles was anticipated in Jesus' teaching well before the Great Commission. Jesus affirmed that Gentiles were welcome and included in the kingdom of God.

How Did Jews Get Along with
Non-Jewish Neighbors?

The earliest layers of conversation in the *Mishnah* and *Tosefta* provide a window into life in first century Palestine. Daily life in a world shared by Jews and Gentiles can be seen in a conversation about work begun just before the sunset that marks the start of the Sabbath. As often happens, this dialog takes place between the more lenient Pharisees who were followers of Hillel and the stricter sect who followed Shammai.

> 1.7 IV A The House of Shammai say, "They do not sell [anything] to a gentile or bear a burden with him,
> B "and they do not lift up a burden onto his back,
> C "unless there is sufficient time for him to reach a nearby place [while it is still day]."
> D And the House of Hillel permit.

> 1.8 V A The House of Shammai say, "They do not give hides to a [gentile] tanner,
> B "or clothing to a gentile laundryman,
> C "unless there is sufficient time for them to be done while it is still day."
> D And in the case of all of them,
> E the House of Hillel permit,
> F while the sun is still shining.[99]

The additional comments in the *Tosefta* build on the passage in the *Mishnah*:

> 1.22 A The House of Shammai say, "They do not sell [anything] to a gentile or bear a burden with him, and they do not lift up a burden onto his back, unless there is sufficient time for him to reach a nearby place" [M. Shab. 1.7A–C]
> B And what is the definition of a nearby place?

C [sufficient time for him] to reach the house nearest
the town-wall.

D R. 'Aqiba says, "Sufficient time for him to go out the
door before the day is sanctified [through sunset]."

E Said R. Eleazar b. R. Sadoq, "Members of the
household of Rabban Gamaliel had the habit of
giving white clothes to a gentile laundryman three
days before the Sabbath [M. Shab. 1.9A],

F "and colored ones on the eve of the Sabbath."

G Accordingly we infer that white ones are harder to
do than colored ones.[100]

These passages show Jews and Gentiles living together cooperatively.
The regulations of the Torah were in force; there was no question
about the importance of honoring the Sabbath. The question was how
to honor the Sabbath properly. This interchange shows consideration
for the Gentile, to prevent an inadvertent violation of the Sabbath.
Shammai's followers, being stricter, forbid putting the Gentile into a
difficult position, while Hillel's followers, traditionally more lenient,
avoid a restriction. The reference to the practice of Gamaliel the Elder
demonstrates his model of thoughtfulness when giving work to non-Jews.

From this example, we can infer that living and working with
Gentile neighbors was not a matter of hostility or avoidance, but of
accommodation and consideration. Compliance with Sabbath-keeping,
purity codes, and festival celebration was required. The concern was
with how to live out those requirements in a way that was considerate
of all parties.

How Did Jews Relate to Potential Converts?

Pharisees were aggressive in promoting Judaism to potential
converts. Several stories attributed to the great Pharisee leader Hillel
attest to his enthusiasm for conversion. He is quoted in the *Mishnah*:

1.12 V A Hillel and Shammai received [it] from them.

    B Hillel says, (1) "Be disciples of Aaron, loving peace and pursuing peace, loving people and drawing them near to the Torah."[101]

The following story shows a group of Pharisees struggling to find a way to accept a convert descended from the ancient enemies of Israel:

4.4 IV A On that day:

    B Judah an Ammonite proselyte came and stood before them in the *bet hamidrash.*

    C He said to them, "Am I allowed to enter the congregation?"

    D Rabban Gamaliel said to him, "You are forbidden [to enter the congregation]."

    E R. Joshua said to him, "You are permitted."

    F Rabban Gamaliel said to him, "Scripture says, *An Ammonite or a Moabite shall not enter into the assembly of the Lord, even to the tenth generation* (Deut. 23:4)."

    G R. Joshua said to him, "And are there Ammonites and Moabites in this place?

    H "Already has Sennacherib, king of Assyria, come up and mixed up all the nations.

    I "As it is said, *I have removed the bounds of the peoples and have robbed their treasures and have brought down as a valiant man them that sit on thrones* (Is. 10:13)."

    J Rabban Gamaliel said to him, "Scripture says, *But afterward I will bring again the captivity of the children of Ammon* (Jer. 49:6). "And indeed they have returned."

    K R. Joshua said to him, "Scripture says, *And I will return the captivity of my people Israel and Judah, says the Lord* (Amos 9:14). "And as yet they have not returned."

    L And they permitted him to enter into the congregation.[102]

Clearly, it was worth reasoning to find a way for this well-intentioned and respectful descendant of the Ammonites to join the congregation of Israel.

In the highly stratified society of the first century, converts (proselytes) were not quite equal to natural-born Israelites. For example, as a general principle,

> 3.8 A A priest takes precedence over a Levite, a Levite over
> an Israelite, an Israelite over a *mamzer*, a *mamzer*
> over a *Netin*, a *Netin* over a proselyte, a proselyte
> over a freed slave.
> B Under what circumstances?
> C When all of them are equivalent.[103]

Because a proselyte was not truly a descendant of Abraham, the language of his prayers needed to be slightly different:

> 1.4 A These [people] bring [firstfruits] but do not recite:
> B a proselyte brings but does not recite,
> C because he is not able to say, "[I have come into the
> land] which the Lord swore to our fathers to give
> us," (Deut. 26:3).
> D But if his mother was an Israelite, he brings and
> recites.
> E And when he [the proselyte] prays in private, he
> says, "God of the fathers of Israel."
> F And when he prays in the synagogue, he says, "God
> of your fathers."
> G [But] if his mother was an Israelite, he says, "God
> of our fathers."[104]

A further restriction prevents women who are descended from proselytes in particular ways from marrying into a priestly family.

In general, Pharisees were happy to encourage proselytes to make the journey into membership in the people of Israel. Even Jesus, who was not being particularly polite to the Pharisees at the time, said, "You cross sea and land to make a single convert" (Matt 23:15). The Jewish reputation for encouraging conversion was so well known that the Roman poet Horace used it in a joke at the very end of his first satiric poem, published around 32 BCE:

> This is one of those lesser frailties I spoke of, and if you would make no allowance for it, then would a big band of poets come to my aid—for we are the big majority— and we, like the Jews, will compel you to make one of our throng.[105]

Whether the stories attributed to Hillel are authentic or not, the spirit they capture was part of the Pharisees' reputation for encouraging conversion. When Jesus encouraged and accepted non-Jews, he was acting like other teachers of his time.

How Did Jews Relate to Foreign Military?

The most visible non-Jews in Palestine in the first century were the soldiers of the occupying Roman army. Strangely, there seem to be mixed feelings about this foreign presence. When rebellion erupted, Pharisees found themselves on both sides of the revolt against Rome— both active in the fighting and advocating for peace. On the eve of the revolt in 66 CE, Pharisees were united with other leaders in trying to preserve peace.

Our best source for information about this time is the historian Josephus. Josephus was a Jewish army commander who was captured, taken to Rome, and adopted into the emperor's family. Here are some excerpts from his account of the conflict:

> Hereupon the men of power got together, and conferred with the high priests, as did also the principal of the Pharisees; and thinking all was at stake, and that their calamities were becoming incurable, took counsel what was to be done. Accordingly they determined to try what they could do with the seditious by words, and assembled the people[106]

Simon ben Gamaliel, son of the Pharisee Gamaliel the Elder and a leader in the early stages of the revolt, was part of a delegation sent to Josephus when he was a commander in Galilee.

> Two of these were of the populace, Jonathan and Ananias, by sect Pharisees; while the third, Jozar, was of the stock of the priests, and a Pharisee also; and Simon, the last of them, was of the youngest of the high priests.[107]

We see that he Pharisees as a group were not of one mind about the revolt, with some playing an active part on each side.

The Pharisee Johanan ben Zakkai had the most historically critical and unexpected role in the revolt against the Romans. He began as an advocate for peace with the Romans. When the conflict was so intense that Jerusalem was under siege, he had himself smuggled out of the city in a coffin and taken to the Roman camp. He negotiated with the Roman commander Vespasian for permission to safely move to Yavneh with some of his students and to continue to teach there.[108] When the people of the temple organization died in the destruction of the temple, traditions were preserved by R. Johanan and his disciples away from the fighting to become the basis for rabbinic Judaism.

Some voices captured in the *Mishnah*, dating from before the destruction of the temple, have an extremely negative view of their Gentile opponents.

3.2 A R. Hananiah, Prefect of the Priests, says, "Pray for
the welfare of the government.

B "For if it were not for fear of it, one man would
swallow his fellow alive."[109]

Gentiles at war simply were assumed to rape captive women, and the
burden of proof was on the women to prove that rape did not happen.

2.9 A The woman who was taken prisoner by gentiles—

B [if it was] for an offence concerning property, she
is permitted [to return] to her husband.

C [If it was for] a capital offense, she is prohibited to
her husband.

D A city which was overcome by siege—all the priest
girls found therein are invalid [to return to their
husbands].

E But if they have witnesses, even a man slave or a
girl slave, lo, they are believed.

F But a person is not believed to testify in his own
behalf.

G Said R. Zekhariah b. Haqqasab, "By this sanctuary!
Her hand did not move from mine from the time
that the gentiles entered Jerusalem until they
left it."

H Said they to him, "A person cannot give testimony
in his own behalf."[110]

In the case of Zekhariah ben Haqqasab, this ruling was binding. Even
though he set aside a house for his wife and supported her from his
property, he was never alone with her again.[111] As well as showing
the low opinion of Gentile soldiers, this story shows the absolute
seriousness with which the Pharisees took rabbinic rulings.

Was Galilee Really Jewish Territory?

Our information about the Gentiles in Palestine during the teaching ministry of Jesus comes from both written material and archeological work. Among the written evidence are the writings of Josephus and the New Testament itself. The collection of archeological evidence has been growing over the last several decades.

In prophetic times, after the conquest of the northern kingdom by the Assyrians, Galilee was described by Isaiah as Gentile territory.

> [I]n earlier times He treated the land of Zebulun and the land of Naphtali with contempt, but later on He shall make *it* glorious, by the way of the sea, on the other side of Jordan, Galilee of the Gentiles. (Isa 9:1 NASB)

By the time of the Maccabean revolt in the second century BCE, Jews were living among the Gentiles in Galilee and were subject to violence from their neighbors during the conflict.

> [M]essengers, with their garments torn, came from Galilee and made a similar report; they said that the people of Ptolemais and Tyre and Sidon, and all Galilee of the Gentiles, had gathered together against them "to annihilate us." (1 Macc 5:14–15)

Josephus describes continuing conflict between Jews and their Gentile neighbors in Galilee before the revolt against Rome:

> [T]wo great men, who were under the jurisdiction of the king [Agrippa], came to me out of the region of Trachonitis, bringing their horses and their arms, and carrying with them their money also; and when the Jews would force them to be circumcised, if they would stay among them[112]

Archeological evidence shows a mixture of Jews and Gentiles in Galilee at the time of Jesus' ministry. Evidence of a Jewish presence is found in Jewish inscriptions, the remains of synagogues, stone vessels, ritual baths, and coins from both Hasmonean and Herodian eras.[113] Finding pagan artifacts mixed in indicates pagan presence even in largely Jewish villages, and signs of Jewish communities are found within largely pagan cities.[114] Although Josephus wrote about bandits and brigands, there are relatively few remains of watchtowers and fortresses in northern Galilee.[115] Based on this evidence, it appears that Jews and Gentiles accommodated each other well enough to live together peacefully, if not affectionately, in the Galilee.

Nevertheless, the area of the Galilee was known to be Gentile territory, and for Jesus to spend much of his ministry time there was to make a political statement. In addition, specific locations mentioned in his travels have Gentile connections. His trip to the region of Tyre and Sidon (Mark 7:24; Matt 15:21), for example, took him far to the northwest of Galilee into the northern part of Phoenicia in Syrian territory. The people who listened to his teaching came from Gentile as well as Jewish territories, "from Galilee, the Decapolis, Jerusalem, Judea, and from beyond the Jordan (Matt 4:24–25)" and "from Judea, Jerusalem, Idumea, beyond the Jordan, and the region around Tyre and Sidon" (Mark 3:7–8).

The contemporary view of Gentiles and their practices, as reflected in the words of Jesus, was far from favorable. Gentiles were very concerned with their day-to-day practical needs.

> Do not worry then, saying, "What will we eat?" or "What will we drink?" or "What will we wear for clothing?" For the Gentiles eagerly seek all these things (Matt 6:31–32)

Gentiles were dominated by and subject to the whims of their rulers.

> The kings of the Gentiles lord it over them (Luke 22:25)

Gentile prayer was a formal and presumably meaningless flow of words.

> And when you are praying, do not use meaningless repetition as the Gentiles do, for they suppose that they will be heard for their many words. (Matt 6:7)

Gentiles were known to be the instruments of pain, destruction and punishment for the people of Israel time after time.

> [T]hey will fall by the edge of the sword, and will be led captive into all the nations; and Jerusalem will be trampled under foot by the Gentiles until the times of the Gentiles are fulfilled. (Luke 21:24)

Finally, for Jesus, Gentiles would be the agents through whom he would die.

> For he will be handed over to the Gentiles; and he will be mocked and insulted and spat upon. After they have flogged him, they will kill him (Luke 18:32–33)

Stereotypical Gentiles were, and always had been, the villains in the story of the people of Israel.

Overall, Jews and non-Jews were living in close proximity in the regions where Jesus taught, but there was significant prejudice and friction between the two groups.

How Did Jesus React to Faithful Gentiles?

The gospels record several encounters between Jesus and people identified as Gentiles. These conversations moved beyond the neighborly separation of Jews and Gentiles into active engagement with each other. The Syrophonecian woman, the Samaritan woman at the well, the Roman centurion looking for help, and the Samaritan leper are all clearly identified as Gentiles; and all impress Jesus with the strength of their faith. In each case, Jesus agreed to the requests they made of him, but he also made an unexpected positive statement of respect for the requester. These conversations between a male Jewish religious teacher and non-Jews—women, lepers, or occupying soldiers—go against all Jewish cultural expectations.

Jesus met the Syrophonecian woman (Matt 15:21–28; Mark 7:24–30) in her own home territory on his trip to Tyre and Sidon. The woman, desperate with her concern for her daughter, heard of his arrival and came begging for help. Jesus tried, unsuccessfully, to ignore her. It is not clear, between the accounts from Matthew and Mark, whether it was Jesus or the woman who first introduced the analogy of children and dogs at mealtime, but Jesus accepted the analogy and the woman built on it. The children of Israel were the first recipients of the ministry of Jesus, and he was focused on them. Outsiders, Gentile "dogs," were not members of the family, but they did have their place in the food chain. Jesus acknowledged that Gentiles have a place in his ministry, admittedly after that of the children of Israel. Because of the faith this woman shows, her request for healing was granted.

The Samaritan woman at the well (John 4:1–42) also met Jesus in her own territory as he was passing through Samaria. This time, Jesus initiated the conversation, and she was shocked that he, as a man and a Jew, would speak to her at all. Jesus accepted that she, in spite of being a woman and a Gentile, had the right to ask him for living water. He explained to her that salvation is from the Jews, but that, in the time to come, all people could be accepted as true worshippers of God.

Jesus showed her, by reminding her of the sin in her life, that righteousness and obedience to the commandments are required of all non-Jews as well as of Jews. The Samaritan woman responded to Jesus in faith. She told her story to her community, and they also listened to Jesus and learned from him. At his departure, they said, "This One is indeed the Savior of the world." Jesus ministered to this whole community of Gentiles, and they accepted his teaching and came to believe in him.

In the interaction between Jesus and the Roman centurion (Matt 8:5–13; Luke 7:1–10), the Roman initiated the encounter. Matthew reports the conversation as happening directly between the two men, while Luke reports Jewish elders representing the centurion. As an officer in a hierarchical system, the Roman recognized Jesus as a superior and communicated with him deferentially. This indication of respect, shown by a commander in the world's dominant civilization for a member of a subject race, was completely unexpected. The centurion showed respect for Jesus, and Jesus responded with a courtesy and willing cooperation unexpected in a subject people.

The Roman asked for help for his servant in full confidence that Jesus was able to provide it. He showed courtesy by relieving Jesus of the need to come to his own house, knowing that entering a Gentile home would be forbidden to a conscientious Jew. Jesus saw the Roman's understanding, consideration, and faith, and granted his request. He paid the Roman a high compliment: "I tell you, not even in Israel have I found such faith" (Luke 7:9). This Gentile's faith was fully acceptable, and it rivaled what Jesus had seen among his own people.

The Samaritan leper (Luke 17:11–19) demonstrated his faith first in a group of Jewish fellow sufferers who came to Jesus for healing. The other nine accepted their healing and moved on with their lives, but this Samaritan came back to say "Thank you." The response that Jesus gave him shows how Jesus reacted to the difference between the Jewish and Gentile behaviors.

> Were not ten made clean? But the other nine, where are
> they? Was none of them found to return and give praise
> to God except this foreigner? (Luke 17:17–18)

The Gentle responded in faith and gave his gratitude where it belonged, to God.

In each of these encounters, the non-Jewish participants demonstrated the strength of their faith. They stepped out across lines of prejudice and hostility to engage with Jesus, and he crossed lines of ethnic and religious expectations to help them. In each case, Jesus gave the Gentile full credit for the faith he saw, including them as worthy recipients of his healing ministry. In his interactions with these Gentiles, Jesus demonstrated that his ministry was in fact to all people, not just to the children of Israel.

How Were Non-Jews Included in the Gospel Message?

The inclusion of Gentiles in the gospel message is found throughout the gospels. It begins in the links to prophecies that explicitly include Gentiles, continues through the ministry of Jesus, and finds its ultimate expression in the Great Commission.

When Jesus first was brought to the temple as an infant to be presented, Simeon greeted the parents with a reference to the prophecies of Isaiah:

> "[M]y eyes have seen your salvation, which you have prepared in the presence of all peoples, a light for revelation to the Gentiles and for glory to your people Israel." And the child's father and mother were amazed at what was being said about him. (Luke 2:30–33)

Here at the very beginning of Jesus' life, he is recognized as a light for revelation to the Gentiles. His parents had a chance to hear the prophecy from the descriptions of the servant in Isaiah applied to their son.

> I am the LORD, I have called you in righteousness, I have taken you by the hand and kept you; I have given you as a covenant to the people, a light to the nations, (Isa 42:6)

> He says, "It is too light a thing that you should be my servant to raise up the tribes of Jacob and to restore the survivors of Israel; I will give you as a light to the

nations, that my salvation may reach to the end of the earth." (Isa 49:6)

Would Mary and Joseph have shared this link between their son and the suffering servant with him as he was growing up? We can see the expectation of suffering as Jesus came to acknowledge his role, and we also can see his developing sense of his responsibility for all people.

The announcement from John the Baptist also included Isaiah's awareness of salvation for all people, and not just the people of Israel. John quoted Isaiah, saying, "All flesh shall see the salvation of God" (Luke 3:6). John was clear that simply being one of the children of the covenant was not enough. He said,

> Bear fruit worthy of repentance. Do not presume to say to yourselves, "We have Abraham as our ancestor"; for I tell you, God is able from these stones to raise up children to Abraham. (Matt 3:8–9)

All sorts of people, from Pharisees and Sadducees to tax collectors and soldiers, came to hear John the Baptist. His message to all alike was repentance and preparation.

In the early stages of his teaching ministry, Jesus went first to the people of Israel. When he sent his disciples out on their own teaching journey, he gave them the same instructions: "Go nowhere among the Gentiles, and enter no town of the Samaritans, but go rather to the lost sheep of the house of Israel" (Matt 10:5–6). Later in his ministry, Jesus went freely into Gentile towns, some of which were receptive and others that were not.

> When the days drew near for him to be taken up, he set his face to go to Jerusalem. And he sent messengers ahead of him. On their way they entered a village of the Samaritans to make ready for him; but they did not receive him. (Luke 9:51–53)

Jesus did not take the advice of his disciples to punish those who refused to receive him, but simply continued on to another town. The opportunity to hear him was offered to Gentiles, but Jesus accepted their unwillingness to listen.

On the surface, the parable of the mustard seed does not appear to be about the inclusion of Gentiles.

> He also said, "With what can we compare the kingdom of God, or what parable will we use for it? It is like a mustard seed, which, when sown upon the ground, is the smallest of all the seeds on earth; yet when it is sown it grows up and becomes the greatest of all shrubs, and puts forth large branches, so that the birds of the air can make nests in its shade." (Mark 4:30–32)

However, the story is related to passages from Ezekiel and from Daniel.

> On the mountain height of Israel I will plant it, in order that it may produce boughs and bear fruit, and become a noble cedar. Under it every kind of bird will live; in the shade of its branches will nest winged creatures of every kind. (Ezek 17:23)

> Its foliage was beautiful, its fruit abundant, and it provided food for all. The animals of the field found shade under it, the birds of the air nested in its branches, and from it all living beings were fed. (Dan 4:12)

In the context of these passages, the birds of the air that Jesus mentioned can be seen to represent all people, including both Jews and Gentiles, who are welcomed and nurtured in the kingdom of God.

This theme appears again when Jesus, near the end of his ministry, is approached by Gentiles in Jerusalem.

> Now among those who went up to worship at the
> festival were some Greeks. They came to Philip, who
> was from Bethsaida in Galilee, and said to him, "Sir, we
> wish to see Jesus." Philip went and told Andrew; then
> Andrew and Philip went and told Jesus. Jesus answered
> them, "The hour has come for the Son of Man to be
> glorified." (John 12:20–23)

As Jesus speaks to this crowd of Jews and Gentiles, he says, "And I,
when I am lifted up from the earth, will draw all people to myself"
(John 12:32). All people will be included with those who will be drawn
to him in glory.

One final incident in that last visit to Jerusalem also demonstrates
the attitude of Jesus toward Gentiles. There are several interpretations
of the incident between Jesus and the moneychangers in the temple.
It might refer to prophecy about the destruction of the temple, be a
protest against corruption in the priesthood, show resistance against the
temple institution itself, or protest against taking financial advantage
of the poor.[116] Another interpretation identifies the scene as the court
of the Gentiles within the temple precincts and points out that the
moneychangers were using space that should have been available for
Gentile worship.[117] When Jesus talked about the house of prayer, he
used that phrase from Isaiah:

> And the foreigners who join themselves to the LORD,
> to minister to him, to love the name of the LORD, and
> to be his servants, all who keep the Sabbath, and do
> not profane it, and hold fast my covenant— these I
> will bring to my holy mountain, and make them joyful
> in my house of prayer; their burnt offerings and their
> sacrifices will be accepted on my altar; for my house
> shall be called a house of prayer for all peoples. (Isa
> 56:6–7)

His protest against the business activities in the one place where Gentiles were permitted in the temple may be considered support for their ability to worship there.

Will Jews and Non-Jews Be Together in the End?

The illustration that Jesus uses most often for the experience of people in the kingdom of God is the messianic banquet. The guests are welcome to enjoy the company, which includes the patriarchs Abraham, Isaac, and Jacob, and even God himself. Jesus says, "I tell you, many will come from east and west and will eat with Abraham and Isaac and Jacob in the kingdom of heaven" (Matt 8:11). This banquet includes the coming together of the people of Israel from all the corners of the world (Ps 107:3; Isa 43:5; Isa 49:12; Zech 2:6–7) and the worship of God by all nations (Isa 59:19; Mal 1:11). It is an image that Isaiah describes as including all people.

> On this mountain the LORD of hosts will make for all peoples a feast of rich food, a feast of well-aged wines, of rich food filled with marrow, of well-aged wines strained clear. And he will destroy on this mountain the shroud that is cast over all peoples, the sheet that is spread over all nations; he will swallow up death forever. Then the Lord God will wipe away the tears from all faces, and the disgrace of his people he will take away from all the earth, for the Lord has spoken. (Isa 25:6–8)

When Jesus speaks about the narrow door and how difficult it is to enter through it, he says,

> There will be weeping and gnashing of teeth when you see Abraham and Isaac and Jacob and all the prophets

in the kingdom of God, and you yourselves thrown
out. Then people will come from east and west, from
north and south, and will eat in the kingdom of God.
(Luke 13:28–29)

Many Gentiles will be feasting at the messianic banquet while some of
those who were born into the chosen people will not be there.

Jesus tells a parable about a wedding feast as a metaphor for the
messianic banquet (Matt 22:8–10). The first group of invited guests
declines to come to the feast, so a second group is recruited from all
possible people in the area.

But when the king came in to see the guests, he noticed
a man there who was not wearing a wedding robe, and
he said to him, "Friend, how did you get in here without
a wedding robe?" And he was speechless. Then the
king said to the attendants, "Bind him hand and foot,
and throw him into the outer darkness, where there
will be weeping and gnashing of teeth." For many are
called, but few are chosen. (Matt 22:11–14)

Even for those given the general invitation, the basic courtesy of putting
on dress clothes provided for the festivities is required. Jesus was clear
that many are invited to the banquet, first through the chosen invitation
list and then through the general invitation. Still, all must be willing to
cooperate with the host's party plans.

At the time of judgment, Jews and Gentiles both will be judged
together.

When the Son of Man comes in his glory, and all the
angels with him, then he will sit on the throne of his
glory. All the nations will be gathered before him, and
he will separate people one from another as a shepherd
separates the sheep from the goats, (Matt 25:31–32)

There is no indication that Jews and Gentiles will be treated differently as they come to the decision of whether to go to the left or to the right. In fact, Jesus sometimes compared his Jewish listeners unfavorably with some of the Gentiles who appear in Scripture:

> The Queen of the South will rise up with the men of this generation at the judgment and condemn them, because she came from the ends of the earth to hear the wisdom of Solomon; and behold, something greater than Solomon is here. The men of Nineveh will stand up with this generation at the judgment and condemn it, because they repented at the preaching of Jonah; and behold, something greater than Jonah is here. (Luke 11:31–32)

Jesus praised the faithfulness he found in the Gentile territories Tyre and Sidon by comparison with his reception in Jewish towns such as Chorazin and Bethsaida (Matt 11:20–24; Luke 10:10–14). His neighbors in Nazareth were offended by his implication that certain Gentiles— the widow of Zarephath and the Syrian Naaman—were as able to receive God's prophets as any in Israel (Luke 4:24–27). In the promised judgment that comes with the end times, Jesus was clear that there will be no partiality between Jews and Gentiles. All are included, and there will be no preferential treatment when all come together in the end.

Did Jesus Intend to Reach Out to Non-Jews?

Jesus' interest in Gentiles, in spite of the mentions in the prophets, was by no means an obvious direction for his ministry to take. When Jesus was in Jerusalem for the Festival of Booths, he said that people would not be able to find him when they searched for him. The reaction was incredulity:

The Jews then said to one another, "Where does this man intend to go that we will not find Him? He is not intending to go to the Dispersion among the Greeks, and teach the Greeks, is He?" (John 7:35 NASB)

The form of the question shows how unlikely they think this is. "He doesn't think he's going to teach Greeks?" is almost a sneer at anyone who would be so foolish. Unexpected as it might be, Jesus did intend to teach Gentiles, even if indirectly.

When Jesus taught the parable of the good shepherd, he focused primarily on the role of the shepherd and the relationship between the shepherd and those in his care. In the middle of the parable, though, he included a brief and cryptic statement:

I have other sheep that do not belong to this fold. I must bring them also, and they will listen to my voice. So there will be one flock, one shepherd. (John 10:16)

What did he mean? Those listening at the time may have assumed that he meant other people from other towns, other members of the Jewish community. Later information about generations of non-Jews that have come to believe in him shows that the Gentile nations were included in this phrase as well.

Jesus made one statement from the cross that is often misunderstood.

Jesus cried out with a loud voice, "Eloi, Eloi, lema sabachthani?" which means, "My God, my God, why have you forsaken me?" (Mark 15:34)

We know that when someone says, "The Lord is my shepherd," they are referring to Psalm 23. In the same way, someone familiar with all the psalms would know that Jesus is quoting the beginning of Psalm 22. With no time or breath for long speeches, Jesus in this one phrase conveys all the lament and poignancy of this psalm. The final lines include three promises:

> All the ends of the earth shall remember and turn to the
> LORD; and all the families of the nations shall worship
> before him. For dominion belongs to the LORD, and he
> rules over the nations. (Ps 22:27–28)

> To him, indeed, shall all who sleep in the earth bow
> down; before him shall bow all who go down to the
> dust, and I shall live for him. (Ps 22:29)

> Posterity will serve him; future generations will be told
> about the Lord, and proclaim his deliverance to a people
> yet unborn, saying that he has done it. (Ps 22:30–31)

In this one allusion, with almost his last breath, Christ conveys that all nations will come to worship God together, that continuing life will be for himself and others, and that generations to come are included in the promise of salvation. The inclusion of all people, including Gentiles and all generations, including our own, is there for all to see.

After his death, the encounter between Jesus and the two travelers on the road to Emmaus shows the way Jesus chose to tell his own story. The travelers were full of all the exciting and alarming news, and Jesus took the opportunity to put the events in context: "Then beginning with Moses and all the prophets, he interpreted to them the things about himself in all the Scriptures" (Luke 24:27). Jesus began at the beginning—with Moses, the Exodus, and the covenant promises that created a chosen people. Then he explained the messianic prophecies and the way they applied to himself and the events of his life. He opened the Scriptures to them, giving them a coherent picture of the way all the threads tied together.

The Great Commission was not some sudden shift for a teacher with an exclusively Jewish audience. It is the logical extension of a ministry that began in the traditions of a single people and was offered to all others based on that people's experience of relationship with God. Jesus said,

> Go therefore and make disciples of all the nations,
> baptizing them in the name of the Father and the Son
> and the Holy Spirit, teaching them to observe all that
> I commanded you; and lo, I am with you always, even
> to the end of the age. (Matt 28:19–20)

The message is clearly to all people of all nations, Jews and Gentiles. The instructions are to go and find those who need to hear the news, to include them with baptism, and to teach them a new way of life.

Jesus knew that not all the recipients of his message would be enthusiastic, especially with his Jewish perspective on the behavior of the Gentiles in the world. Even as he sent out the disciples during his lifetime, he warned, "you will be dragged before governors and kings because of me, as a testimony to them and the Gentiles" (Matt 10:18). Those Jesus sent out would be facing all possible listeners, from the highest to the lowest in all the lands, Jews as well as Gentiles.

Was Righteousness Expected of Non-Jews?

What did Jesus expect of the Gentiles who were to hear his message? At a minimum, he expected inclusion, that Gentiles would all be included as potential recipients of the good news of the kingdom of God. He spoke to Gentiles as well as Jews, and he instructed those who followed him to include both Jews and Gentiles in their work of sharing his words. He expected that Gentiles would be welcome to participate in the messianic banquet at the end of time and that they would stand in judgment with no partiality or prejudice alongside the people of Israel.

Jesus also expected that Gentiles were capable of great faith, as great as any shown by the people of the covenant. In his encounters with believing Gentiles, Jesus always pointed out that it was their faith that made the difference, that made their healing possible. Faith, which would come to be recognized as the single critical element for salvation, was equally available to Jews and Gentiles. Jesus made sure that each Gentile heard from him its critical importance.

Finally, Jesus expected righteousness from Gentiles, just as he did from Jews. He ordered his disciples to teach all people "to observe all that I commanded you." Although Jesus rearranged the priorities of some provisions within the Mosaic covenant, this included the provisions of the moral law. Repentance, turning away from sin, was always the first step on the road to the kingdom of God.

The struggle with different cultural backgrounds and different understandings of how life should be lived caused conflicts that coalesced around the differences between Jews and Gentiles. The leaders of the church met to provide guidelines for the newcomers into the church communities. This meeting was held in Jerusalem roughly twenty years after the death and resurrection of Jesus, and its discussion and decision will be the topic of the next chapter.

Questions for Reflection and Discussion

1. How would you describe the different attitudes of Jews toward Gentiles?
2. What evidence do we have that first-century Jews were evangelistic?
3. Consider Mark 7:24–30. Does Jesus exclude non-Jews from his ministry? How do he and this woman agree on the positions of Jews and Gentiles?
4. How did Jesus show that he was open to all those who had faith?

5. How many ways did Jesus include Gentiles in the gospel message?

6. In the encounters between Jesus and Gentiles, what different kinds of boundaries did he cross?

7. Did Jesus expect that Gentiles would be capable of repentance and righteousness?

8. How do you picture the messianic banquet at the end of time?

6

What Did Non-Jews Have to
Do to Become Christians?

The Jerusalem council described in Acts 15 met to consider a single question: Should non-Jews who were followers of Jesus be required to convert to Judaism and be circumcised? Unfortunately, the decision of the council can have two different and almost contradictory meanings. One meaning is about behavior, while the other is about food. When James states the decision, he uses the term "defilements." As we saw in chapter 3, the work of Jonathan Klawans, provides a new perspective for understanding defilements.

The separate distinctions of purity/impurity and sacred/profane as they relate to Gentile believers are both addressed in the council discussion. James provides a scriptural rationale showing that Gentiles are to be accepted into the people of God as they are—as Gentiles—but that moral purity, rather than ritual purity, is still required of them. Translation of the full form of the decision supports this perspective, especially when the term associated with strangulation in Acts 15:20 is seen to reflect human violence.

I propose a new translation of the council's decision which may reflect the original intent more closely.

> We should write to them to only stay away from
> impurities caused by idols and sexual immorality and
> oppression and bloodshed.

This chapter will explore the rationale behind this alternative translation.

James follows the decision with a reference to the synagogues where Moses is proclaimed, pointing Gentiles to learn more about the Mosaic law, especially as it relates to their situation as non-Jews living among the people of Israel.

How Should We Look at the Jerusalem Council Decision?

The apostolic council held in Jerusalem was the one place that the leaders of the early church came together to talk about the relationship between Jews and Gentiles in the church. The council met to consider one question: Should non-Jews who were coming into the new churches be required to convert to Judaism and be circumcised? All perspectives were represented in the council, and all took turns presenting their arguments. The usual procedure in a council was that a final decision be made by majority rule. However, a critical part of the decision-making process was listening for the guidance of the Holy Spirit.[118] After listening to Peter, Paul, and Barnabas talk about the power of God working through the Gentiles, James proposed a resolution to the question, which was accepted by everyone.[119] The requirements of the decision were expressed in a single sentence in Greek,

$$\text{ἀπέχεσθαι τῶν ἀλισγημάτων τῶν εἰδώλων καὶ τῆς}$$
$$\text{πορνείας καὶ τοῦ πνικτοῦ καὶ τοῦ αἵματος}^{[120]}$$

We are left to struggle, after all these years, with what that decision actually meant.

Unfortunately, this single set of words can have two distinctly different meanings. The most widely accepted interpretation in recent centuries is that this decision deals primarily with food—about what may or may not be eaten by followers of Jesus in the churches. The other interpretation, which had strong advocates at different times in history, is that the decision is primarily about morality, about what behavior is or is not acceptable among followers of Jesus.

Each interpretation is based on a problem in the early church. If the main problem in the church at that time was how to make it possible for the Jewish and Gentile believers to share meals together, then a declaration about eating practices would solve the problem. However, if the primary issue was what life changes Gentiles were expected to make to accept the teachings of Jesus, then a declaration about acceptable and unacceptable behavior would be appropriate. The words of the decision can be interpreted either way.

When the group of apostles and elders in Jerusalem met together, their purpose was specifically to consider the question of whether Gentile followers of Jesus should be circumcised and submit to the whole law of Moses (Acts 15:1–6).[121] Nowhere in the events leading up to the meeting is there any indication that dietary regulations or problems in table fellowship prompted the discussion. The difficulty comes from the attempt to relate the action of the council to the conflict between Peter and Paul described in Galatians (Gal 2:11–12). Scholars even differ on the possible order in which the events actually occurred. If the conflict over meals in Antioch occurred before the council meeting, it might imply that food issues were a significant part of the discussion there. If it occurred later, then the council resolution must not have fully resolved the potential for conflicts over food.

The conflict over the two alternative meanings of the council decision is as old as the source documents that we have for the book of Acts.[122] The eastern Alexandrian text has only the statement of the decree with four items, while some western texts do not include the mention of strangling but do have additional words included with the decision. The western texts, represented by Codex Bezae (D), include a negative form of the Golden Rule[123] which uses language very similar to that used by Jesus in the Sermon on the Mount (Matt 7:12).[124] The presence of this addition relating to behavior would lead to a moral rather than dietary perspective for the decision. However, since the eastern text is generally considered to be the more authoritative, this insertion is more likely to reflect some later attempt at clarification.

What Was the Problem with Gentiles?

James used the term ἀλίσγημα *(alisgēma)*, which means defilements or impurities, to specify things Gentiles are required to avoid. In order to understand this idea, we need to know what purity and impurity meant to the Jewish followers of Jesus. We saw the way to tell the difference between ritual and moral impurity in chapter 3.[125] Now, we need to understand what kind of impurity was forbidden by James and the council.

What did the members of the Jerusalem council think was the problem with Gentiles in the early church? A clue comes from the way the phrase "Gentile sinners" (Gal 2:15) is used as a statement of the obvious. Gentiles are assumed to be in a state of sin, with their sinfulness a part of their identity as not being the people of God. Gentiles are condemned for their sinful practices in many places in Scripture. The non-canonical Book of Jubilees, written in the second century BCE, shows a perspective on Gentiles from shortly before the first century.

> [The Israelites] will forget all of my commandments, everything which I shall command them, and they will walk after the gentiles and after their defilement and shame. And they will serve their gods, and they will become a scandal for them and an affliction and a torment and a snare. (Jub 1:9)[126]

The risk here is that association with Gentiles will lead to the moral impurity of idolatry and sexual sin.[127]

Gentiles were corrupting because Gentiles were sinful. Their sin was not contagious in the same way that ritual impurity was, but it was dangerously attractive because Jews could be led into sin by their example. The laws that resulted in separation (forbidden foods, intermarriage, etc.) symbolized the differentiation of the people of Israel from others' immorality, and the laws also enforced social separation from those who might lead them into sinful behavior. Gentiles joining the people of Israel through Christ needed to leave behind the sinful practices identified under the moral provisions of the Mosaic law that had always applied to non-Jews living among the people.

Was Lack of Holiness also a Problem for Non-Jews?

Even if Gentiles were not inherently impure, they still would not be holy in the same way that the people of Israel were holy to the Lord (Lev 20:26). Richard Bauckham points out that, just as the opposite of purity is impurity, so the opposite of holy or sacred is profane. Both sets of distinctions, between the sacred and the profane and between the clean and the unclean, are critically important (Ezek 22:26).[128] Even though Gentiles can turn away from sinful behaviors, this repentance does not make them holy people belonging to God (Lev 10:8, 10). Gentiles, even "good," repentant Gentiles, were still ordinary people.

It takes something more than simple repentance to bring about the holiness that comes from being one of God's chosen people. Before the coming of Jesus, only joining the people of Israel and living under the Mosaic covenant could make this possible. However, when the Holy Spirit came to Gentiles as well, it was clear that this situation had changed. Peter's vision of different kinds of animals to be eaten had been accompanied by the message, "What God has made clean, you must not call profane." (Acts 10:15)

When Peter went to the home of the Gentile Cornelius, he said, "You yourselves know that it is unlawful for a Jew to associate with or to visit a Gentile; but God has shown me that I should not call *anyone* profane or unclean" (Acts 10:28). Note that Peter does not say "any*thing*," but "any*one*." He concluded that, like the animals in the vision, the *people* he is called to see are neither profane nor unclean.

When Peter was criticized for his actions, he reported back to the leaders in Jerusalem, "The Spirit told me to go with them and not to make a distinction between them and us" (Acts 11:12). At that meeting, which preceded the Jerusalem council, the concern about maintaining separation was raised, and the gathered leaders agreed that Gentiles were included in the community of those who received the Holy Spirit.[129]

Peter related the incident with Cornelius and his family again during the council's deliberations because it demonstrated the status of distinctions between Jews and Gentiles. He said,

> God, who knows the human heart, testified to them
> by giving them the Holy Spirit, just as he did to us;
> and in cleansing their hearts by faith he has made no
> distinction between them and us. (Acts 15:8–9)

Receiving the Holy Spirit implies a change in the status of Gentiles from profane to holy. They receive holiness through the Spirit that is given to them and lives within them. The presence of the Holy Spirit (1 Cor 6:19) ultimately removed the last of the distinctions separating Christian Jews and Christian Gentiles as the people belonging to God.

How Does James Announce the Decision?

In the end, it was not the miraculous confirmation alone, but the witness of Scripture that led to the final decision. Bauckham[130] explains that James presented an argument based in Scripture, the way a Jewish sage of his time would, to address the question of the minimum requirements for inclusion in the people of God.[131] James based his thinking on the idea of the Christian community as the temple, and he responded to the issue of the Gentiles in a way that upheld the continuing authority of the Mosaic law.[132] James's quotation of Amos

9:11–12 in Acts 15:16–18 is a conflation that includes other texts used to interpret the Amos passage.

> This agrees with the words of the prophets, as it is written, "After this I will return, and I will rebuild the dwelling of David, which has fallen; from its ruins I will rebuild it, and I will set it up, so that all other peoples may seek the Lord—even all the Gentiles over whom my name has been called. Thus says the Lord, who has been making these things known from long ago." (Acts 15:15–18)

James begins with "prophets" in the plural rather than singular, to indicate that the perspective includes more than simply the Amos passage. For James, the "dwelling of David" refers to the eschatological temple, and "the nations over whom my name has been called" to the Gentiles who acknowledge God.

In the form of interpretation used at the time, repeated words were used to identify links between related passages. The Greek passage in Acts uses quotations from the *Septuagint* with slight changes in the wording of Amos to create word associations. James used this technique to include references to Hosea 3:5, Jeremiah 12:15, and Isaiah 45:21. The crucial elements for the point that James made to the council are that (1) the Christian community, including its Gentile participants as they are, has become the people of God, and (2) all the nations who are called are to be included in the covenant, as they are.[133]

However, even though Gentiles are to be accepted as they are, it is still necessary for Gentile Christians to separate themselves from the moral pollution of their previous lives.[134] Purity is still required, and righteousness is still the goal for all, Jews and non-Jews. To discover how this is expressed in the decree of the Jerusalem council, it is necessary first to examine some issues with how the council decree is translated.

What Are the Translation Issues in the Decision?

Translating the two verses (Acts 15:20 and 29) that contain the council decision is problematic at best. I accept the scholarly consensus that the four-item version of the Alexandrian text is original, but I do not believe that this decides the question of the ritual, as opposed to moral, nature of the restrictions. The translator's perspective determines which set of alternative word meanings are chosen. When the perspective changes, the elements of the passage snap into a completely different, but internally consistent, set of meanings. There are many potential meanings for the critical words in the passages:

Ἀλισγημάτων (ἀλίσγημα [*alisgēma*] pollution) is the noun form of the verb ἀλισγέω which means to pollute or to make something ceremonially impure.[135] The noun form means that which has been ritually defiled—"a thing defiled."[136] When used in the plural, as in Acts 15:20, the plural indicates multiple separate acts.[137] Translators have assumed that the pollution is caused only by idols, although it is possible that the pollution may be caused by any or all items in the following list.

Αἵματος (αἷμα [*haima*] blood or bloodshed) carries a wide variety of different potential meanings, including actual blood; the death of a person as the result of violence;[138] and depriving a person of life by violent means—"to kill, killing, to commit murder."[139] The word used here is simply "blood," with no implication of blood as food or meat in which the blood remains.

Πνικτοῦ (πνικτός [*pniktos*] strangled or suffocation) a rare word referring to cutting off breath, the experience of being choked, strangled, throttled, drowned, stifled, suffocated, afflicted, or tormented.[140] It comes from Greek tragic drama, where its forms are used to mean "to stifle," "to choke," "to strangle," "to throttle," and figuratively "to afflict" or "to alarm."[141] It is not used in the Greek translations of Levitical food regulations in the Septuagint, and words with this root only appear there with the meanings of "tormenting" Saul (1 Sam 16:15), "hanging" himself (2 Sam 17:23), a lion "strangling" prey (Nah 2:12), Job's choice of "strangling" (Job 7:15), and "killing" seven husbands (Tob 3:8). In the gospels, related words are used when swine "drowned" (ἐπνίγοντο [*epnigonto*] Mark 5:13), seeds are "choked" (ἔπνιξαν [*epnixan*] Matt 13:7), a servant is "seized by the throat" (ἔπνιγεν [*epnigen*] Matt 13:7), and when crowds "pressed in" on Jesus (συνέπνιγον [*synepnigon*] Luke 8:42).

Πνικτός [*pniktos*] is the noun form of the verb πνίγω, which is translated as to choke or strangle, which is in turn derived from the root verb πνέω which means blowing, as does the wind.[142] When translated in the context of the apostolic decision, context alone has been used to assert that this term refers to animals that have not been properly slaughtered.

As a result, depending on the perspective, the items in the decree can take on different but internally consistent meanings:

ἀλισγημάτων (ἀλίσγημα [*alisgēma*] pollution)

> Ritual perspective: something that has been ritually defiled
> Moral perspective: impurity caused by some violation of moral law

εἰδώλων (εἴδωλον [*eidōlon*] idol)

> Ritual perspective: meat sacrificed to idols
> Moral perspective: idols, sacrifices to idols

αἵματος (αἷμα [*haima*] blood or bloodshed)

> Ritual perspective: meat with blood in it
> Moral perspective: bloodshed

πνικτοῦ (πνικτός [*pniktos*] strangled or suffocation)

> Ritual perspective: meat from an animal which has been strangled
> Moral perspective: suffocation, choking, cutting off breath

πορνείας (πορνεία [*porneia*] sexual immorality)

> Ritual perspective: some explicitly forbidden sexual relationships
> Moral perspective: sexual immorality

The choice of a food-related perspective typically is based on context, either because impurity is assumed only to refer to ritual impurity or because the "majority" of items on the list can be applied consistently to foods. Those who have argued for the moral perspective usually work with a list of three items, without strangulation, since the other three prohibitions can be seen most easily in their moral interpretations. However, the word πνικτός, which has been seen as only viable from a ritual perspective, actually has more significant implications and New Testament usage relating to human to human violence.

When we understand pollution to refer not only to ritual impurity, but also moral impurity, the structure of Acts 15:20 changes. The following shows this alternative interpretation, first in the original Greek and then with a basic word-by-word translation.

20 ἀλλὰ ἐπιστεῖλαι αὐτοῖς τοῦ
ἀπέχεσθαι
   τῶν ἀλισγημάτων
     τῶν εἰδώλων
     καὶ τῆς πορνείας
     καὶ τοῦ πνικτοῦ
     καὶ τοῦ αἵματος

20 but we write to them
to hold back (present tense, middle voice, infinitive)[143]
   (from) the pollutions(genitive case, plural for multiple acts)[144]
     of the idols (genitive plural)
     and of the sexual immorality (genitive singular)
     and of the strangulation (genitive singular)
     and of the bloodshed (genitive singular)

29 ἀπέχεσθαι
  εἰδωλοθύτων
  καὶ αἵματος
  καὶ πνικτῶν
  καὶ πορνείας

29 to hold back (present tense, middle voice, infinitive)
  (from) idol sacrifices (genitive plural)
  and (from) blood/bloodshed (genitive singular)
  and (from) strangulations (genitive plural)
  and (from) sexual immorality (genitive singular)

If the genitive of the word "pollutions" connects it grammatically to all elements on the list that follows, as opposed to just the first item, then James's proposal has to do with listing the sources of moral impurity, identified in the Mosaic law, that Gentiles will have to observe.

The written decision sent to the churches eliminated the word "pollution" which, based on the original structure of the sentence, was the reason for avoiding the behaviors listed. If this omission was intentional, the council's intent may have been to transmit only the specific requirements to the Gentile churches without confusing them with issues of purity that would be familiar only to Jews. In any case, the fact that the decision had to do with moral behavior rather than ritual purity was lost in transmission.

What Does the Decision Mean?

My new proposed translations of the two passages are:

> but we should write to them to only stay away from impurities caused by idols and sexual immorality and oppression and bloodshed. (Acts 15:20, author's paraphrase)

and

> that you stay away from idol sacrifices and bloodshed
> and oppression and sexual immorality. If you keep
> yourselves from these, you will do well. Farewell. (Acts
> 15:29, author's paraphrase)

Gentile Christians were to avoid idolatry, violence against others by bloodshed or cutting off breath, and sexual immorality. There are no references to eating in any of these restrictions, and food laws were not part of the debate chronicled in these passages. In the injunction to "stay away" is an implication that there has already been more than enough of the pollutions listed, and that, in the new life in Christ, these sins no longer have a place.

The question asked of the council was whether circumcision and following the entire Mosaic law was required of Gentile Christians. The response of the council was to say no—one did not have to become an Israelite and enter the full Mosaic covenant to belong to the God of Israel. A place had been prepared already for the Gentiles, and the specifics of the moral law for non-Jews had already been spelled out in the Torah.

Immediately following the statement of the decision of the council, James concluded with a reference to the availability of the Mosaic law: "For in every city, for generations past, Moses has had those who proclaim him, for he has been read aloud every sabbath in the synagogues" (Acts 15:21). If a Gentile is looking for the basis of the decision, he need only go as far as the local synagogue to hear the reading of the law that forbids idolatry, blasphemy, bloodshed, and sexual immorality. As Christians, these Gentiles would already be aware of the prohibition of insult to God by blasphemy. The council of elders reinforced the other major provisions of the law given through Moses as it already existed and applied to Gentiles.

If the Gentile problem was addressed by the council, why would there still be a conflict between Peter and Paul in Galatians? The policy issue of circumcision had been decided, but the details about how the groups within the church should live together in practice had not been worked out. In addition, the faction that had lost the circumcision question may not have been completely won over by the result. Gentiles were assured by the decision that they were considered free and equal members of the church, but the kind of fellowship that could cross the Jewish-Gentile divide was still to be worked out.

Shortly after this time, Paul writes about the importance of sensitivity to the convictions of others, and the fact that what one chooses to eat can lead to difficulties for others (Rom 14:1–3). If the council's decree had clearly forbidden all meat involved in idol worship, why would Paul later say that it is permitted to eat such meat? Paul's concern in 1 Corinthians 8:9–10 is for the effects on others of eating meat of questionable origin. Even when one is free to eat foods that cause concern to others, one should not do so out of respect for the other's conscience.

What Do Non-Jews Need to Do?

When the question was raised in the early church about whether Gentile Christians were required to become Jews, the answer was a clear "no." Non-Jewish Christians were only directed to observe those critical portions of the Mosaic law that applied to Gentiles—the ones forbidding idolatry, violence, and sexual immorality. Jewish and Gentile Christians were to be one people without distinctions before God or with each other.

Bruce Metzger, in his analysis of the language of the decree, came much of the way down this path but stopped short of this conclusion. He says,

> In conclusion, therefore, it appears that the least unsatisfactory solution of the complicated textual and exegetical problems of the Apostolic Decree is to regard

the fourfold decree as original (foods offered to idols, strangled meat, eating blood, and unchastity—whether ritual or moral), [145]

In rejecting the alternative moral interpretation of the decree, he says,

[T]his reading can scarcely be original, for it implies that a special warning had to be given to Gentile converts against such sins as murder, and that this was expressed in the form of asking them to "abstain" from it—which is slightly absurd![146]

Since all elements of the fourfold decree can have moral interpretations, and since the topic of the decree is the minimum requirements Gentile Christians must satisfy, it is far from absurd to require them to avoid the major moral defilements of idolatry, violence, and sexual immorality.

The decree of the Jerusalem council was not an odd exception to the lack of concern for dietary regulations in Gentile churches. It was, rather, an affirmation that moral law as understood through the Mosaic covenant continued to matter to all those who belong to the people of God through Jesus. This is no statement of exemption from the law, but rather a statement that the righteousness defined by the law had not gone out of fashion, particularly in the face of the idolatrous, violent, and immoral practices of the surrounding Gentile cultures. The righteousness of the resident alien was still required of the newly invited Gentiles in the early church.[147]

Questions for Reflection and Discussion

1. How do you picture the groups of Jews and Gentiles getting along together in Paul's churches? What did they agree on? What did they disagree about?

2. What customs established Jewish identity? How could those customs create factions in a church?

3. Read through chapter 15 of Acts. Who participated in the council? What perspectives were included in the debate?

4. What are the factors James used to arrive at his decision?

5. Compare Acts 15:8–9 with Acts 11:11–18. What does the action of the Holy Spirit tell Peter and James?

6. Read the letter in Acts 15:22–29. What is meant by "having become of one mind"? How did the council come to consensus?

7. How do you understand Acts 15:28?

8. Do you think that "essentials" are more likely to describe what foods not to eat or what kinds of behavior are not allowed?

7

What Did Paul Expect of Christian Lifestyles?

Paul described himself as a Pharisee, a Jew who was intensely active in his faith: "I advanced in Judaism beyond many among my people of the same age, for I was far more zealous for the traditions of my ancestors" (Gal 1:14).

Paul's intense engagement in his faith led him to oppose and arrest followers of Jesus when he believed they were his enemies. After his conversion, his enthusiasm led him to an energetic and aggressive ministry among them. Some parts of Paul's early background and education carried forward into his missionary life, while he left behind other aspects of his Jewish roots. Paul's conversion changed him from a Jew earnestly waiting for the Messiah to a Jew for whom the Messiah had come.

Paul's expectations of the Messiah came out of his Jewish heritage and education. For him, Jesus fulfilled rather than invalidated the law and prophecy of the Hebrew Scriptures. Paul's understanding of the crucifixion and resurrection of Jesus radically changed his expectations of what it meant to live in a relationship with God now that it was mediated through the presence of Christ.

What kind of behavior did Paul expect of those who were part of the largely Gentile churches he founded? How closely did those expectations match the provisions of the law that applied to non-Jews?

How similar were they to the evolving Jewish understanding of what righteousness meant for the children of Noah? At the point of his conversion, Paul was a fully observant Jewish Pharisee. As Paula Fredrickson points out, Paul experienced two major miracles—his experience of Jesus on the road and the unexpected positive response of pagans to his gospel.[148] Because of these experiences, Paul's instructions for living in Christ reflect both his preconversion Judaism and his experiences dealing with the behavior of Gentile converts.[149]

Many, many books and papers have been written about Paul and law. W. D. Davies in the 1950s was the first to pick up the thread begun by Albert Schweitzer considering the impact of Paul's Jewish background on his way of thinking. Davies was the first, between the 1950s and the 1980s, to take Paul's Judaism seriously. He began to incorporate Jewish ideas into understanding Paul, although not to the extent of including Paul's Jewish way of thinking. Over the last several decades, scholars have included this wider understanding of Paul's origins.[150] Scholars needed to rethink their assumptions about Paul rejecting aspects of his Jewish origins. Krister Stendahl saw Paul as one who was called into a new role rather than converted away from his Jewish faith—one who spoke about the law "from the perspective of traditional Jewish thought as it was known to him."[151] I agree.

Apparent inconsistencies among Paul's letters have led to different approaches to understanding them. We can (1) accept that Paul is inconsistent in his positions, (2) assume that Paul held a consistent core of convictions that were applied differently in different circumstances, or (3) expect that Paul's positions on specific issues developed over the time. I hold that his positions developed over time. Regarding the Judaism of his early life, Paul may have (1) rejected his Jewish background at his conversion and opposed it in his ministry, (2) become a radical Jew and continued his work of reformation from a new perspective, or (3) continued as a believing Jew living in the messianic age. I consider the last alternative the most likely.

Rather than follow a particular scholar's line of thought, we will look at Paul's opinions in his own words from the letters agreed by the widest range of scholars to have been written by Paul himself. These are the letters to the Galatians, Philippians, Romans, Corinthians, Thessalonians, and Philemon.

How Can We Follow the Way Paul Thinks?

We do not know, although scholars argue about it, exactly how much of Paul's early education happened in Tarsus and how much in Jerusalem. Paul was fluent in Hebrew as well as Greek, as we learn when he addresses the people in Acts 21:40. In spite of his birth into a family living in the Diaspora, Paul considered himself to be completely an observant member of the people of Israel:

> circumcised on the eighth day, a member of the people of Israel, of the tribe of Benjamin, a Hebrew born of Hebrews; as to the law, a Pharisee; as to zeal, a persecutor of the church; as to righteousness under the law, blameless. (Phil 3:5–6)

When Paul came to Jerusalem to continue his education, he would have been welcomed by relatives living in the city (Acts 23:16). The information Paul gave about himself in Jerusalem can be accepted as accurate, since his readers would have had connections who confirmed the material. He claimed to be "a Jew, born in Tarsus in Cilicia, but brought up in this city at the feet of Gamaliel, educated strictly according to our ancestral law, being zealous for God, just as all of you are today" (Acts 22:3).

As a student of Gamaliel the Elder, Paul was squarely in the middle of Pharisaic life as it was known before the destruction of the temple. The founders of the two great schools of Pharisees, Hillel and Shammai, were a generation older than Paul. In his time, their schools would have been well established with numbers of students in each house.

When Paul encountered Jesus on the road to Damascus, his acceptance of the call of Jesus was not an alternative to his faith. On the contrary, his experience of Jesus only made sense in the context of his scriptural background. Scripture provided the context and meaning for the arrival of the Messiah, and Paul's acceptance of Jesus as Messiah was a result of his early faith rather than a rejection of it. He said, "Do we then overthrow the law by this faith? By no means! On the contrary, we uphold the law" (Rom 3:31).

The word Paul chooses, translated as "uphold," is ἵσταμαι (*histamai*), which implies putting something in place, acknowledging the validity of something, or even establishing or authorizing something.[152] Far from leaving the law behind, Paul saw this faith in Christ as solidifying, strengthening, and reinforcing the law that was already in place.[153] This understanding of Torah is an integral part of Paul's foundation in Judaism.

Paul was not a systematic theologian whose reasoning was based on an ordered set of principles. Rabbinic thinking two centuries later had become systematic, but, in Paul's time, Pharisees argued directly from Scripture about practical applications. The Scripture and traditions Paul had internalized were the center of the convictions he brought to specific situations. These were not completely consistent with each other, and he used a Pharisee's reasoning process to work through potential problems and inconsistencies. Paul's reasoning did not begin from central principles or from an integrated body of reference material. He worked from relevant parts of a body of Scripture, chosen and prioritized in response to particular situations.[154] As a Pharisee would, Paul used Scripture as his authority, adapting and applying it as needed to different situations that came up in the churches.[155]

How Are Salvation and Righteousness Connected?

For Paul, the resurrection of Jesus marked the critical turning point in the history of creation and in the relationship between God and human beings.

[S]ince all have sinned and fall short of the glory of God; they are now justified by his grace as a gift, through the redemption that is in Christ Jesus, whom God put forward as a sacrifice of atonement by his blood, effective through faith. He did this to show his righteousness, because in his divine forbearance he had passed over the sins previously committed; (Rom 3:23–25)

Human beings were freed from the consequences of their sin, the result of their self-focused disobedience to the will of God. God offered them reconciliation as an unconditional gift, just as if they had been righteous all along: "For our sake he made him to be sin who knew no sin, so that in him we might become the righteousness of God" (2 Cor 5:21). This righteousness makes possible a restored relationship with God that leads to eternal life.

Salvation through Christ results in righteousness, or at least the attribution of righteousness, to human beings through his death and resurrection: "I do not nullify the grace of God; for if justification comes through the law, then Christ died for nothing" (Gal 2:21). Justification, which is not precisely the same in its Greek original δικαιοσύνη *(dikaiosynē)* as in English, refers exclusively to restoring righteousness, restoring human beings to the state that God requires of them. Justified human beings are not excused in their current state, but, over time, they are transformed into the kind of people who naturally choose to do what is righteous, proper, correct, and pleasing to God.

Salvation and righteousness are deeply intertwined. In order to receive salvation, one must be able to approach a relationship with God from the basis of righteousness. Salvation involves transforming human beings, known for their failure to do God's will, into a condition from which they can be accepted as righteous in spite of themselves.

For Christ is the end of the law so that there may be righteousness for everyone who believes. (Rom 10:4)

The word here for end, τέλος *(telos)*, is not the disappearance of something, but its goal, purpose, or completion.

Righteousness is not an outmoded concept that is no longer relevant after the advent of Christ. It is the foundation for the success of the work of Christ on behalf of human beings. For Paul, righteousness was and always had been defined by God in communication with people through the Mosaic covenant. The chosen people were expected to be a light to the nations and to pass this understanding on to others. Righteousness itself, as a concept and a goal for human behavior, did not go out of fashion at the coming of Christ.

> But now, apart from law, the righteousness of God has been disclosed, and is attested by the law and the prophets, the righteousness of God through faith in Jesus Christ for all who believe. (Rom 3:21–22)

The presence of Christ is a separate and independent witness to what it means to be righteous, as well as the way that we, who are unable to live righteously on our own, can come to be considered righteous before God.

How Does Law Relate to Sin?

Paul uses the Greek word for law, νόμος *(nomos)*, to mean different things in different contexts and sometimes with more than one meaning. For example, in Romans 3:21, he uses it to mean both "the provisions of the Mosaic law" and "the books of Scripture which contain the law" in a single sentence. Some of the different meanings of the word include:

- Something parceled out or assigned
- A law, rule, principle or norm prescribing what a person must do
- Anything prescribed by custom, usage, or law

- The first five books of Moses (the Torah)
- The entire Hebrew Bible (the Tanakh)[156]

Paul's letters were written close together in time, so differences in usage or perspective do not imply changes in Paul's thought. On the other hand, Paul's letters usually are addressed to particular situations for particular groups of people with his message tailored to his audience. As a result, we would expect to find different nuances and implications in the use of the word "law" in various places in Paul's writings.

Where Paul talks about the law in general or in principle as a set of requirements for behavior he is most likely referring to the Mosaic law, e.g., "through the law comes the knowledge of sin" (Rom 3:20). Knowledge of sin—knowledge of the difference between good and evil—can only exist in the presence of some form of standard: "where there is no law, neither is there violation" (Rom 4:15). Violation or transgression is only meaningful when there is some kind of standard that a person can either comply with or reject. This is the reality of the nature of any kind of standard.

> What then should we say? That the law is sin? By no means! Yet, if it had not been for the law, I would not have known sin. I would not have known what it is to covet if the law had not said, "You shall not covet." (Rom 7:7)

I might have coveted often, but I would not have known that it was a sin.

One recurring concern in rabbinic conversations is whether or not we can be held responsible for violation of a law if we were not aware of the provisions of that particular law. Paul addresses the issue of ignorance of moral law in the first chapter of Romans. Those who have not heard the words of the law may still be aware of its provisions.

> For what can be known about God is plain to them, because God has shown it to them. Ever since the creation of the world his eternal power and divine

nature, invisible though they are, have been understood
and seen through the things he has made. (Rom 1:19–20)

Knowledge of God is visible in creation for those who have not received
the direct communication available to the children of the covenant.

When Gentiles, who do not possess the law, do instinctively
what the law requires, these, though not having the law, are
a law to themselves. They show that what the law requires
is written on their hearts, to which their own conscience
also bears witness; and their conflicting thoughts will
accuse or perhaps excuse them (Rom 2:14–15)

The knowledge of righteousness, of what the law requires, is available in
our hearts and by the internal conflict we experience when we choose
not to follow it.

Paul struggled with the relationship between law and sin. If there
was no sin before the law existed to define it, then is the law somehow
evil because it defines what sin is? Paul says no, but then he has to
account for the fact that knowing about a restriction leads human
beings to want to do exactly what is forbidden. His reasoning is this:

[T]he law is holy, and the commandment is holy and just
and good. Did what is good, then, bring death to me?
By no means! It was sin, working death in me through
what is good, in order that sin might be shown to be
sin, and through the commandment might become
sinful beyond measure. (Rom 7:12–13)

Paul describes the normal human tendency to rebelliousness in terms
of the dichotomy between mind and body:

I see in my members another law at war with the law
of my mind, making me captive to the law of sin that

> dwells in my members. . . . So then, with my mind I
> am a slave to the law of God, but with my flesh I am a
> slave to the law of sin. (Rom 7:23–25)

The mind, or intention, or will, is opposed to the desires of the "flesh" for sensual gratification.[157] This description of the inclination to sin is typical of the tendencies (יֵצֶר, *yetzer*) to good and evil in Jewish tradition, and very different from the introspective examination of motive that appears in later Western thought. The fact that knowing the restrictions of law exacerbates the tendency to do evil is not a reason to ignore or eliminate law altogether.

God's desire is that all, Jew and Gentile, will do good and not evil.

> There will be anguish and distress for everyone who
> does evil, the Jew first and also the Greek, but glory and
> honor and peace for everyone who does good, the Jew
> first and also the Greek. For God shows no partiality.
> (Rom 2:9–11)

God alone evaluates behavior, and even when the evaluation is negative, it serves the ultimate good of the one being evaluated.

> For all who eat and drink without discerning the body,
> eat and drink judgment against themselves. For this
> reason many of you are weak and ill, and some have
> died. But if we judged ourselves, we would not be
> judged. But when we are judged by the Lord, we are
> disciplined so that we may not be condemned along
> with the world. (1 Cor 11:29–32)

For Paul, the function of the law changed with the coming of the Messiah. The law continued to express the nature of the righteousness God required, but with the presence of Christ, the law no longer needed to function as a disciplinarian.

> Now before faith came, we were imprisoned and
> guarded under the law until faith would be revealed.
> Therefore the law was our disciplinarian until Christ
> came, so that we might be justified by faith. But now
> that faith has come, we are no longer subject to a
> disciplinarian, for in Christ Jesus you are all children
> of God through faith. (Gal 3:23–26)

When children have grown old enough to accept responsibility for
their own actions, they no longer need supervision to enforce the rules.
Adults ultimately internalize the principles behind the rules and use
them as a guide for behavior. In the end, behavior that conforms to
the rules becomes a natural practice. When we outgrow the need for
a disciplinarian, it does not mean that we are free to violate the law at
will. Rather it means that our conformance with the law has become
natural, normal, and intentional.

Paul, like Jesus, has hard words for those who know what the law
says, but do not follow it: "They know God's decree, that those who
practice such things deserve to die—yet they not only do them but
even applaud others who practice them" (Rom 1:32). It is not enough
simply to have heard or learned the way we should behave. We must
act according to that guidance as well—"For it is not the hearers of
the law who are righteous in God's sight, but the doers of the law who
will be justified" (Rom 2:13).

Simply having been one of the people who originally received the
law is not enough. The law is of no value if its lessons are ignored.

> Circumcision indeed is of value if you obey the law;
> but if you break the law, your circumcision has become
> uncircumcision. . . . Then those who are physically
> uncircumcised but keep the law will condemn you that
> have the written code and circumcision but break the
> law. (Rom 2:25, 27)

For Paul, as for Jesus, those who do the will of the Father, whether they were born Jews or not, are conforming to God's righteousness.

What Are the Roles of Grace and Faith?

There are two ways of understanding the way law works: either we have to comply with the law in order to earn God's favor, or we choose to comply with the law in gratitude for God's kindness. In either case, the law describes the kind of behavior God desires for human beings. In the first case, we can be proud of our ability to achieve what God requires (and boast about it). In the second case, we can only acknowledge that the loving goodness of God has nothing to do with our own merit. Paul cited Abraham's example to demonstrate this distinction:

> For if Abraham was justified by works, he has something to boast about, but not before God. For what does the scripture say? "Abraham believed God, and it was reckoned to him as righteousness." Now to one who works, wages are not reckoned as a gift but as something due. (Rom 4:2–4)

The promise to Abraham preceded the Mosaic law, and the promise made through faith to those who believe cannot be modified by the later provisions of the law.

> My point is this: the law, which came four hundred thirty years later, does not annul a covenant previously ratified by God, so as to nullify the promise. For if the inheritance comes from the law, it no longer comes from the promise; but God granted it to Abraham through the promise. (Gal 3:17–18)

Grace, and the faith that makes it possible to accept grace, come first; and the law with its provisions and requirements comes second.

Jews and Gentiles all are made righteous by God's grace through their faith. This is a spiritual activity and not the physical action of doing the works of the law.

> For I am not ashamed of the gospel; it is the power of God
> for salvation to everyone who has faith, to the Jew first
> and also to the Greek. For in it the righteousness of God
> is revealed through faith for faith; as it is written, "The
> one who is righteous will live by faith." (Rom 1:16–17)

The provisions of the law came with consequences—rewards and punishments, blessings and curses—which are results of the relationship with God rather than its preconditions. If we try to comply with the law as a way to win God's favor, inevitably we will fail and receive the negative consequences.

> For all who rely on the works of the law are under a
> curse; for it is written, "Cursed is everyone who does
> not observe and obey all the things written in the book
> of the law." Now it is evident that no one is justified
> before God by the law; for "The one who is righteous
> will live by faith." But the law does not rest on faith; on
> the contrary, "Whoever does the works of the law will
> live by them." (Gal 3:10–12)

If we depend entirely on doing the works of the law and not on faith, we cannot attain the righteousness God commands.

Paul recognized that, even though righteousness is defined by the law, we cannot become righteous through the law—only through faith.

> We ourselves are Jews by birth and not Gentile sinners;
> yet we know that a person is justified not by the works

of the law but through faith in Jesus Christ. And we
have come to believe in Christ Jesus, so that we might
be justified by faith in Christ, and not by doing the
works of the law, because no one will be justified by
the works of the law. (Gal 2:15–16)

The law describes what righteousness and holiness look like, even
though it does not provide the path for us to use to attain righteousness.

Now we know that whatever the law says, it speaks
to those who are under the law, so that every mouth
may be silenced, and the whole world may be held
accountable to God. For "no human being will be
justified in his sight" by deeds prescribed by the law,
(Rom 3:19–20)

The law makes it possible for all people to learn what it means to be
accountable to God, even though they cannot be made righteous by
attempting righteous behavior on their own.

Since we have these promises, beloved, let us cleanse
ourselves from every defilement of body and of spirit,
making holiness perfect in the fear of God. (2 Cor 7:1)

This desire and effort to pursue the righteousness described in the law
is only engaged in response to the free grace of God, and is never a
condition for it.

It was clear to Paul that Jesus is the one through whom human
beings can be made righteous before God.

For just as by the one man's disobedience the many were
made sinners, so by the one man's obedience the many
will be made righteous. But law came in, with the result
that the trespass multiplied; but where sin increased,

137

grace abounded all the more, so that, just as sin exercised dominion in death, so grace might also exercise dominion through justification leading to eternal life through Jesus Christ our Lord. (Rom 5:19–21)

By joining with Christ in faith, ordinary sinful human beings can receive the power to acquire the righteousness of God.

The death he died, he died to sin, once for all; but the life he lives, he lives to God. So you also must consider yourselves dead to sin and alive to God in Christ Jesus. Therefore, do not let sin exercise dominion in your mortal bodies, to make you obey their passions. No longer present your members to sin as instruments of wickedness, but present yourselves to God as those who have been brought from death to life, and present your members to God as instruments of righteousness. For sin will have no dominion over you, since you are not under law but under grace. (Rom 6:10–14)

This leads to a process in which we participate through faith and through which righteousness becomes more and more part of our daily reality.

Was Paul Still Jewish When He Became Christian?

After becoming a follower of Jesus, Paul continued Jewish practices in a number of different ways. He assumed that the legal procedures specified in the Mosaic law were still in force,[158] and used them.

This is the third time I am coming to you. "Any charge must be sustained by the evidence of two or three witnesses." (2 Cor 13:1)

He turned to the Mosaic law as a basis for his arguments about support for those who are active in missionary work.

> Do I say this on human authority? Does not the law also say the same? For it is written in the law of Moses, "You shall not muzzle an ox while it is treading out the grain." (1 Cor 9:8–10)

His concern for sexuality within family relationships was based on the restrictions of Leviticus.

> It is actually reported that there is sexual immorality among you, and of a kind that is not found even among pagans; for a man is living with his father's wife. (1 Cor 5:1)

> You shall not uncover the nakedness of your father's wife; it is the nakedness of your father. (Lev 18:8)

Paul summarized the teaching of Jesus on love by saying, "the whole law is summed up in a single commandment, 'You shall love your neighbor as yourself'" (Gal 5:14). This is very similar to the way that Hillel responded when he was asked by a non-Jew to summarize the whole Torah as he stood on one foot: "What you dislike do not do to others; that is the whole Torah. The rest is commentary. Go and learn" (B. Shab. 31a)[159].

Paul did not abandon the Hebrew Bible, his process for interpreting Scripture, or his conviction that the Scripture represented God's communication with human beings when he became a follower of Jesus.

With his commitment to Christ, Paul's highest priority became sharing the coming of Jesus as the Messiah to Jews and to the nations. As a missionary and evangelist, Paul put a higher priority on the success of his message than he did on his specifically Jewish practices: "For though I am free with respect to all, I have made myself a slave to all, so that I might win more of them" (1 Cor 9:19), He was willing to tailor all aspects of his life, from his communication style to his lifestyle, to match those he was trying to reach.

> To the Jews I became as a Jew, in order to win Jews. To those under the law I became as one under the law (though I myself am not under the law) so that I might win those under the law. To those outside the law I became as one outside the law (though I am not free from God's law but am under Christ's law) so that I might win those outside the law. (1 Cor 9:20–21)

He was free to do this because living by the law of Christ made it possible for him to follow or not to follow the ritual provisions of the law as the situation demanded.

Paul honored the role of the people of Israel in the process of God's ongoing revelation. Their place in the historical unfolding of God's plan is unique.

> They are Israelites, and to them belong the adoption, the glory, the covenants, the giving of the law, the worship, and the promises; to them belong the patriarchs, and from them, according to the flesh, comes the Messiah, who is over all, God blessed forever. Amen. (Rom 9:4–5)

Their position as the first chosen, the first to be in direct relationship with the living God, can never be taken away: "Then what advantage has the Jew? Or what is the value of circumcision? Much, in every way. For in the first place the Jews were entrusted with the oracles of God" (Rom 3:1–2).

Even the rejection of the Messiah in Paul's time was seen as a way by which the message was spread to Gentiles.

> So I ask, have they stumbled so as to fall? By no means! But through their stumbling salvation has come to the

Gentiles, so as to make Israel jealous. Now if their stumbling means riches for the world, and if their defeat means riches for Gentiles, how much more will their full inclusion mean! (Rom 11:11–12)

Paul sees the separation between the people of Israel and the followers of Jesus to be only temporary, one stage in a process that ends with full inclusion of both groups:

I can testify that they have a zeal for God, but it is not enlightened. For, being ignorant of the righteousness that comes from God, and seeking to establish their own, they have not submitted to God's righteousness. (Rom 10:2–3)

The issue for Paul, as always, is righteousness. He sees the Jews who do not recognize Jesus as Messiah as rejecting the gift of God to their generation.

In practice, Jews and Gentiles come to the gospel from the same basis in human nature. "What then? Are we any better off? No, not at all; for we have already charged that all, both Jews and Greeks, are under the power of sin" (Rom 3:9). The blessing of righteousness through faith is available to Jew and Gentile, just as is was offered to Abraham before the Mosaic law was received.[160]

Is this blessedness, then, pronounced only on the circumcised, or also on the uncircumcised? We say, "Faith was reckoned to Abraham as righteousness." How then was it reckoned to him? Was it before or after he had been circumcised? It was not after, but before he was circumcised. (Rom 4:9–10)

In short, all are equal, Jews and Gentiles alike, in receiving the righteousness that comes through faith. "For in Christ Jesus neither circumcision nor uncircumcision counts for anything; the only thing that counts is faith working through love" (Gal 5:6).

For a follower of Jesus, Jewish observance is an option that one may or may not choose. Paul recommends that no change be made in one's status—that one who was a Jew remain a Jew and one who was not a Jew not seek to become one.

> Was anyone at the time of his call already circumcised? Let him not seek to remove the marks of circumcision. Was anyone at the time of his call uncircumcised? Let him not seek circumcision. Circumcision is nothing, and uncircumcision is nothing; but obeying the commandments of God is everything. Let each of you remain in the condition in which you were called. (1 Cor 7:18–20)

If a person chooses to accept circumcision, then he commits himself to take full responsibility under the law for all of its requirements, moral and ritual. "Once again I testify to every man who lets himself be circumcised that he is obliged to obey the entire law" (Gal 5:3).

Circumcision does not become a substitute for faith in Christ, however, since salvation is not received through complying with the requirements of the law. "You who want to be justified by the law have cut yourselves off from Christ; you have fallen away from grace" (Gal 5:4). If we choose to follow the whole law instead of, and not in addition to, faith in Christ, this becomes a rejection of the grace of God offered in Jesus.

What Did Paul Mean by "Old" and "New" Israel?

Since God is equally the God of Jews and Gentiles, both are justified, made righteous, on the same basis.

> Or is God the God of Jews only? Is he not the God of Gentiles also? Yes, of Gentiles also, since God is one; and he will justify the circumcised on the ground of faith and the uncircumcised through that same faith. (Rom 3:29–30)

Those who belong to God are one people without internal distinctions based on their cultural origins. "For there is no distinction between Jew and Greek; the same Lord is Lord of all and is generous to all who call on him. For, 'Everyone who calls on the name of the Lord shall be saved'" (Rom 10:12–13). This single new people is defined, not by their original ethnicity or outward appearance, but by their faith.

> For a person is not a Jew who is one outwardly, nor is true circumcision something external and physical. Rather, a person is a Jew who is one inwardly, and real circumcision is a matter of the heart—it is spiritual and not literal. Such a person receives praise not from others but from God. (Rom 2:28–29)

Paul chose to use words that originally referred to the people of the covenant—Israel, Jew, circumcised—to refer to the people brought together into the new covenant in Christ.

> This means that it is not the children of the flesh who are the children of God, but the children of the promise are counted as descendants. (Rom 9:8)

> Just as Abraham "believed God, and it was reckoned to him as righteousness," so, you see, those who believe are the descendants of Abraham. (Gal 3:6–7)

> And if you belong to Christ, then you are Abraham's offspring, heirs according to the promise. (Gal 3:29)

There was no question for Paul that the hereditary people of Israel were the ones to whom the Messiah had been sent. For "when the fullness of time had come, God sent his Son, born of a woman, born under the law, in order to redeem those who were under the law, so that we might receive adoption as children" (Gal 4:4–5).

However, Paul identified Christ the Messiah as the foundation of the earlier covenant relationships, even before Jesus was born or lived in the world.

> I do not want you to be unaware, brothers and sisters, that our ancestors were all under the cloud, and all passed through the sea, and all were baptized into Moses in the cloud and in the sea, and all ate the same spiritual food, and all drank the same spiritual drink. For they drank from the spiritual rock that followed them, and the rock was Christ. (1 Cor 10:1–4)

Christ's presence confirms and strengthens the promises made in the covenants, and it is the mechanism for the extension of the promises to the Gentiles.

> For I tell you that Christ has become a servant of the circumcised on behalf of the truth of God in order that he might confirm the promises given to the patriarchs, and in order that the Gentiles might glorify God for his mercy. As it is written, "Therefore I will confess you among the Gentiles, and sing praises to your name" (Rom 15:8–9)

When Paul talked about the new Israel, he was not creating a new entity. The role of the people of the covenant was not changed or confused. Paul used this terminology as a metaphor to illustrate that the new, larger group—Jews and Gentiles brought together in Christ—are now one people in a similar relationship with God.

Paul's Goal Is Pleasing God

Paul explained that distinctions between Jews and Gentiles, like those between men and women and slaves and free people, no longer mattered in the new church communities. "Circumcision is nothing, and uncircumcision is nothing; but obeying the commandments of God is everything" (1 Cor 7:19). Throughout his letters, the primary authority that Paul cites is Scripture. He often uses references and outright quotations from the Greek *Septuagint* translation of the law, the prophets, and the writings. These materials are his primary source of information about God's actions in the world, God's relationship with the people of Israel, and God's nature.

Scripture is still his primary source when Paul says,

> Finally, brothers and sisters, we ask and urge you in the Lord Jesus that, as you learned from us how you ought to live and to please God (as, in fact, you are doing), you should do so more and more. For you know what instructions we gave you through the Lord Jesus. (1 Thess 4:1–2)

In most cases, the teachings of Jesus, even when they involve a change in priority (as with the second greatest commandment), are in conformity with Torah. In the rare instances where the teaching of Jesus differs from Torah, as we saw in the instructions on divorce, Paul accepts the teaching of Jesus as having precedence over the instruction in the Torah.

Paul believed that guidance on living a holy life reflects God's intent for the people, whether that guidance comes from Scripture or from the teaching of Jesus—"For God did not call us to impurity but in holiness. Therefore whoever rejects this rejects not human authority but God, who also gives his Holy Spirit to you" (1 Thess 4:7–8). Rejection of the teachings on behavior, Paul believed, was a rejection of the will of the God who provided and motivated them. If human beings are to live in relationship with God, we must live in a way that is worthy of that honor.

For we are the temple of the living God; as God said,
"I will live in them and walk among them, and I will
be their God, and they shall be my people. (2 Cor 6:16)

In Philippians 1:27, Paul urges the Christians to "conduct yourselves
in a manner worthy of the gospel (Μόνον ἀξίως τοῦ εὐαγγελίου τοῦ
Χριστοῦ πολιτεύεσθε)". This verb πολιτεύομαι (*politeuomai*) means to
live, to conduct oneself, and to lead one's life. It also has an additional
sense from its root form πόλις (*polis*) of citizenship or even having one's
home base grounded in the news of the gospel. Paul expected that those
who were in Christ would behave in a particular way, living out the
gospel in their behavior. Life in the church had a behavioral component
that went along with the faith that united the people.

Paul shared this behavioral standard with each of the churches he
founded and visited: "For this reason I have sent to you Timothy, who
is my beloved and faithful child in the Lord, and he will remind you
of my ways which are in Christ, just as I teach everywhere in every
church" (1 Cor 4:17). Paul says that Timothy will be reminding the
Corinthians of the ways of living in Christ that Paul taught in his visits
to all of the churches.

The word Paul uses for "ways" is ὁδός (*hodos*), which can mean a
road, path, route, or way, but which also carries the extended meaning
of a way of life. As Edwin Freed points out,

> Here the word translated as "way" (*hodos*) refers to the
> moral/ethical standards Paul required of himself and his
> converts. It is the equivalent of the Hebrew word *halakah*
> ("rule of conduct") and of the Greek *peripateo* in its moral/
> ethical sense of "conduct of one's life" or "live."[161]

This ὁδός is the same word which Moses' father-in-law uses in Exodus
18:20 in the *Septuagint*, when he advises that Moses make known to the
people "the way" (τὰς ὁδούς [*hodos*]) in which they are to walk under
the statutes and laws that God provides.

The way to follow involves a choice.

> Happy are those who do not follow the advice of the wicked, or take the path that sinners tread, or sit in the seat of scoffers; but their delight is in the law of the LORD, and on his law they meditate day and night. (Ps 1:1–2)

For those who have accepted salvation through faith in Christ, Paul has continuing expectations about present and future behavior.

> [H]owever, let us keep living by that same *standard* to which we have attained. Brethren, join in following my example, and observe those who walk according to the pattern you have in us. (Phil 3:16–17 NASB)

As did the leaders of the Jerusalem church, Paul had a strong sense of the immediacy of the expected return of Christ. He expressed that expectation when he said,

> [T]he night is far gone, the day is near. Let us then lay aside the works of darkness and put on the armor of light; let us live honorably as in the day, not in reveling and drunkenness, not in debauchery and licentiousness, not in quarreling and jealousy. Instead, put on the Lord Jesus Christ, and make no provision for the flesh, to gratify its desires. (Rom 13:12–14)

The time of darkness is nearly gone, and the day, that day, the day of the Lord, was expected momentarily. How would we behave on the day we expect the Lord? This is the way Paul expects every one of us to behave every day.

Let us behave properly, just the way we will behave on the day we meet Christ face to face, so that we will not need to be embarrassed in front of him. What would we rather not have Jesus catch us doing? Would we want to have Jesus find us out-of-control drunk, messing around where we should not be messing, or having a spiteful bickering match? Paul did not want any of his people ashamed on that day, which might come at any moment. Behaving properly every day mattered.

Idolatry Leads to Craving Evil

Paul touched on a wide variety of behaviors in his letters, from the very good to the very bad. He described the behavior of the Israelites while Moses was up on the mountain.

> Now these things occurred as examples for us, so that we might not desire evil as they did. Do not become idolaters as some of them did; as it is written, "The people sat down to eat and drink, and they rose up to play." (1 Cor 10:6–7)

Paul cites the consequences of this past idolatry as a warning for all of us in the present.

Those who give themselves up to the desires of the flesh, not even offering token resistance, become addicted to their evil behavior. Paul's description of those who reject the righteousness of God comes from the first chapter of the letter to the Romans.

> Therefore God gave them up in the lusts of their hearts to impurity, to the degrading of their bodies among themselves, because they exchanged the truth about God for a lie and worshiped and served the creature rather than the Creator (Rom 1:24–25)

Paul saw idolatry, placing any created object before God, as a source of all other forms of corruption.

And since they did not see fit to acknowledge God, God gave them up to a debased mind and to things that should not be done. They were filled with every kind of wickedness, evil, covetousness, malice. Full of envy, murder, strife, deceit, craftiness, they are gossips, slanderers, God-haters, insolent, haughty, boastful, inventors of evil, rebellious toward parents, foolish, faithless, heartless, ruthless. (Rom 1:28–31)

The specific people Paul talks about are not identified, but their primary sin, the one that leads to the others, is rejecting God and substituting created things for the Creator. The resultant behavior, while bad in itself, is the consequence of the depraved mind that flourishes in the absence of God.

Sensuality Results from the Flesh Being Hostile to God

In Paul's own time, many chose to reject the gospel and continue to enjoy physical desires and their satisfaction. Paul said,

For many live as enemies of the cross of Christ; I have often told you of them, and now I tell you even with tears. Their end is destruction; their god is the belly; and their glory is in their shame; their minds are set on earthly things. (Phil 3:18–19)

Physical satisfaction is transitory and not supposed to dominate a person's attention.

"All things are lawful for me," but not all things are beneficial. "All things are lawful for me," but I will not be dominated by anything. "Food is meant for the stomach and the stomach for food," and God will destroy both one and the other. (1 Cor 6:12–13)

These earthly activities, as we see in Romans 13:13, included debauchery, licentiousness, drunkenness, reveling, quarreling, and jealousy.

Paul draws the contrast between flesh σάρξ *(sarx)* and Spirit πνεῦμα *(pneuma)*. Daniel Boyarin points out that this is not a typical Platonic dualism, in which the body and all that is associated with it are disposable while the spirit represents a more valuable, higher form of reality. Paul's dualism is not rejection of the body, as we know from his insistence on bodily resurrection. The contrast of flesh and Spirit allows him to articulate two different ways of living.[162]

The flesh is whatever does not subject itself to God. He says,

To set the mind on the flesh is death, but to set the mind on the Spirit is life and peace. For this reason the mind that is set on the flesh is hostile to God; it does not submit to God's law—indeed it cannot, and those who are in the flesh cannot please God. (Rom 8:6–8)

This hostility goes back to the disobedience and rebellion of original sin, and it provides the motivation for ordinary sin in Paul's own life and the lives of those around him. The ultimate cause of sin is the innate self-centeredness of human nature. This is consistent in scientific terms with natural selection and in biblical terms with the disobedience of the first two human beings.

Does Paul then condemn all bodily desires and pleasures, or only some expressions of them? He says, "those who belong to Christ Jesus have crucified the flesh with its passions and desires" (Gal 5:24). Does this mean that all passions and desires are to be eliminated?

Edward Ellis studied sexual desire in Jewish literature around Paul's time and found that desire itself was condemned in only a few places, including the Sibylline Oracles and 2 Baruch. He also found distrust of desire in the Apocalypse of Moses and the Testaments of the Twelve Patriarchs. Many more sources, including the *Septuagint*, Tobit, Sirach, 1 Enoch, Jubilees, 4 Maccabees, Wisdom of Solomon, Psalms of Solomon, and the letter of Aristeas, condemn sexual immorality and excessive, uncontrolled desire. In light of Paul's Jewish background and his affirmation of marriage, Ellis concludes that Paul does not condemn all desire, but only that which is overpowering, uncontrolled, and likely to lead to sinful behavior.[163] Paul expects the believers to reject and eliminate this kind of excessive passion and desire.

Paul takes sexual immorality especially seriously, and this is because of the effect of sexual sin on the body. He says, "Shun fornication! Every sin that a person commits is outside the body; but the fornicator sins against the body itself" (1 Cor 6:18). Because of the presence of the Holy Spirit, a person is no longer alone in his or her own body. Everything that affects the body also affects the Spirit who is joined with it. Paul is horrified by the implications:

> Do you not know that your bodies are members of Christ? Should I therefore take the members of Christ and make them members of a prostitute? Never! Do you not know that whoever is united to a prostitute becomes one body with her? For it is said, "The two shall be one flesh." But anyone united to the Lord becomes one spirit with him. (1 Cor 6:15–17)

Paul's readers must have been shocked by his using the same word, κολλάω (*kollaō*), for joining with God and joining with a prostitute. The word's original meaning is to glue or to cement things together, and its use expanded to include tightly joining or bonding people or things. Paul's comments are very similar to the modern warning about sexually transmitted diseases: "You're having sex with everyone that person ever had sex with." Paul explains that both types of joining have a physical and spiritual component linking the prostitute (τῇ πόρνῃ [*pornē*]) and the Lord (τῷ κυρίῳ [*kyriō*]) that is degrading to the Lord.

151

Paul sees conflicts within the Christian community as symptoms of desires of the flesh, whether for comfort, possessions, partying, status, power, or sexual pleasure. Competition leads to envy and conflict, revealing evidence of the desires underneath. He asks, "as long as there is jealousy and quarreling among you, are you not of the flesh, and behaving according to human inclinations?" (1 Cor 3:3). The desires behind envy and conflict, if left unchecked, are also those that lead eventually to the larger violations of theft and murder.

What Is Appropriate Sexuality?

The alternative to life under the domination of the flesh is life in the way of Christ, and each person must grow into living in this way as one becomes more mature in Christ.

> I am speaking in human terms because of your natural limitations. For just as you once presented your members as slaves to impurity and to greater and greater iniquity, so now present your members as slaves to righteousness for sanctification. (Rom 6:19)

As the Spirit comes to live in believers, we each bear an additional level of responsibility for our own body.

> Do you not know that you are God's temple and that God's Spirit dwells in you? If anyone destroys God's temple, God will destroy that person. For God's temple is holy, and you are that temple. (1 Cor 3:16–17)

Our own behavior, even our treatment of our own body, becomes a part of our worship.

> I appeal to you therefore, brothers and sisters, by the mercies of God, to present your bodies as a living sacrifice, holy and acceptable to God, which is your spiritual worship. (Rom 12:1)

A mature person of faith will choose not to engage in sexual immorality, not because the activity is forbidden, but because it would tarnish the holiness required for the presence of God. "The body is meant not for fornication but for the Lord, and the Lord for the body" (1 Cor 6:13).

Since sexual morality is particularly important for Paul, he felt the need to explain not just what is forbidden, but also what is acceptable.

> For this is the will of God, your sanctification: that you abstain from fornication; that each one of you know how to control your own body in holiness and honor, not with lustful passion, like the Gentiles who do not know God; that no one wrong or exploit a brother or sister in this matter (1 Thess 4:3–6)

Those who are not as self-sufficient as Paul is, each should each have his or her own spouse, who will be treated with fairness and honor. In addition, no one should interfere in the marriage relationships of others. Living with the full expression of male and female in one bonded pair is appropriate and holy, just as the Creator intended from the beginning.

> If anyone thinks that he is not behaving properly toward his fiancée, if his passions are strong, and so it has to be, let him marry as he wishes; it is no sin. Let them marry. But if someone stands firm in his resolve, being under no necessity but having his own desire under control, and has determined in his own mind to keep her as his fiancée, he will do well. So then, he who marries his fiancée does well; and he who refrains from marriage will do better. (1 Cor 7:36–38)

In Paul's time, Greek romantic novels characterized desire as a form of madness or a sickness that could overcome people and drive irrational thoughts and behavior. In the novels, as in Paul's letters, this powerful force could be channeled properly in the relationship of marriage.[164]

According to Edward Ellis, Paul's view of marriage in 1 Corinthians 7 consisted of several elements:

1. Approval of marriage, sex, and the sexual pleasure involved
2. Belief that the responsibilities of marriage can be a distraction from service to God
3. Understanding sexual desire as a powerful and potentially dangerous force
4. Marriage being the place where sexual desire can be satisfied in a safe and godly way
5. Equality of husbands and wives in marriage[165]

Therefore, those who received Paul's advice about marriage would not think that Paul was condemning sexual desire or pleasure, but only that he was condemning their uncontrolled expression.

Peter Tomson also analyzed Paul's teaching on marriage in 1 Corinthians 7 in detail. He sees this chapter as Paul's answer to questions about whether we should abstain from sexual activity, divorce or separate, or remain unmarried in order to devote ourselves to the gospel. Tomson sees several different forms of authority in Paul's response: "I say by way of concession, not of command" (1 Cor 7:6), "I say" (1 Cor 7:8), "I give this command—not I but the Lord" (1 Cor 7:10), and "I say—I and not the Lord" (1 Cor 7:12).

The truly surprising teaching is on divorce, in which Paul is stricter than any of the precedents at the time.

> To the married I give this command—not I but the Lord—that the wife should not separate from her husband (but if she does separate, let her remain unmarried or else be reconciled to her husband), and

that the husband should not divorce his wife. To the rest I say—I and not the Lord—that if any believer has a wife who is an unbeliever, and she consents to live with him, he should not divorce her. And if any woman has a husband who is an unbeliever, and he consents to live with her, she should not divorce him. (1 Cor 7:10–13)

This prohibition on divorce is stricter than any ruling from the Pharisees and closer to the strictness of the Essenes. On this issue, Paul did not move from the legalism of a Pharisee to a more permissive liberal position. Instead, he moved to a stricter position held by the disciples.[166] This shows, among other things, that Paul was in communication with the other apostles and that he participated in aspects of the apostolic tradition that were different from those of his earlier Pharisaic background.

How Do We Manage to Do Good?

Doing good, living out actions that are good and not evil, is not automatic or instinctive. It takes thought and care. Paul says, "test everything; hold fast to what is good; abstain from every form of evil" (1 Thess 5:21–22). Each of us must seek carefully to find good things to be done and valued, and hold onto those good things. Each of us must be committed to doing good, time after time, whenever there is an opportunity, simply because we belong to Christ. Paul exhorts,

Let us not lose heart in doing good, for in due time we will reap if we do not grow weary. So then, while we have opportunity, let us do good to all people, and especially to those who are of the household of the faith. (Gal 6:9–10)

Our motivation for doing good also matters. We are supposed to do good because we belong to Christ and not for any other reason. We are not to do good in order to get a reward from others, although trading favors was part of all social relationships in the Roman Empire. We are not to do good out of pride or for self-promotion either. Paul says, "Do nothing from selfish ambition or conceit, but in humility regard others as better than yourselves. Let each of you look not to your own interests, but to the interests of others" (Phil 2:3–4).

Doing good to others is part of the law of love for one's neighbors, and the law of love is the underlying guide and criterion for all action among the followers of Christ—"For the whole law is summed up in a single commandment, "You shall love your neighbor as yourself" (Gal 5:14). Practicing love for others is a new kind of behavior pattern, a change from the usual human focus on self-satisfaction.

> For you were called to freedom, brothers and sisters; only do not use your freedom as an opportunity for self-indulgence, but through love become slaves to one another. (Gal 5:13)

How Do We Keep from Judging Others?

Paul is clear that bad behavior is common in the world, and that we cannot avoid encountering it.

> I wrote to you in my letter not to associate with sexually immoral persons—not at all meaning the immoral of this world, or the greedy and robbers, or idolaters, since you would then need to go out of the world. (1 Cor 5:9–10)

Paul explains that God will judge those who behave badly outside of the community of faith, but that such behavior is simply not acceptable for those who belong to Christ.

> But now I am writing to you not to associate with
> anyone who bears the name of brother or sister who
> is sexually immoral or greedy, or is an idolater, reviler,
> drunkard, or robber. Do not even eat with such a one.
> For what have I to do with judging those outside? Is
> it not those who are inside that you are to judge? God
> will judge those outside. "Drive out the wicked person
> from among you." (1 Cor 5:11–13)

The wording that Paul uses, "ἐξάρατε τὸν πονηρὸν ἐξ ὑμῶν αὐτῶν",
"Drive out the wicked person from among you" is a quotation from
Deuteronomy 19:19 in the *Septuagint* "ἐξαρεῖς τὸν πονηρὸν ἐξ ὑμῶν
αὐτῶν," which is translated "So you shall purge the evil from your
midst" (Deut 19:19).

Bringing the offender to repentance and restoration, of course, is
the preferred option.

> My friends, if anyone is detected in a transgression, you
> who have received the Spirit should restore such a one
> in a spirit of gentleness. Take care that you yourselves
> are not tempted. (Gal 6:1)

However, if this is not possible, improper behavior is in no way
acceptable within the community. Condoning the behavior might make
it likely that others would follow, or the community itself might become
associated with the particular behavior.

Those outside the community, either by choice or exclusion, are
only to be judged by God.

> Therefore do not pronounce judgment before the
> time, before the Lord comes, who will bring to light
> the things now hidden in darkness and will disclose
> the purposes of the heart. Then each one will receive
> commendation from God. (1 Cor 4:5)

157

Only God has full information about the secrets of the heart, and only God has enough information to judge correctly. He warns, "in passing judgment on another you condemn yourself, because you, the judge, are doing the very same things" (Rom 2:1). Those who impose judgment on others can expect to receive the same strictness or harshness that they themselves impose on others.

Paul shows concern for the effect that being judgmental can have on the recipient: "Let us therefore no longer pass judgment on one another, but resolve instead never to put a stumbling block or hindrance in the way of another" (Rom 14:13). Each follower of Jesus should be careful not to put any kind of obstacle between another person and Christ.

God is patient with each of us to allow us to find the way to repentance—"do you despise the riches of his kindness and forbearance and patience? Do you not realize that God's kindness is meant to lead you to repentance?" (Rom 2:4). We should follow that example of patient love and kindness with others who are struggling in sin.

> Those who eat must not despise those who abstain, and those who abstain must not pass judgment on those who eat; for God has welcomed them. Who are you to pass judgment on servants of another? It is before their own lord that they stand or fall. And they will be upheld, for the Lord is able to make them stand. (Rom 14:3–4)

No one is to impose any particular custom or way of worship on another, because only God has the authority over what is appropriate for each individual.

> Those who observe the day, observe it in honor of the Lord. Also those who eat, eat in honor of the Lord, since they give thanks to God; while those who abstain, abstain in honor of the Lord and give thanks to God. (Rom 14:6)

Each is to worship God sincerely to the best of his ability with the best understanding available of what is pleasing to God. Interference with the form of worship or service of another can only create a separation from God or within the community.

For Paul, as for Jesus, acting out of love was critically important. In his chapter on love in the letter to the Corinthians, Paul explains both the importance and character of love.

> Love is patient; love is kind; love is not envious or boastful or arrogant or rude. It does not insist on its own way; it is not irritable or resentful; it does not rejoice in wrongdoing, but rejoices in the truth. It bears all things, believes all things, hopes all things, endures all things. (1 Cor 13:4–7)

Evidence of love in action should be seen in interactions with friends, neighbors, strangers, and enemies.

> Let love be genuine; hate what is evil, hold fast to what is good; love one another with mutual affection; outdo one another in showing honor. . . . Contribute to the needs of the saints; extend hospitality to strangers. Bless those who persecute you; bless and do not curse them. (Rom 12:9–10, 13–14)

How Is Character Formed through Practice?

Becoming a follower of Jesus involves transformation—a new life and a new perspective. Paul exhorts, "Do not be conformed to this world, but be transformed by the renewing of your minds, so that you may discern what is the will of God—what is good and acceptable and perfect" (Rom 12:2). In a very real sense, human beings become what they do. A person who behaves well or poorly establishes a habit of that particular kind of behavior and grows into the sort of person who habitually behaves well or poorly.

In physiological terms, any repeated behavior strengthens the nerve and muscle pathways that support that behavior. The kind of practice that Paul recommends makes a real physical and psychological difference: "The things you have learned and received and heard and seen in me, practice these things, and the God of peace will be with you" (Phil 4:9). Paul commands continual learning and vigilance to assure that one's character is developing in the right direction.

Those who choose to follow the direction of the flesh—led by impulse, pleasure, and desire—are participants in a lifestyle that leads to an increasing taste and craving for certain kinds of experiences.

> Now the deeds of the flesh are evident, which are: immorality, impurity, sensuality, idolatry, sorcery, enmities, strife, jealousy, outbursts of anger, disputes, dissensions, factions, envying, drunkenness, carousing, and things like these, of which I forewarn you, just as I have forewarned you, that those who practice such things will not inherit the kingdom of God. (Gal 5:19–21)

As each impulse is indulged and reinforced, the behavior pattern becomes habitual and the resultant "fruits" of habit and attitude are established. Paul extends the injunctions against forbidden behaviors beyond the actual behaviors to the motivations leading to them. Thus, he includes sensuality as well as immorality and jealousy as well as strife. In this, Paul reflects Jesus' concern about small sins leading to larger sins.

The process of habituation also works for the positive. Those who practice righteous behavior become experienced in it and good at it. They also have the benefit of seeing the positive results of their behavior in relationships with others and in the lives of those around them.

Increasing self-control is an outgrowth of practice in responding to and overcoming passions and desires. Gentleness and kindness grow out of an increasing awareness of the needs of others. The capacity for patience and faithfulness grows with experience. The ability to love grows in those who act out of love, and the capacity for joy grows as joy is experienced and savored. Reducing and eliminating the clamor of conflicting desires makes the experience of internal peace a reality. The positive reinforcement of these behaviors solidifies habits and internalizes a personal preference for godly behavior.

Paul Led His Converts into Righteousness

Paul did not reject or abandon the original role of the people of Israel or the Hebrew Scriptures in his evangelistic ministry. They were the basis for his convictions about the Messiah. Paul extended the understanding, already present in the Hebrew Scriptures, about the movement of God's presence outward from Israel to the nations. Justification by faith as the basis for salvation still had to do with righteousness, with making it possible for human beings to enter a relationship with a holy God. Paul saw this righteousness as available through faith to Abraham even before the Mosaic covenant and also available by faith to those outside of Israel.

The righteousness that God requires was described in the law, and Paul assumed that the law provided the basis for proper behavior. He recognized that the presence of standards leads to both an awareness of violation and to the human resistance to standards in general. Nevertheless he says that the existence of standards in the law is "holy and just and good" (Rom 7:12). Careful conformance to the law is not sufficient for salvation, of course, since salvation depends on faith alone, but this does not make the provisions of the law irrelevant. One who chooses the route of circumcision voluntarily makes himself responsible for the full ritual and moral provisions of the law. One who does not make that choice is nevertheless subject to the law of Christ, and the behavior expected of those who belong to Christ is still righteousness. Law still matters, because law defines what righteousness means, and righteousness does not stop being relevant with the coming of Christ.

As we can see from the behaviors he encouraged and forbade, Paul did not reject or eliminate the moral teachings of his Jewish background. As Peter Tomson says,

> [T]he cumulative evidence that Paul based his practical instructions on elements of halakha can not be dismissed as a relic of his Jewish past gone out of use with his revelation of Christ. It must imply that rules functioning in some variety of Jewish community life informed his authoritative teaching as an Apostle.[167]

Although there is much commonality between the law and the fruit of the Spirit, the former does not necessarily define the latter. Steven Westerholm points out,

> Paul's understanding of the moral behavior which the Spirit induces corresponds nicely with the moral demands of the Mosaic law. But this does not mean that Paul derives Christian duty from the law. The ethical instruction of the epistles would have looked very different had Paul continued to find the will of God in the way he did as a Pharisee, by interpreting and applying the relevant statues from Torah.[168]

Paul does not discuss specific commandments, apply specific statutes to particular situations, consider the details of practical application, or use the tension of contrasting points of view, which are all typical of the discussion of behavior in rabbinic Judaism. Nevertheless he based his directions for behavior on the core moral provisions of the Mosaic law. The commonality we observe comes from the underlying ideal of the righteousness of God expressed through the Mosaic and new covenants.

Questions for Reflection and Discussion

1. What does the word "righteousness" mean to you? What negative connotations does it have?

2. What kind of person was Paul before he met Jesus on the road? How do you think the meeting changed him?

3. What do you think Paul was like as a pastor in the churches he founded? What would you like to learn from him if you could talk with him directly?

4. Consider Romans 7:14–25. How do you relate to Paul's experience of sin? How right is he about the way sin works in your life?

5. What way of life does Paul believe is pleasing to God? What behaviors are not pleasing to God?

6. What does grace mean to you personally? Has there been an event in your life when your sense of grace was particularly strong?

7. How and when in your life have you experienced repentance? What made it possible for you to turn away from sin and establish a different pattern of behavior?

8. How have you experienced the presence of the Holy Spirit?

PART III

Recovering the Legacy
in the Church

The lost legacy of the early church was a clear understanding of righteousness grounded in the moral law of the Scriptures. Repentance, turning away from something and turning toward something else, was the first step in accepting the gospel. If we in the present day church are to receive the gospel, we need to know clearly what we are turning toward and what we are turning away from. The law as it applied to non-Jews, the moral provisions of the law of Moses, provides us the reference point we need.

How can we recover what was lost? How can we recapture the knowledge of righteousness for today's church? Whether they are psychological, sociological, or political, clear standards and guidelines in contemporary terms are critical for healing the things that hurt us or divide us. Of course knowing the moral principles is only the beginning. Acting on them is up to us.

8

Do We Still Need Guidelines?

Why has the Chinese communist government allowed the controlled growth of the church inside China? A Chinese scholar tells how the government tried to figure out what made the West so successful. At first, they thought it was better weapons. Then they thought it might be a better political system. Then they looked at the economic system. In the end they realized that it was the Christianity built into Western culture that made the difference. Christian moral foundations made possible the success of both capitalism and democratic government.[169] The Chinese government permits Christianity because Christians make good citizens. So what is it about Christianity that makes such a difference?

This chapter considers the impact of moral practices in our contemporary life. This perspective grows out of the Reformed stream of the mainline Protestant tradition, but the underlying principles are shared with other Protestant denominations as well as with the Roman Catholic and Orthodox traditions.

Moral choices are available to almost all people, not only to those in privileged positions. The only exceptions are those subject to some kinds of mental illness. Our circumstances determine which moral choices confront us, but choices are available in even the most difficult or constrained circumstances. For example, Viktor Frankl described behavior among people whose choices were extremely restricted— guards or prisoners in a concentration camp. These people showed themselves to be either decent or not in how they treated others. Both types were found in each group. There were prisoners as well as guards who behaved decently to those around them, and there were prisoners and guards who did not.[170] Even within this kind of severely constrained environment, individuals have some range of moral choice in their behavior, especially toward other people.

No matter how much a person may be influenced by a group, responsibility for individual sin remains with the individual. When I find myself part of an organization that is behaving in ways I cannot condone, I feel that I have a responsibility to take action—to confront and/or separate from the group. I have known others who have made the same choice, even in very difficult financial circumstances. Rene Girard has described the way group dynamics lead to scapegoating,[171] and Scott Peck has described the way specialization, stress, group narcissism, and diffusion of responsibility lead people in groups to behave less well than they would as individuals.[172] Nevertheless, in spite of the influences of the surrounding group, individuals are still accountable for their own behavior.

In the Reformed tradition, John Calvin described three uses of moral law:

1. A mirror: by exhibiting the righteousness of God, it shows us our own unrighteousness, convicts and condemns us, and leads us to take refuge in God's mercy.
2. A bridle: by the dread of punishment, it curbs those who, unless forced, have no regard for righteousness and justice.
3. A schoolmaster: in the perfection to which it exhorts us, it points out the goal toward which, during the whole course of our lives, it is our duty to aim.

In contemporary terms, the law serves to

1. Break through the denial of those of us who think we are good, but do not notice when we behave badly

2. Keep people who are out of control from doing damage to others or even to themselves
   a. People who like being out of control hate law because it gets in the way of their doing what they want.
   b. Those who wish they could do better can practice doing the right thing by obeying the law.
3. Show those of us who would like to become better people which way to go

Law can function as a rating scheme for people to measure themselves, as a leash that forcibly keeps people from misbehavior, and as a coach to guide people through the process of change and improvement. In order to understand how law does this, we will look at how the use of law relates to current understanding of psychology.

The law as a rating system is intended only to help an individual become aware of the impact of sin in his or her own life as each looks at his or her own heart and behavior. The coach is only for helping an individual make changes to move into a more godly path. The law is misused when we apply it to other people's business.

What Are the Effects of Sin on Understanding?

If living by the law's direction is so good for us, why is it so hard? How do we become confused about the direction the law gives? The stumbling block is our human sin. Every human being has some knowledge of good and evil—part of the image of God built into us. Sin is our normal human tendency to choose evil rather than good. Sin is defined as acting against God's will, either willfully or in willful ignorance.

Sin can have many forms, depending on the way we understand God's will. Some people act against God through idolatry, by placing something else—money, sex, another person, status, fame, etc.—before the love and loyalty that God requires. Others sin by disobedience, by not submitting to and following God's direction as they understand it. Some sin through alienation from their true selves, by not accepting and being the selves that God intended them to be. Still others resist acting in love and behave in ways that are not for the good of others. Regardless of the form, sin is a resistance to God through which we, in our self-absorption, foolishness, or rebellion, separate ourselves from God. Sin begins with attitude and ends in action. James says, "Anyone, then, who knows the right thing to do and fails to do it, commits sin" (Jas 4:17).

It is important to distinguish between individual sin and corporate or group sin. After years of working in financial business organizations known for their corporate sin, I believe that the sin of a group is the combination of the sins of its individual members, made stronger by the support and power that the group provides. Additional factors reinforce sin in a group. For example, we can feel that a behavior is "normal" because it is shared or acceptable because it is supported by organizational structures.

In fact, each individual must make the choice either to go along with a group's behavior and standards, or to stand outside of them. It may not be easy to disassociate from some groups. For example, a teenage conscript into the German army in 1944 or a young father whose income depends on a pornographic product may have to plan carefully before taking action. The effects of group sin are magnified beyond the number of individuals involved, but, for this study, corporate sin is addressed through the individual sin of the participants.

While some make a distinction between individual and corporate sin, in my experience, that which appears from the outside to be the action of a system can be seen from the inside as a group of individuals acting co-operatively in a constellation of sinful behaviors. Individuals may facilitate sinful behavior by encouraging it, protecting perpetrators from discovery, scapegoating victims, rationalizing it, distracting attention away from it, etc. No system creates sin, although almost any system can be adapted to support sin. Institutionalized sin gains power and momentum from the number of participants as well as by processes that engage our normal human tendencies to enjoy sin.

The phenomenon of sin is not well understood in the modern world, but the concept of addiction can serve as a model for the way sin works. In their early stages, both sin and addiction are a source of pleasure and relief. In their later stages, they dominate a person's attention and activities. A person in the grip of sin or addiction cannot think clearly or see his or her situation from the outside. Aspects of life that were valued—family, work, faith, and other interests—are overwhelmed and forgotten in the urgency of indulging in the behavior. Self-deception and rationalization infect the person's perceptions, emotions, and ability to reason.

For example, drug addiction has been defined as a disorder that includes

1. A compulsion to seek and take the drug
2. Loss of control in limiting intake
3. Emergence of a negative emotional state (e.g., dysphoria, anxiety, irritability) when access to the drug is prevented.[173]

Drugs provide temporary gratification of ordinary human needs by making a person feel better or distorting awareness of the present situation.[174] The addictive behavior develops its own momentum and is very hard to interrupt, even with persuasion, punishment, or self-control.[175] Under the influence of addiction, a person is dominated by strong and sometimes conflicting motivations. How does this feel? Those in the grip of addiction experience craving, broken resolutions, restraint, resisting temptation, compulsion, and impaired control.[176] This subjective experience fits Paul's description of the action of sin in his letter to the Romans:

> I do not understand my own actions. For I do not do what I want, but I do the very thing I hate. . . . I can will what is right, but I cannot do it. For I do not do the good I want, but the evil I do not want is what I do. (Rom 7:14, 18–19)

Both sin and addiction are able to dominate a person's behavior and attention.[177] Under the influence of an addiction, we are unable to see our own behavior accurately and unable to recognize the negative impact it is having on our lives. Calvin describes the domination of sin in terms that closely parallel addicts' inability to see their own condition:

> he is so puffed up with haughtiness and ambition, and so blinded with self-love, that he is as yet unable to look upon himself, and, as it were, to descend within himself, that he may humble and abase himself, and confess his own miserable condition.[178]

The impact of sin on a person's judgment is as variable as the impact of addiction can be in different situations. Some people happily enjoy their sin and their horizon is defined by their successes in providing for it. Some are in recovery, consciously fighting and avoiding the sins to which they are particularly vulnerable. Many flirt with sin, enjoying tasting it while resisting selective parts, refusing to think about the future progression or wider implications of their behavior.

Sin has the effect of clouding the minds of those caught in it, interfering with our ability to think and see the situation clearly. This is known as the noetic effect of sin because it refers to the way sin disrupts the reasoning processes. This disruption can be caused by the distracting anticipation of pleasure, driven by the compulsion of strong passions, and fomented by the imagined justifications of wishful thinking. Our ability to think clearly is impaired at the very moment when we need it most—when we are faced directly with a strong temptation.

Part of the time, and away from our greatest personal vulnerabilities, people are able to hear our conscience, coming from the original image of God within each of us. This comes to us through the movements of conscience. This is the way that natural law is made available to human beings through our own direct experience. However, our ability to access our conscience depends on our capacity for self-awareness.

When we are in denial about our sin, when we believe ourselves to be basically good without looking too closely, we no longer have accurate perceptions of good and evil. Those who struggle with their own self-centeredness and who try to see themselves as others see them are more likely to be able to see God's image in the created world and sense it in themselves.

Law Is a Wake-up Call

The first and most important use of moral law is as a standard, as a rating scale against which we can evaluate ourselves. This is a theological use that forces us to look at ourselves from the outside to see ourselves as others see us or as God sees us. The scale shows us where we fit on a ruler that goes all the way from divine goodness to ultimate evil. This rating is for our individual and personal use. It is up to each of us to look at our own lives and behavior to compare them with the standard.

The rating scale has a theological base because it requires us to understand what good and evil look like in practice. It implies that we have an awareness of moral standards, whether we get them from observing the natural world or from divine revelation. The law we receive through revelation and covenant is the expression of the will of God for human beings. Calvin says that

> [T]he purpose of the whole law [is] the fulfillment of righteousness to form human life to the archetype of divine purity. For God has so depicted his character in the law that if any man carries out in deeds whatever is enjoined there, he will express the image of God, as it were, in his own life.[179]

This first use of the law is to motivate change, to bring attention to what it would take for a human being to change from a self-centered, self-directed person to one who demonstrates the image of God. By showing the righteousness of God, according to Calvin, the law "admonishes every one of his own unrighteousness," "convicts and finally condemns him" in order that he can "be brought at once to know and to confess his weakness and impurity."[180] Calvin sees the law as

- Demonstrating the holiness of God as a standard
- Giving each person grounds for personal comparison and recognition of failure
- Leading each to turn to mercy and forgiveness in Christ

Only by recognizing our failings and helplessness are we motivated to turn to God through Christ. This, of course, is hard for us to notice when our bad behavior is part of a reinforcing system. The law can break through each person's false belief in his or her own goodness and motivate us to turn to Jesus for help to change.

Contemporary psychologists have studied how people make changes in their lives, and have found that motivation is a critical requirement for effective change. By studying the process of change, scientists have identified five stages of change and the activities that happen in each stage, whether it is to break an addiction, change a habit, manage a chronic disease, or recover from a health crisis.

1. *Precontemplation:* when people are content and unaware of a problem in their situation.
2. *Contemplation:* when people recognize that there is a potential for change.
3. *Action:* when people take specific steps to make the change.
4. *Maintenance:* when the change is established and it is time to put in place new supporting practices.
5. *Resolution:* when the previous issues and behavior are no longer present.[181]

The first use of the law is for those who are in the precontemplation and contemplation stages of dealing with the sin in their lives. These are people comfortable in their current situation and those who are thinking about the possibility of changing it.

Those in precontemplation do not recognize that they have a problem or have any reason to begin the work of change. In the case of rehabilitation or addiction treatment, action-based programs do not help those who do not recognize that they have a problem.[182] A person cannot be "helped" to make a change in life, even a change for the better, unless he or she actually wants to make that change.[183] The first use of the law motivates a person to turn away from sin and toward a relationship with God through Christ. This commitment, like other commitments for behavioral change, must be made freely by the person involved, and not under duress.[184]

Studies have identified the relative contributions that different factors make to the success of attempts to change. Although there were many arguments about which psychological model or form of therapy was best, no one was found to be more effective than another. The factors that contribute to successful change are:

> 40% characteristics of the client (character, motivation, life situation, etc.)

> 30% supporting relationship (the presence of a counselor or therapist or helping listener of some kind)

> 15% hope (confidence that some kind of change is possible)

> 15% approach (a specific program or technique to be used for change).[185]

More than half of the potential for change comes directly from the circumstances of the person involved and from his or her confidence in the possibility of change. Another third comes from the presence of a supportive relationship during the change. A person's motivation and hope for change, combined with empathetic relationships with other Christians, can provide the preconditions that secular psychology has identified for the effectiveness of this first use of law.

Considering the critical role that people play in their own potential for change, what works against a person's ability to make changes? Awareness of one's own failings—one's own sinfulness—is a painful experience, and human beings tend to avoid thinking about the negative. Denial works in a number of layers:

- Denial of facts: "forgetting" or lying to oneself or others about what actually happened
- Denial of implications: rationalizing the causes or minimizing the consequences of what has happened
- Denial of change: refusing responsibility or claiming inevitability of the situation
- Denial of feelings: shutting out feelings that threaten self-worth and identity

When thinking about their own bad behavior, people may deny that they ever did such a thing, insist that it was not that big a deal, claim that they could not help it, or refuse to believe that they are the kind of people who would behave that way. Denial protects us against painful threats to our self-image as good people.[186]

Denial is more than simply letting an issue slide into unimportance and out of our conscious awareness. It also involves active avoidance. We refuse to look at things we do not want to see, even things that are conspicuous and obvious to those around us. Denial is not simply about forgetting trivial details; it is about avoiding thinking about truly important issues that impact our lives.[187] Many of us have plenty of help avoiding noticing the effects of our bad behavior. There is strong social pressure to avoid bringing up embarrassing issues and to pretend we did not hear them when someone else mentions them.[188] In commenting on the effects of denial in the political arena, C. Fred

Alford observes, "The best way to disrupt moral behavior is not to discuss it and not to discuss not discussing it."[189]

Calvin's first use of law provides an external standard that we can use to become aware of our own situation and realize the need for change:

> For until his vanity is made perfectly manifest, he is
> puffed up with infatuated confidence in his own powers,
> and never can be brought to feel their feebleness so long
> as he measures them by a standard of his own choice. So
> soon, however, as he begins to compare them with the
> requirements of the Law, he has something to tame his
> presumption. . . . He, then, who is schooled by the Law,
> lays aside the arrogance which formerly blinded him.[190]

Norms and standards against which we can measure ourselves are particularly effective, and the objective validity of these norms is critically important.

People often compare themselves with those around them. When the use of alcohol, drugs, or sex is frequent in a group, change is unlikely. This is sometimes called the false consensus effect, because it leads us to believe that our own bad behavior is not out of the ordinary. Law provides an objective standard, separate from the behavior of our social networks—a standard not subject to the distortion made possible by self-selected peer groups.

After recognizing the distance each person is from living a godly life, the next step is to reach out for help. Calvin says,

> In order to instruct the people in the doctrine of
> repentance, it was necessary for him to teach what
> manner of life was acceptable to God; and this he
> included in the precepts of the law. . . . [then] being
> thus led to despair as to their own righteousness, they
> might flee to the haven of divine goodness, and so to
> Christ himself.[191]

Recognizing the demands of true holiness and realizing the impossibility of satisfying them lead one to reach for outside help, look for rescue, and depend on God's mercy and grace.

We can see a parallel in the first three steps of twelve-step recovery programs. These programs began as a way to address alcohol abuse and have since been used successfully for many kinds of addictions.

1. We admitted we were powerless over alcohol—that our lives had become unmanageable.
2. Came to believe that a Power greater than ourselves could restore us to sanity.
3. Made a decision to turn our will and our lives over to the care of God as we understood Him.[192]

Recognizing our own helplessness in the face of sin or addiction and turning to God has been shown to be the most effective way to begin the process of change.

Law Is a Guide for Progress

Calvin's third use of law, which he describes as its "principal use, and more closely connected with its proper end,"[193] is as a coach or guide for behavior. For Calvin, the law is "the best instrument for enabling [people] daily to learn with greater truth and certainty what that will of the Lord is which they aspire to follow, and to confirm them in this knowledge."[194] The law describes the destination that people of faith are striving to achieve.

> It will not now be difficult to ascertain the general end
> contemplated by the whole Law—viz. the fulfillment of
> righteousness, that man may form his life on the model
> of the divine purity. For therein God has so delineated
> his own character, that any one exhibiting in action

what is commanded, would in some measure exhibit a living image of God.[195]

It also serves as a day-to-day motivator and reminder, to keep people of faith conscious of their goal and constantly careful to be moving toward it.

> this further advantage from the Law: by frequently meditating upon it, he will be excited to obedience, and confirmed in it, and so drawn away from the slippery paths of sin.[196]

> in the case of a spiritual man, inasmuch as he is still burdened with the weight of the flesh, the Law is a constant stimulus, pricking him forward when he would indulge in sloth.[197]

Thus the law provides both guidance, showing the direction one should go, and motivation to make the daily choices that lead in that direction.

In the busy modern world we can go well down the path against the law without even noticing it. Sometimes we need an interruption to remind us to look at our behavior and see what is going on from a wider perspective. For example, in our business environment with teams of men and women working closely together, it is easy for relationships of admiration and affection to develop between coworkers. From time to time, this kind of innocent friendship can become a sexual relationship. Often it only takes a reminder of the possible outcomes to keep someone from crossing the line. I remember seeing one coworker developing feelings for our wonderful boss. All I needed to say was, "It's easy to have a crush on Charlie," for her to realize that she did not want to drift into this particular misbehavior. In this kind of situation, the law provides a clear, independent, and constant standard of the behaviors we need to avoid.

From a modern psychological point of view, if we are motivated to change our behavior, we need a way to measure, or at least be aware of, our progress in the right direction. Psychological research on people who were successful in making changes shows that these people

- Learn from consequences
- See the difference between their current behavior and their goals
- Use this understanding to change their decision making[198]

In modern terms, having a goal and norm for behavior contributes to motivation by providing a clear direction toward which one is aiming, showing clearly which behaviors are not good, reinforcing the importance of good choices, and providing grounds for identifying problems.[199]

The consequences of sin may be relatively minor or completely catastrophic. One man I know lost his job, home, and the respect of his community when he was publicly caught in misbehavior. He later said that being caught, horrible as it was, actually turned out to be a blessing because it forced him to take his particular sin seriously. He has focused his attention on using the guidance of law, under the protection of repentance and grace, to rebuild his life and relationships. Using the law this way, in the face of great personal cost, demonstrates strength and growing maturity.

Calvin recognized that compliance with all the principles of the law all of the time is impossible for ordinary human beings.

> We ought not to be frightened away from the law or to shun its instruction merely because it requires a much stricter moral purity than we shall reach while we bear about with us the prison house of our body. For the law is not now acting towards us as a rigorous enforcement officer who is not satisfied unless the requirements are met. But in this perfection to which it exhorts us, the law points out the goal which throughout life we are to strive.[200]

The impossibility of complete success should not keep anyone from working toward the goal of holiness.

> No one will travel so badly as not daily to make some degree of progress. This, therefore, let us never cease to do, that we may daily advance in the way of the Lord; and let us not despair because of the slender measure of success.[201]

Even without reaching the final destination, regular improvement is within human capability.

> How little soever the success may correspond with our wish, our labour is not lost when to-day is better than yesterday, provided with true singleness of mind we keep our aim, and aspire to the goal, not speaking flattering things to ourselves, nor indulging our vices, but making it our constant endeavor to become better, until we attain to goodness itself. [202]

In this way, the law becomes an internal motivator for better behavior on a daily basis.

Law Is a Tool for Internal Transformation

The human goal is not merely behavior in compliance with the law, but internal transformation into the kind of person for whom the behavior described in the law is natural. Calvin said, "in the Law human life is instructed not merely in outward decency but in inward spiritual righteousness."[203] The outward manifestation of compliance with law is not the only issue. The inward habits of mind and heart matter as well.

> God, whose eye nothing escapes, and who regards not the outward appearance so much as purity of heart,

under the prohibition of murder, adultery, and thefts
includes wrath, hatred, lust, covetousness, and all other
things of a similar nature. Being a spiritual Lawgiver,
he speaks to the soul not less than the body.[204]

In presenting the provisions of the moral law, Calvin extends the
implications of a particular behavior into expectations about the
character of the individual.

The best rule, in my opinion, would be, to be guided by
the principle of the commandment—viz. to consider
in the case of each what the purpose is for which it was
given. For example, every commandment either requires
or prohibits; and the nature of each is instantly discerned
when we look to the principle of the commandment as its
end. . . . So in each of the commandments we must first
look to the matter of which it treats, and then consider
its end, until we discover what it properly is that the
Lawgiver declares to be pleasing or displeasing to him.[205]

Not only does Calvin extend a particular commandment into its
underlying principle, he also sees a commandment as either requiring
or forbidding the opposite of the behavior specified.

When the particular virtue opposed to a particular vice
is spoken of, all that is usually meant is abstinence from
that vice. We maintain that it goes farther, and means
opposite duties and positive acts.[206]

we must reason from the precept to its contrary in this
way: If this pleases God, its opposite displeases; if that
displeases, its opposite pleases: if God commands this,
he forbids the opposite; if he forbids that, he commands
the opposite.[207]

For Calvin, the specific requirements or restrictions of the law include both living by the principles leading to each and rejecting any behavior or attitude that opposes those principles.

What Are Inappropriate Uses of Law?

Just as the law is a great guide and support when we use it correctly, it can result in some extremely negative consequences when used in the wrong way. We need to be aware of and guard against three primary dangers in our use of law: legalism, perfectionism, and judgmentalism.

- *Legalism* applies the bare law, the words of the regulations, outside the context in which the law was given and exacts obedience in detail. This is contrary to the intent of the law as a gift of grace meant to give loving guidance to those who want to come closer to God.
- *Perfectionism* expects complete and constant compliance with all the law's provisions, which leads to despair over the impossibility of success. On the contrary, progress is what matters, not instant perfection, as long as each person pays attention and works toward the ultimate although unattainable goal.
- *Judgmentalism* looks to others in comparison, allowing a person to feel better about his or her own situation by criticizing the visible weaknesses of others. In reality, law within the community of faith is for guiding one's own behavior and intentions. The only appropriate role of law in looking to others is to inspire compassionate support as they struggle along as companions on the same path toward holiness.

These three misuses have contributed to the great dissatisfaction with moral law in present culture. Legalism is perceived as an obsession with rules in the absence of consideration for human feelings. This makes it anathema to modern secular humanism and seen as a tool for oppression. Perfectionism is perceived as a self-righteous confidence in moral superiority. This makes it repulsive to the aggressive egalitarianism of popular culture and seen as a mechanism for establishing and justifying some form of elite. Judgmentalism is perceived as arbitrary condemnation of others based on ordinary human differences. This puts it at the core of racial prejudice, discrimination against marginalized people, and all kinds of hate crimes.

Moral law is so identified with these three abuses that the term "righteousness" has become a negative term associated with pride, superficiality, and social domination instead of describing desirable behavior. If moral law is to return to being a positive influence for the growth of goodness and virtue in society, we need to address these three abuses and return to appreciation of the value of moral law in supporting healthy standards of behavior.

Jesus is quite emphatic about preventing obstacles like these three abuses from getting in the way of the gospel message.

> If your hand or your foot causes you to stumble, cut it off and throw it away; it is better for you to enter life maimed or lame than to have two hands or two feet and to be thrown into the eternal fire. And if your eye causes you to stumble, tear it out and throw it away; it is better for you to enter life with one eye than to have two eyes and to be thrown into the hell of fire. (Matt 18:8–9)

Terrible as it is to have something get in the way of one's own journey of faith, it is far worse to put an obstacle in the way of someone else's chance for salvation.

> If any of you put a stumbling block before one of these little ones who believe in me, it would be better for you if a great millstone were fastened around your neck and you were drowned in the depth of the sea. Woe to the world because of stumbling blocks! Occasions for

> stumbling are bound to come, but woe to the one by
> whom the stumbling block comes! (Matt 18:6–7)

Because moral law is intended to be a blessing that leads people into godly lives, turning it into an obstacle is particularly heinous.

How Do We Avoid Legalism?

Legalism is what happens when rules have gotten out of control. Rules themselves can actually be a good thing, because they tell us what to expect and what not to expect in different situations. In baseball and football, the rules tell us how to play the game, and umpires and referees make sure the rules are followed. When driving, we know we are supposed to do particular things when we see different colored lights, and we use painted lines on the ground to tell us where we are allowed and not allowed to put our cars. Rules can be helpful and reassuring, because they provide structure in our complicated and chaotic world.

Usually we choose to follow the rules, but sometimes we choose to break them, for good reasons or bad reasons. An ambulance on the way to the hospital does not wait for a light to change from red to green. Other times when we ignore the light, we may suffer the consequences: either a fine or a crash. Each system of rules has a purpose and a set of situations where they apply. Since rules cannot cover every possible situation, sometimes we need to go back to the purpose of the rules to decide what to do.

The problem of legaism occurs when following the rules becomes more important than satisfying the purpose for which the rules were created. Rules make us feel safe, since they make the world around us feel more understandable. Rules help us feel in control because they tell us what we should do next. Rules can also make us feel that we are better than our neighbors, because we are more careful to follow the rules well. Because of these feelings we can become attached to the rules themselves, and this attachment turns into legalism.

Legalism strips the law of its meaning by stripping it of its purpose. What remains—the set of rules—is empty of intent and appears to be an arbitrary list of prohibitions. We know that the natural human tendency is to resist when it comes to obeying rules. Put a child into a room full of toys and tell them they can play with anything except Grandma's fragile glass vase. What will the child be attracted to? If the vase were not forbidden, it might never have been interesting. Adults have had the same kind of problem, beginning with Adam and Eve. The most attractive, delicious-looking fruit in the garden was the kind that they were told specifically not to take.

Paul talks about the way rules naturally lead people to want to do the opposite of what they are told. He says,

> I know that nothing good dwells within me, that is, in my flesh. I can will what is right, but I cannot do it. For I do not do the good I want, but the evil I do not want is what I do. . . . So I find it to be a law that when I want to do what is good, evil lies close at hand. For I delight in the law of God in my inmost self, but I see in my body another law at war with the law of my mind, making me captive to the law of sin that dwells in my body. Wretched man that I am! (Rom 7:18–24)

That law of sin that leads people to behave badly is a natural problem for all of us. The more intently we focus on the rules, the more we want to give up, stop thinking about it, and go out and have a good time.

This tendency of law to lead to rebellion is why the law has been called "dead," "killing," and a "curse." Calvin says that Paul uses the terms law and gospel to contrast the rebellion-inciting and life-giving aspects of law.

> For this reason [Paul] gives to the law the name of the letter, because it is in itself a dead preaching; but the gospel he calls spirit, because the ministry of the gospel

is living, nay, lifegiving. . . . these things are not affirmed absolutely in reference either to the law or to the gospel, but in respect of the contrast between the one and the other; for even the gospel is not always spirit.[208]

Even at its worst, of course, the bare law is a tool that God can use to bring people to salvation.

[H]owever much [the law] may point out true righteousness, yet, owing to the corruption of our nature, its instruction tends only to increase transgressions, until the Spirit of regeneration come, who writes it on the heart; and that Spirit is not given by the law, but is received by faith.[209]

Only in the context of faith and with the accompaniment of the Spirit does the law bring life, and not through the law itself, but by faith.

Legalism is the bare law—the rules only with rewards and punishments—while the alternative is the whole law in the context of its purpose in the covenant. Calvin sees this in Psalm 19 where David speaks of the law, "he not only means the rule of living righteously . . . but he also comprehends the covenant by which God had distinguished that people from the rest of the world, and the whole doctrine of Moses."[210]

Legalism is law that leads to wrath and punishment, since human beings will fail to keep it. The alternative is law that leads to acceptance, as Paul describes it, since failure is justified by grace through faith. Legalism is law that curses and kills; the alternative is law that guides and gives life. Both can be seen in the same set of bare words of Scripture, but the law that gives life is supplemented by faith and by the ongoing presence of the Holy Spirit.

Calvin describes the difference that God's living presence makes in his commentary on Psalm 19:7–9: "It is, therefore, necessary that God should employ the law as a remedy for restoring us to purity; not that the letter of the law can do this of itself . . . but because God employs his word as an instrument for restoring our souls."[211] The distinction is whether the law is a set of external rules or an internal conviction in the context of a full relationship with God.

> [R]ighteousness consists of two parts; first, that God is reconciled to us by free grace, in not imputing to us our sins; and, secondly, that he has engraven his law in our hearts, and, by his Spirit, renews men within to obedience to it; from which it is evident that the Law is incorrectly and falsely expounded, if there are any whose attention it fixes on itself, or whom it hinders from coming to Christ.[212]

The context of the whole relationship transforms the role of law from a killing standard into a loving guide.

> The object of the Psalmist is to celebrate the advantages which the Lord, by means of his law, bestows on those whom he inwardly inspires with a love of obedience. And he adverts not to the mere precepts, but also to the promise annexed to them, which alone makes that sweet which in itself is bitter. For what is less attractive than the law, when, by its demands and threatening, it overawes the soul, and fills it with terror?[213]

Legalism is the first and fastest way to turn people away from the gospel. If the gospel is presented as a set of rules—one must do this and one must not do that—things are put in the wrong order. The rules must not come first. If one may not come to Christ until one is living by the law, and since living up to the law takes a lifetime of effort, then no one will ever be able to come to Christ. Obeying the rules is not the price of admission to God's family. Rules are not the most important issue in accepting the gospel. If they are treated that way, they become the very kind of stumbling block Jesus warned about.

How Do We Avoid Perfectionism?

Living with perfectionism is not fun. I know this because my parents were perfectionists. If I brought home a report card with mostly As, they would ask why I got the one B. There was no way I could do enough to please them.

While it is hard to live with perfectionists, having one inside your head can be even worse. Not only are you criticized for the things you did wrong, you are criticized for your thoughts and feelings as well. You should not be jealous of your friend's new outfit. You should not get mad at the person who swerved in front of you on the highway. You should not want to leave early just because the meeting is boring. Perfectionism is a taskmaster that is easy to hate.

Perfectionism is the second misapplication of moral law that can become a stumbling block. From the perspective of Jesus or Paul, perfection is surely the goal for each human being. Jesus says, "Be perfect, therefore, as your heavenly Father is perfect" (Matt 5:48). Paul says to the church in Corinth, "Since we have these promises, beloved, let us cleanse ourselves from every defilement of body and of spirit, making holiness perfect in the fear of God" (2 Cor 7:1). There is no question that commitment to Jesus leads his followers to try to live up to a very high standard in all aspects of their lives. Unfortunately, when this quest for perfection gets out of hand, perfection itself becomes an obstacle.

Perfectionism acts as an obstacle at two different levels. It presents a barrier with standards set too high for those who are first coming to faith, and for others it can lead to despair of ever being good enough to satisfy its requirements. In both cases, it causes a misdirection of attention: perfectionism leads us to focus on what is wrong in the smallest detail while taking attention and energy from doing what is right.

For those at the beginning of their acquaintance with the gospel, perfectionism can be discouraging. How do you react when you think you can never be good enough for something you really want? No matter how much you want it, you are likely to give up. What is the point of trying if you know you can never succeed? Why bother? If you are convinced that you will never be good enough for God, you can easily walk away from all the love God offers in spite of our human sinfulness.

For those struggling on their path of discipleship, perfectionism has a different course that also can lead to loss of hope. Some of us who are trying to follow Christ set too high standards for our own behavior in the process. We count the slightest infractions of behavior, or even of feeling, as failures in righteousness. Instead of accepting forgiveness for these sins, we can become obsessed with trying to avoid or prevent them. This, of course, leads to a continuing round of failures and further discouragement. This form of scrupulousness, encouraged by an overly sensitive conscience, can also lead to despair over any hope of change or progress.

Dietrich Bonhoeffer wrote about those who take too little responsibility for their behavior as well as those who take too much responsibility. In the end, after trying our best to avoid sin, we need to come to understand that there is no way we can solve the problem completely. At a certain point, we need to accept that we cannot be free of sin and accept that we can rely on grace. This does not mean that we can simply go on enjoying our sin, but, rather, that after we have done our human best, we can trust that the rest is in God's hands.[214] The quest for perfection involves a gut-level acceptance of the fact that complete success on that quest is not possible within present human circumstances.

Since progress toward the goal matters, and since we know that the destination is not achievable in this life, aiming at this distant target truly can be discouraging. But this is not an excuse for not following Christ:

> there is no man who is not far removed from this perfection, while many, who have made but little progress, would be undeservedly rejected. What then? Let us set this before our eye as the end at which we ought constantly to aim. Let it be regarded as the goal towards which we are to run.[215]

Calvin is quite clear that he does not expect perfection in this present life.

> I insist not that the life of the Christian shall breathe nothing but the perfect Gospel, though this is to be desired, and ought to be attempted. I insist not so strictly on evangelical perfection, as to refuse to acknowledge as a Christian any man who has not attained it. In this way all would be excluded from the Church[216]

Even Paul, when he talks about himself, says, "Not that I have already obtained this or have already reached the goal; but I press on to make it my own, because Christ Jesus has made me his own" (Phil 3:12). Progress toward the goal is what matters, and not the perfection of being there already. Christians should not let themselves be distracted by how far they are from perfection, but instead to keep their attention focused on progress toward the goal. When telling others about the love of God, they must never let the perfection they strive for change from a goal to an obstacle for others who are coming to Jesus.

Whether called self-confidence, self-esteem, or self-efficacy, a person's own positive confidence in his or her ability to act is critical for taking action and making changes.[217] For example, self-efficacy has been linked to successful change in a variety of health-related behaviors, including coping with stress, recovery from cardiac surgery, and dealing with the chronic pain of rheumatoid arthritis.[218] Studies have shown that confidence in one's own capabilities is necessary to be able to use those capabilities.[219] Perfectionism undermines self-efficacy because it destroys a person's confidence in his or her own ability to make progress.

How Do We Avoid Judgmentalism?

Judgmentalism is the third and most common obstacle people encounter in their engagement with moral law. Often, moral law is used in conversation to show off and demonstrate superiority over someone else. Listeners get tired of hearing critical gossip and come to associate moral law with self-righteousness, pettiness, envy, and lack of compassion.

Jesus is very clear about whether or not we are supposed to judge the behavior of others. He says,

> Do not judge, so that you may not be judged. For with the judgment you make you will be judged, and the measure you give will be the measure you get. Why do you see the speck in your neighbor's eye, but do not notice the log in your own eye? Or how can you say to your neighbor, "Let me take the speck out of your eye," while the log is in your own eye? You hypocrite, first take the log out of your own eye, and then you will see clearly to take the speck out of your neighbor's eye. (Matt 7:1–5)

We are not supposed to pronounce a decision about right and wrong the way a court does, coming to our own conclusions about the behavior or character of the people involved. This kind of judgment is imposed and communicated in the form of criticism or correction. The implication is that the corrector is somehow superior to the one being corrected.

This is different from the idea of assessment, which uses objective criteria and does not include a conclusion enforced on the person being assessed. Judgment differs from discernment because discernment tries to understand multiple factors, some of which may be qualitative, while judgment implies approval or disapproval on a single scale. Judgmentalism is not thinking about relative values, but imposing negative evaluations on others.

The way Jesus felt about those stuck in sin is equally clear:

> And as he sat at dinner in Levi's house, many tax collectors and sinners were also sitting with Jesus and his disciples—for there were many who followed him. When the scribes of the Pharisees saw that he

was eating with sinners and tax collectors, they said to his disciples, "Why does he eat with tax collectors and sinners?" When Jesus heard this, he said to them, "Those who are well have no need of a physician, but those who are sick; I have come to call not the righteous but sinners." (Mark 2:15–17)

Jesus did not excuse bad behavior, but he did not attack or criticize people for it either. He said, "Go and sin no more," to the woman caught in her sinful life (John 8:1-11), but he did not gossip about her afterward. He showed the woman at the well that he knew what she was up to, but he still welcomed her and offered her the living water (John 4).

Even Paul says to the Corinthians that they cannot avoid contact with all sinners, "meaning the immoral of this world, or the greedy and robbers, or idolaters, since you would then need to go out of the world" (1 Cor 5:10. We cannot simply tell those we meet what is wrong with the way they are living their lives. Telling the truth at the wrong time creates obstacles to being able to accept that same truth at the right time. As Paul says, "We who are strong ought to put up with the failings of the weak, and not to please ourselves. Each of us must please our neighbor for the good purpose of building up the neighbor" (Rom 15:1–2).

What does this look like in practice? Paul talks about the way people who are strong in their faith should get along with those who are just beginning:

> Welcome those who are weak in faith, but not for the purpose of quarreling over opinions. Some believe in eating anything, while the weak eat only vegetables. Those who eat must not despise those who abstain, and those who abstain must not pass judgment on those who eat; for God has welcomed them. Who are you to pass judgment on servants of another? It is before

their own lord that they stand or fall. And they will be upheld, for the Lord is able to make them stand.

Some judge one day to be better than another, while others judge all days to be alike. Let all be fully convinced in their own minds. Those who observe the day, observe it in honor of the Lord. Also those who eat, eat in honor of the Lord, since they give thanks to God; while those who abstain, abstain in honor of the Lord and give thanks to God. . . . Let us therefore no longer pass judgment on one another, but resolve instead never to put a stumbling block or hindrance in the way of another. (Rom 14:1–13)

It is not up to individual Christians to put our own judgments in between Jesus and someone who is struggling to come to him. Our job is to welcome all those he calls. Any and all judgment belongs exclusively to the Lord.

Law Must Be Used Properly.

The law is a blessing because it reveals God's intentions for us. It defines the kind of people God hopes we will become and provides waypoints on our journey to Christlike life. When we lose our way, the law can wake us up and remind us of our goal. As we struggle with the ordinary and exceptional challenges of daily life, the law provides criteria to help us in our choice of actions. As we grow into the kind of people God intends us to be, the law leads us to practice righteousness more consistently, transforming us from the outside in. Law leads us into a godly life, and in the process supports us as we grow into becoming Christlike people.

The law is still valid and useful for Christians, even though its reputation has been tarnished by those who have fallen into legalism, perfectionism, and/or judgmentalism. Nevertheless, "the Law has lost none of its authority, but must always receive from us the same respect and obedience."[220] Practicing Christians are challenged to accept its guidance in a way that advances their own journey of faith, but not to allow that law to become an obstacle to themselves or others who are coming to or growing as disciples of Jesus.

Questions for Reflection and Discussion

1. What makes it hard to see our own bad behavior the way others see it?

2. Can you remember a time when you knew that you were doing something wrong but could not seem to deal with it? How did the situation turn out?

3. Consider Romans 1:18–21. How do we know what God expects of us? How does understanding God's idea of goodness help break through our own denial of sin?

4. Consider Psalm 19:7–13. How does this reflect modern psychology's understanding of denial and the process of changing behavior?

5. Consider Romans 2:5–11. How and when will we be held accountable for the way we live?

6. How have you encountered legalism as an obstacle? What effect did it have?

7. How have you encountered perfectionism as an obstacle? What effect did it have?

8. How have you encountered judgmentalism as an obstacle? What effect did it have?

9. What are the key standards you live by? Where did you learn them? How are they changing as you grow in faith?

10. When in your own experience have your standards helped you find a safe way through dangerously tempting situations?

9

A Godly Life Is Always a Choice

Even though Paul said that followers of Jesus are not under the discipline of law, he did have expectations for righteous behavior among believers. Knowing the provisions of the law, no matter how much you want to follow them, is not enough. The presence of the Holy Spirit is required to make it possible for believers to live righteously. This presence of the Spirit was a living experience for the people of Paul's churches. The people of the church in Galatia received the Spirit (Gal 3:2), experienced the Spirit's presence (Gal 3:4), and witnessed miracles in their community (Gal 3:5). The Spirit was a real felt presence and not just a theoretical ideal in Paul's churches.

Christians are not people without guidance, but people who have the law as a guide. Law is given by a loving Parent in the hope that, by following it, we become more like Jesus, our older brother in the family. As John Calvin explained,

> That Christians are under the law of grace, means not
> that they are to wander unrestrained without law, but
> that they are engrafted into Christ, by whose grace they
> are freed from the curse of the Law, and by whose Spirit
> they have the Law written in their hearts.[221]

The law serves each of us, both as internal map and as external road signs, on our individual journeys toward God's own righteousness.

We have seen so far that moral law as a guide for living has been consistent from the earliest Jewish roots of our faith. In each time period, this law consistently includes provisions forbidding idolatry, violence, and sexual immorality while requiring equal treatment and justice for all. We have seen how important it is for us to have the guidance that the law provides. The remaining issue is how we choose to hear and follow this guidance.

How Can We Hear the Message of Scripture?

Scripture is the result of the work of many different people living in different cultures and different historical contexts. Each contribution is directed by the Holy Spirit, but each piece is expressed through the language and culture of the writer. Thus, each passage needs to be understood in terms of what it meant for the original writer and readers as well as what that message means in our modern cultural context.

Scripture must be available and accessible for all people because nobody has a special position or point of view that is automatically more accurate than anyone else's. Scripture is full of detail and nuances, and it is meaningful both in what it says and in what it does not say. The use of experiences and parables allows each passage to carry more than one possible message. Since the messages of Scripture come into each of our personal contexts, this richness allows parts of the text to convey multiple messages. Interpretation is the process of bringing God's message into a particular context, to a particular person or group of people in a particular situation with particular issues or questions.

Each passage of Scripture is a plain text capturing God's revelation, but it is heard by people with many different perspectives and communication styles. One whole passage may include a variety of ideas, some of which have higher priority for one particular situation than others. Several different passages may be applied by the listener to a single situation; we may need to resolve the relationship between their messages. We also need to address, rather than gloss over, inconsistencies between different writers based on their individual perspectives and the limitations on the information available to them at the time of writing.

Since hearing a message from God is always part of a two-way communication, listening for the voice of God in Scripture must be done in the context of prayer. Whatever tools of interpretation we use, whether they are highly analytical or deeply intuitive, we must use them with full awareness of the One whose message is being sought. The ability to use the words of Scripture to justify ungodly behavior has been a source of humor and tragedy over many centuries. As a result, we depend on the active presence and participation of the Holy Spirit for accurate understanding of divine communication.

The work of the Spirit is not to give us new ideas outside of the text itself, but to open our hearts to receive what is already there in a passage. Jesus described this work of the Spirit on the night of his arrest:

> When the Spirit of truth comes, he will guide you into all the truth; for he will not speak on his own, but will speak whatever he hears, and he will declare to you the things that are to come. He will glorify me, because he will take what is mine and declare it to you. (John 16:13–14)

The Spirit is a trustworthy assistant because the Spirit is not inventing, but passing along whatever comes from God directly and from Christ. The Spirit is deeply engaged in both sides of the communication process.

> Likewise the Spirit helps us in our weakness; for we do not know how to pray as we ought, but that very Spirit intercedes with sighs too deep for words. And God, who searches the heart, knows what is the mind of the Spirit, because the Spirit intercedes for the saints according to the will of God. (Rom 8:26–27)

In interpreting a particular passage in a particular context, the Spirit directs our attention and makes the connections that evoke the message.

Every message coming from interpretation of Scripture must be validated for consistency with the whole body of Scripture. It also must be validated against the explicit teaching and lived example of Jesus. There must be no creative expansion of the communication in order to ensure that it represents the scriptural voice and not the wishful thinking of the interpreter. As Calvin warned,

> We must consider, I say, how far interpretation can be permitted to go beyond the literal meaning of the words, still making it apparent that no appending of human glosses is added to the Divine Law, but that the pure and genuine meaning of the Lawgiver is faithfully exhibited.[222]

How Does Interpretation Form Us?

Engagement with the Scripture is a developmental experience. As we practice it, we receive experience in the skills that add up to wisdom. We obtain practice in extracting principles from parables and stories in the Scripture. We gain practice in applying principles to situations, those presented in Scripture and the situations of our own lives. As we work through our interpretation, we practice anticipating the purposes and intentions of God. Why would God have acted in a particular way? What guidance did God give, and in what kind of situations? How does God's action toward human beings show God's character? When we listen carefully, we find ourselves better able to think and act in godly ways.

The goal of this practice in interpretation is developing a character that naturally prefers to choose righteous actions.[223] Our ethical behavior includes both discerning our alternatives and choosing what to do. Practicing by working through scriptural situations enhances our ability to see options as well as to make good choices among them. Whether our criteria for making choices are based on authority (deontological—"God said it"), goal oriented (teleological—"growing into the image of Christ"), or results based (consequential—"exhibiting the kingdom of God in the world"), growing in wisdom through interpretation increases our ability to choose well.

Life presents us with a continuing stream of issues in which we need to make moral decisions. The attempt to do the right thing— and the struggle to figure out what that is—requires sorting through many potential alternatives.[224] In the process, our understanding of God's moral guidance is continually challenged. This helps our decision making process by refining it in response to experience, examination, and criticism.[225] When we practice applying our convictions to specific situations, we integrate those convictions into internal habits of thought.

Listening to God through Scripture in the context of prayer opens us to a further level of formation and transformation. Dietrich Bonhoeffer makes an important distinction between formation that results from human activity and formation that is God-directed.

> Formation occurs only by being drawn into the form
> of Jesus Christ, by being conformed to the unique form
> of the one who became human, was crucified, and is
> risen. This does not happen as we strive "to become
> like Jesus," as we customarily say, but as the form of
> Jesus Christ himself so works on us that it molds us,
> conforming our form to Christ's own (Gal 4:9). Christ
> remains the only one who forms.[226]

Making space for this internal transformation, through the work of the Holy Spirit, is at the heart of our engagement with Scripture. Through whichever techniques in prayer and in listening we use, the goal is to come closer to God—to know God better and to know Christ better.

We put ourselves in the place where this transformation can occur through patient receptivity and active listening. We will not suddenly find that the Person we seek is inconsistent with the one we have known through reading Scripture. As Bonhoeffer explained,

Even the conscience freed in Jesus Christ confronts responsible action with the law that, when obeyed, keeps one in unity with oneself as grounded in Jesus Christ. . . . This is the law to love God and neighbor as spelled out in the Decalogue, in the Sermon on the Mount, and in the apostolic admonitions.[227]

We put ourselves in a place where we can be changed so that this law is expressed in the core of our being.

This opportunity for formation is available to all who engage with Scripture, to all who search for the relationship between God's revelation and the circumstances of daily life through interpretation. It is open to all who want to deepen their understanding of and relationship with God.

How Does the Spirit Help Us?

The good news is that we are not alone in our struggle with sin and that we have God's active help through the presence of the Holy Spirit.[228] Turning to Jesus for mercy and forgiveness not only brings us strength, but also brings us an ally in the struggle to improve and move toward the divine image.[229] The Holy Spirit truly becomes an active participant in the daily life of the believer.

[T]he Spirit is called the Spirit of sanctification, because he quickens and cherishes us, not merely by the general energy which is seen in the human race, as well as other animals, but because he is the seed and root of heavenly life in us.[230]

Only this presence, this help from the outside, gives human beings the strength to do what our sinful inclination makes impossible otherwise.

Divine initiative changed the way human beings relate to law.

> God has done what the law, weakened by the flesh,
> could not do: by sending his own Son in the likeness of
> sinful flesh, and to deal with sin, he condemned sin in
> the flesh, so that the just requirement of the law might
> be fulfilled in us, who walk not according to the flesh
> but according to the Spirit. (Rom 8:3–4)

Righteousness and the just requirements of the law have not changed, but sin itself has been condemned. Human beings have been freed from the power of sin, from the domination and control of sin, by the work of Christ and through the Spirit. "And [wrongdoers are] what some of you used to be. But you were washed, you were sanctified, you were justified in the name of the Lord Jesus Christ and in the Spirit of our God" (1 Cor 6:11).

The effect of this work is both a present movement toward righteousness and also a hope for the future, since the future in eternity depends on our transformation into people who can live compatibly with a righteous God. "But if the Spirit of Him who raised Jesus from the dead dwells in you, He who raised Christ Jesus from the dead will also give life to your mortal bodies through His Spirit who dwells in you" (Rom 8:11). This transformation is not a result of our attempts to conform to the law but a result of faith. "Well then, does God supply you with the Spirit and work miracles among you by your doing the works of the law, or by your believing what you heard?" (Gal 3:5).

The Holy Spirit becomes part of all human beings who belong to Christ, regardless of any distinctions among them. "For in the one Spirit we were all baptized into one body—Jews or Greeks, slaves or free—and we were all made to drink of one Spirit" (1 Cor 12:13). The gifts and effects of the presence of the Spirit are only relevant and effective for those who are in a spiritual relationship with God, because they make no sense to those who do not participate in the spiritual life. "Those who are unspiritual do not receive the gifts of God's Spirit, for they are foolishness to them, and they are unable to understand them because they are spiritually discerned" (1 Cor 2:14). Those who are in

Christ are able to transcend the sinfulness integral to life in the body only because the Spirit helps their redirection toward righteousness. "But if Christ is in you, though the body is dead because of sin, the Spirit is life because of righteousness" (Rom 8:10).

Paul experienced this conflict between his bodily desire for independence and rebellion and his own intellectual commitment, as a Pharisee or a follower of Jesus, to try to live by God's law. He saw the conflict between body and mind (Rom 7:23) as impossible to resolve without outside help, which is available from the Holy Spirit.

> But I say, walk by the Spirit, and you will not carry out the desire of the flesh. For the flesh sets its desire against the Spirit, and the Spirit against the flesh; for these are in opposition to one another, so that you may not do the things that you please. (Gal 5:16–17)

The work of the Spirit is not to help individuals get what they want, but to help them to want and to act in accordance with God's will.

The presence of the Spirit opposes the willful desire to enjoy all of the pleasures of this world, and we each must take action to walk away from those pleasures and follow the Spirit. Following the direction of the Spirit is active and not passive. We must choose to obey the Spirit's direction, and that obedience does not happen automatically.[231] A battle is going on, and the pleasures and temptations of the flesh are promoted and advertised all around us.

Paul was fully conscious that his desire to do the will of God led to this ongoing struggle with his flesh. He could not win that struggle without help. The real, effective power to win this struggle comes from Christ.

> For I joyfully concur with the law of God in the inner man, but I see a different law in the members of my body, waging war against the law of my mind and making me a prisoner of the law of sin which is in my members. Wretched man that I am! Who will set me

free from the body of this death? Thanks be to God through Jesus Christ our Lord! (Rom 7:22–25)

Miraculously, the Spirit actually does provide, in spite of all resistance, the power to comply with the will of God and to recognize and turn back from our mistakes.

> Do not be deceived; God is not mocked, for you reap whatever you sow. If you sow to your own flesh, you will reap corruption from the flesh; but if you sow to the Spirit, you will reap eternal life from the Spirit. (Gal 6:7–8)

This combination, human being working with indwelling Spirit, makes it possible for us to grow into what is promised to us.

> So then, brothers and sisters, we are debtors, not to the flesh, to live according to the flesh— for if you live according to the flesh, you will die; but if by the Spirit you put to death the deeds of the body, you will live. (Rom 8:12–13)

The key is an active cooperation between believer and Spirit that engages the Spirit in each of our attempts to overcome the power of sin and live righteously.

Walking with the Spirit involves an active commitment on the part of each of us to cooperate with and be directed by the Spirit from day to day. "If we live by the Spirit, let us also be guided by the Spirit" (Gal 5:25). This is not a condition for salvation, since salvation has already been won through the faith in Christ that brought us the Spirit in the first place. We do not have to fulfill the law to be part of the body of Christ, but our living by our faith will result in fulfilling the law.[232]

Walking with the Spirit is part of the ongoing process of transformation and renewal that continues throughout life. As Paul says, "Do not be conformed to this world, but be transformed by the renewing of your minds, so that you may discern what is the will of God—what is good and acceptable and perfect" (Rom 12:2). Following the active direction of the Spirit does not mean following the regulations of the law. It means that we accept the Spirit's ongoing direction and guidance voluntarily. Thus Paul can say to the Galatians, "But if you are led by the Spirit, you are not under the Law" (Gal 5:18) when we are receiving direction from the Spirit about which behaviors to encourage and which to avoid.

Walking by the Spirit does involve work, even though it is not the kind of work on which salvation is based. This work involves constant attention, effort, and action in order to follow the direction of the Spirit. "For those who are according to the flesh set their minds on the things of the flesh, but those who are according to the Spirit, the things of the Spirit" (Rom 8:5).

To walk according to the Spirit involves a series of conscious choices in thought and attention as well as in visible action and behavior. One must *choose* to pay attention to the Spirit, to listen to the Spirit's direction, and to act out of what comes from the Spirit. "Do you not know that if you present yourselves to anyone as obedient slaves, you are slaves of the one whom you obey, either of sin, which leads to death, or of obedience, which leads to righteousness?" (Rom 6:16). There is no question in Paul's mind that obedience to the direction of the Spirit is expected, and that obedience will be expressed in righteous behavior.

Because of the opposition of flesh and Spirit, we can be pretty sure that the guidance of the Spirit will not always be what we "feel like" doing at a particular time. This is especially hard for those of us who are used to the freedom to act on impulse. In order to follow the direction of the Holy Spirit, we have to control our own actions and follow the directions we receive, especially when it is contrary to our natural inclinations.

How Can We Talk about Sin with Respect?

So, how do we have a friendly conversation about sin when we disagree with each other about it? A sin is expressed in action, and some of us may believe that a particular behavior is sinful while others do not. In addition, our egos tend to deny or defend our own sin, because acknowledging sinfulness is personally painful. Attitudes about our own sin can range from "I'm a basically good person," and "I sin some, but I'm not as bad as lots of others," to "I have no control over my sins," and "My sins are horrible; I've hurt so many people." Before we even start, we know that a conversation about moral law and its violation is personal and on very sensitive ground.

The central topics covered in the moral law—idolatry, violence, sexual immorality, and justice—are expressed in the modern world in terms of money, power, sexuality, addictions, crime, war, and many more. "Sins" that can be topics of conversation these days might be driving a gas-guzzling car, visiting the casinos, infidelity, or same-sex sexuality. The kinds of sins that cause conflict are those seen to be sinful by some, but not by others. Typically even within a particular area of moral law, such as sexual immorality, there will be general agreement on some applications of the law, such as pedophilia, while there is disagreement on others, such as homosexuality.

Christians are encouraged to try to help those who are stuck in sin to get out of it.

> My brothers and sisters, if anyone among you wanders from the truth and is brought back by another, you should know that whoever brings back a sinner from wandering will save the sinner's soul from death and will cover a multitude of sins. (Jas 5:19–20)

We are also expected to follow the model of Christ, who welcomed and loved those caught in sin. Nevertheless, Jesus was always clear that the goal should be to leave the sin behind. In trying to do these two things at the same time, we need to both love the person and oppose the sinful action. We need to distinguish between the normal human inclination to sin that we all share and the action or behavior itself. In encouraging the journey out of sin, we need to accept steps aside or steps backward on the path, but not to lose hope in the possibility of progress in the right direction.

The choice of a way to proceed depends on whether we believe that a particular action is a sin or not. The course of a conversation between two people depends on whether or not they agree that a particular action is a sin. Looking at my own behavior, the choices are relatively clear. If I think a particular behavior is a sin, I am responsible to resist it as best I can, and to repent of it when I have fallen into it. If I do not think it is a sin, I have the option to enjoy that behavior as a gift of God, with responsibility to keep that enjoyment within bounds.

When the behavior in question is someone else's, my choices are more complicated. If my friend is doing something he or she believes to be sin, and I agree that it is, I am called to listen and support resistance and repentance. If I think the behavior is not a sin, I should still listen to my friend's struggle, but support what I think is healthy reasoning when I hear it. I am also responsible to respond truthfully if asked what I think. If my friend is doing something that he or she does not think is a sin, and I agree, the choice is pleasant—encourage enjoyment, support awareness of appropriate limits, and encourage giving gratitude to God.

When my friend is doing something that I believe is sin, but he or she does not, things are most difficult. What can I do without intruding and forcing my friend away? I can always listen. I can support awareness of sin, resistance, and repentance when I hear them. I can ask about my friend's awareness of boundaries and control over behavior. Above all, I do not condemn my friend for having engaged in the sin. I listen and support without approving. If I am asked what I think, I tell the truth. However, I respond with my own perspective only if asked, and only in terms that will encourage my friend to find the better path.

The letter to the Ephesians provides a good model of how to do this. "Let no evil talk come out of your mouths, but only what is useful for building up, as there is need, so that your words may give grace to those who hear" (Eph 4:29). Since only some of the many things that are true will actually help and encourage, I need to choose carefully and say that which will be both true and helpful. I must also be clear that my silence is not approval and that my presence is not meant to encourage the behavior in question.

The essence of courtesy is respect for the other person's sense of sin and respect for the differences between our convictions. I do not contradict things my friend says unless invited. I do not insist on what I believe to be good or volunteer what I believe to be bad. I do not impose situations on my friend that presume agreement between us, because it does not help to put my friend into a situation of public embarrassment. I do not condemn my friend for honest and sincere disagreement, and I do not punish my friend by exclusion if I am treated in return with respect. Courtesy is the bare minimum requirement of the love that Christians are called to give to friends, neighbors, strangers, and even enemies.

How does it actually work to talk with a friend about sin with courtesy and respect? In conversation it is critically important to acknowledge the other person's responsibility for making his or her own choices. It is not helpful simply to tell another person what choice to make. It is more helpful to encourage that person to come to a good choice based on their own discernment and judgment.

For example, one young friend, a man in his late teens, started dating a friend of his older sister, a woman in her twenties. One day I asked him casually, "How's the seduction coming?"

"Whose?" he asked.

"Yours."

"[pause] Well, my sister's done it lots of times."

"Yes, but did you ever talk to her about how much she regretted it?" Nothing more was said, but I did hear that the relationship ended shortly afterward.

Another situation involved a man in his early thirties who had to move back in with his parents for a while. His mom had fallen back into the habit of treating him as if he were still in high school. "My mom is giving me grief for hanging around with my old friends," he said.

"You're a grown-up now. You get to pick your own friends," I replied. There was a long pause while light dawned.

"What are the guys up to these days?" I asked.

"They mostly just go drinking. To tell you the truth, we don't have all that much in common anymore." Once the pressure of the need to resist his mother eased up, he could see his own situation more clearly and make choices about how to spend his time that were more in line with his own values.

Respect for the other is critical, especially respect for each person's responsibility to turn away from sin and to avoid the circumstances that lead to it. A friend's job is to support taking responsibility and to help with the process of discerning where sin is found and what practical things can be done to avoid it.

How Do We Follow God's Directions?

How can we tell whether the guidance we feel we are receiving comes from the Holy Spirit or from an underhanded craving for our own satisfaction? It is necessary to check and keep on checking. Paul says, "test everything; hold fast to what is good; abstain from every form of evil" (1 Thess 5:21–22). Each of us is responsible and accountable for our own actions. We are all supposed to check regularly to make sure that we are living as Christ directed both externally and internally. "Examine yourselves to see whether you are living in the faith. Test yourselves. Do you not realize that Jesus Christ is in you?—unless, indeed, you fail to meet the test!" (2 Cor 13:5).

We must not take credit for someone else's good work or good intentions, or blame others for our own lack of them. Each of us must respond to the particular challenges, tasks, and temptations that come along in the course of our own daily life. "All must test their own work; then that work, rather than their neighbor's work, will become a cause for pride. For all must carry their own loads" (Gal 6:4–5). What is the standard for grading this test? It is the standard of righteousness expressed in the Scriptures, in both the old and new covenants.

Each of us is responsible to be sure that what seems to be the guidance of the Holy Spirit is in fact coming from that holy source. "Those who are spiritual discern all things, and they are themselves subject to no one else's scrutiny. For who has known the mind of the Lord so as to instruct him?" But we have the mind of Christ" (1 Cor 2:15–16). Those who are not engaged in a spiritual life do not have the authority to direct those who are, at least in spiritual matters. Since discernment of spirits is one of those manifestations of the Spirit given to individuals for the common good of the community (1 Cor 12:7–12), each believer is provided with a source of support through the community's help in our individual discernment.

Practicing a behavior pattern encourages repetition and can be habit-forming. Practicing righteousness is formative, and making righteous actions "normal" encourages ongoing practice. Paul observes the continuing effect of growth in righteousness when he identifies the fruits of the Spirit: "But the fruit of the Spirit is love, joy, peace, patience, kindness, goodness, faithfulness, gentleness, self-control; against such things there is no law" (Gal 5:22–23). These qualities of character grow in those who practice them, a practice enabled and encouraged by the presence of the Spirit. As we spend more and more of our time in these habits of mind and heart, the presence of the Spirit can be seen by others. Thus real mental and spiritual engagement in faith can be seen through direct observation.

But how does the physical body function differently as a result of this relationship with the Spirit? "The body is meant not for fornication but for the Lord, and the Lord for the body. And God raised the Lord and will also raise us by his power. Do you not know that your bodies are members of Christ?" (1 Cor 6:13–15). The bodies of believers belong to Christ, and each one becomes a real, physical part of Christ's living body on earth. "[A]nyone united to the Lord becomes one spirit with him" (1 Cor 6:17). This unity has two sides: Christ reaching out and into us from above through the Spirit, and the individual opening to and receiving this presence into body, mind, and heart.

As people are joined with Christ, the real physical presence of the Spirit becomes part of our daily lives and experiences. Paul says, "But you are not in the flesh; you are in the Spirit, since the Spirit of God dwells in you" (Rom 8:9). These bodies, which have become rather a mess in the process of life with sin, need to become the home of a new resident, because the Spirit of God is moving in.

> Or do you not know that your body is a temple of the Holy Spirit within you, which you have from God, and that you are not your own? For you were bought with a price; therefore glorify God in your body. (1 Cor 6:19–20)

These human bodies have become a holy sanctuary, the way the temple in Jerusalem was a place for the residence of the glory of God. This temple must be protected from the consequences of moral decay, particularly from dirt, unworthy distractions, and rivals for the reverence and attention God deserves.

> What agreement has the temple of God with idols? For we are the temple of the living God; as God said, "I will live in them and walk among them, and I will be their God, and they shall be my people." (2 Cor 6:16)

Acceptance of life in Christ and the presence of the Spirit involves a commitment to preserve and offer our entire self to God in the best possible condition.

> I appeal to you therefore, brothers and sisters, by the mercies of God, to present your bodies as a living sacrifice, holy and acceptable to God, which is your spiritual worship. (Rom 12:1)

211

How Do We Live a Sanctified Life?

There are several components of the practical process of living a sanctified life from day to day. We need to:

- Maintain an ongoing relationship with God and live a lifestyle that is pleasing to God
- Communicate with God in frequent prayer and listen to God through Scripture and the voices of others
- Worship regularly to keep the big picture active in our minds and hearts
- Contribute our time and money in service to those in need, through the church, charitable organizations, and personal causes
- Use regular and continuing discernment to discover our unique purpose in life, and then find and act in the place where our talents, skills, experience, and passion meet the needs of the world
- Provide the necessities of life (physical, emotional, and spiritual) for ourselves and those dependent on us

If our lives are built around these components, will it show on the outside? Will those who know us and see us regularly be able to tell that we are trying to live a life pleasing to God? The short answer is "not necessarily." We will still be doing many of the same activities we have always done—getting up in the morning, doing our chores, working at our jobs, caring for our families, going to church, trying to resist temptation—but we will see these activities from God's perspective as well as from our own. Those paying attention will be able to see the fruits of the Spirit growing in and around us.

We Are Headed for Holiness.

The goal of the work of the Spirit is true holiness. Paul believed that this is the destination for all people who belong to Jesus. As Paul said in the greetings of his letter to the Romans, "To all God's beloved in Rome, who are called to be saints" (Rom 1:7). The term Paul used over and over for the people of his churches is ἅγιος (*hagios*)—which means sacred, holy, pure, and consecrated—identifies them as belonging to God and holy as the Lord is holy.

The struggle toward holy living is an ongoing experience for every believer in Christ, and the Holy Spirit is the primary ally each of us has in the process. What human beings could not do for themselves, the Holy Spirit makes possible, although as a work-in-progress rather than a completed task.

The people of Paul's churches were in the first enthusiasm of faith, the first to begin the great experiment of living in the already-but-not-yet state of life in Christ. Their efforts to live holy lives together brought out the challenge living with differences in culture, as well as the minefield of life with ordinary sinful human beings. The priority in all these conflicts is the righteousness made possible through the Holy Spirit. "For the kingdom of God is not food and drink but righteousness and peace and joy in the Holy Spirit" (Rom 14:17). The need for righteousness has not been made obsolete by the gospel; it is still our goal and destination, through the power of Christ and the help of the Spirit.

Holiness is part of our identity as people of Christ.

> Therefore prepare your minds for action; discipline yourselves; set all your hope on the grace that Jesus Christ will bring you when he is revealed. Like obedient children, do not be conformed to the desires that you formerly had in ignorance. Instead, as he who called you is holy, be holy yourselves in all your conduct; for it is written, "You shall be holy, for I am holy." (1 Pet 1:13–16)

Holiness is the path we are taking, and it is the way we become qualified to do the work Jesus has called us to do: "you are a chosen race, a royal priesthood, a holy nation, God's own people, in order that you may proclaim the mighty acts of him who called you out of darkness into his marvelous light" (1 Pet 2:9).

Questions for Reflection and Discussion

1. How many different kinds of choices do you make? What kinds of small choices do you make often? What kinds of big choices have influenced the direction of your life?
2. How do you listen for direction from God?
3. How do you approach the Bible when you are looking for guidance or advice? Do you have particular passages that you visit? What sections have been most helpful?
4. Consider Galatians 5:17. How does this compare with the commercial messages of our current culture?
5. Consider 1 Corinthians 6:12–20. Do you have a sense of how precious you are to God, body as well as mind and spirit?
6. How does our response to each challenge help us to be ready for the next challenge?
7. Have you ever tried to warn a friend that what they are planning or doing is sinful? How did that situation turn out?
8. What can we do to increase our awareness of the leading of the Spirit?

Guide for Discussion Leaders

The goal of this study is to show Christians how to identify the commands in the Bible that we should follow. Discussion focuses on the passages that underlie the identification process and on the relationship between Scripture and behavior for the participants. Each participant should become familiar with the biblical basis for making choices and begin the process of internalizing the guidance of Scripture.

Gatherings should be surrounded and steeped in prayer. Since the Holy Spirit is a critical part of our interpretation and understanding of Scripture, engaging and maintaining awareness of the presence of the Spirit should be continuous throughout the gathering. The leader should pray for the presence of the Spirit in preparation for the meeting, before the group comes together, and during quiet moments in the conversation.

A small group for discussion of this material would have nine meetings, one for each chapter. The group should have between six and twelve members in order to allow time for each participant to share his or her perspective. If there is a larger group, it is possible to create several sharing groups of three to six participants. One potential format for the gatherings with approximate times is:

Welcome and opening prayer: 5 minutes
Ice breaker: 10 minutes
Review of main points of chapter; questions: 15 minutes
Discussion of questions from chapter: 40 minutes
Prayer requests and prayer for each participant: 15 minutes
Arrangements and closing prayer: 5 minutes

A discussion session should take between one and one half and two hours altogether.

An ice breaker is suggested to give each participant a chance to feel comfortable speaking in the group. It should be a simple question that most people feel comfortable talking about, but that allows some kind of self-expression. For the first session, it can be introductory, for example—"Introduce yourself and say one thing about yourself that no one here knows." Questions work best if they are simple, light, personal, and offer a chance for participants to become comfortable with each other.

The role of the discussion leader is to engage the participants in thinking about the issues presented in each chapter. In the review of the material, the leader would typically summarize each section of the chapter in two or three sentences and ask for questions about any points the participants found confusing. In the discussion of the questions at the end of the chapter, the leader should feel free to use the questions in whatever order makes sense and also feel free to include other questions based on the participants' needs.

The leader should use open questions to encourage sharing, for example, "What is your experience when you find that you have done something wrong?" rather than "Have you ever done something wrong?" The leader acts as moderator of the discussion, keeping stronger voices from dominating the conversation and encouraging the quieter voices to contribute. The leader needs to be aware of body language in the group, to be sure to invite those who want to say something but are not able to find an opening in the conversation.

At the first meeting, it is important to establish guidelines for the group process. Typically, these include ground rules for confidentiality and acceptable limits on conversation. Confidentiality can exist at a range levels, for example keeping all comments confidential, allowing ideas to be shared but without identifying specific names, and all conversation able to be shared. The leader should restate the agreement about confidentiality regularly to remind participants of their responsibility to limit sharing. Acceptable limits on conversation should reflect the needs of the group, and may include limits on arguments, criticism, or advice in the group discussions.

Logistically, the role of leader can be shared among members of the group. The job can be shared by two people, with one responsible for logistics and prayer while the other reviews the material and facilitates discussion. The role of discussion leader can also rotate among members of the group, either on an assigned schedule or by asking for volunteers for future meetings at the end of a gathering.

Glossary

Antigonos of Sokho: A Jewish sage active in the second century BCE, before the Maccabean revolt. He was the successor of the sage known as Simeon the Righteous.

Apocrypha: Books written between 200 BCE and 100 CE that are not included in the Old Testament. Most were included in the canon by the Roman Catholic Church in 1546, but are rejected by most Protestants. They include Tobit (c. 200 BCE), Judith (c. 150 BCE), Additions to Esther (140–130 BCE), Wisdom of Solomon (c. 30 BCE), Ecclesiasticus (Sirach) (132 BCE), Baruch (c. 150–50 BCE), Letter of Jeremiah (c. 300–100 BCE), Prayer of Azariah (Song of Three Young Men) (second or first century BCE), Susanna (second or first century BCE), Bel and the Dragon (c. 100 BCE), 1 Maccabees (c. 110 BCE), 2 Maccabees (c. 110–70 BCE), 1 Esdras (c. 150–100 BCE), Prayer of Manasseh (second or first century BCE), 3 Maccabees, 2 Esdras (c. 100 CE), and 4 Maccabees.

Bar Kochba: Leader of the failed revolt against Rome between 132 and 135 CE that resulted from Emperor Hadrian's ban on circumcision and plans to build a Roman temple in Jerusalem. Rabbi Akiva supported Bar Kochba since he believed him to be the Messiah, and Akiva was ultimately executed by the Romans.

Bet midrash: A house of study where men and boys studied Torah. Leading teachers such as Hillel and Shammai gathered their students into schools that advocated the scriptural interpretations of their leaders.

Children of Noah: All of humanity before the Mosaic covenant and all those who are not part of the people of Israel after the time of Moses.

Codex Bezae: A manuscript of the gospels and Acts in Greek and Latin written between the fourth and sixth centuries. It was owned by John Calvin and donated by his successor Theodore Beza to the University of Cambridge. It is known as D in the list of ancient biblical manuscripts.

Dead Sea Scrolls: Ancient manuscripts discovered in and around the cliffs on the shore of the Dead Sea beginning in 1947. Many of the nearly eight hundred manuscripts are fragments, but the scrolls represent a diverse library of materials belonging to a community of Essenes who lived at Qumran. The collection includes portions of all but one of the books of the Old Testament, apocryphal books, interpretations of Scripture, calendars, and rule books for the life of the community.

Diaspora: The scattered Jews who lived outside the land of Palestine after 581 BCE. Beginning in Egypt, Jews spread throughout the Hellenistic world until there were more Jews living outside Palestine than inside. The translation of the Hebrew Bible into Greek in Egypt and the collecting and editing of the *Mishnah*, *Tosefta*, and *Talmud* in Babylon were the work of these dispersed people.

Didache: The earliest known manual of church behavior and practices. It includes the ethical choice of one of two "ways" of life; a section on fasting, prayer, baptism, and the Lord's supper; and organization of church life with qualifications and responsibilities for various roles. It is likely that it was first written in Greek around 100 BCE by a Jewish convert in Syria.

Exegesis: The process of bringing out the meaning of a passage of Scripture. It includes establishing the base text, considering issues in translation, identifying historical and sociological surroundings, and putting the passage into its scriptural context. Methods of exegesis have included literal, allegorical, moral, analogical, and mystical approaches, as well as various modern forms of biblical criticism.

Gamaliel: The name of three important rabbis in early rabbinic Judaism. Rabban Gamaliel the Elder was Paul's teacher, known for his humane interpretation of law. Rabban Gamaliel II was the grandson of Gamaliel the Elder and followed Johannan ben Zakkai as the leader of the community in Yavneh after the destruction of the temple. Rabban Gamaliel III was the son of Rabbi Judah the Patriarch, and he completed the editing of the *Mishnah* in the early third century CE.

Gentile: Any non-Jewish (non-Israelite) person. Israel was set apart from the Gentiles as a people chosen by God, and this religious distinction was the reason for the other restrictions that kept them separate from others.

Halakhah: The way, derived from the word translated as walk or go. Halakhah is a principle or teaching that acts as a practical guide for living. It came to be a word for the whole set of rules and regulations developed by the rabbis from interpreting the law of Moses in specific situations. The Halakhah were collected in the *Mishnah*, which was then the basis for further interpretation. As a result, Halakhah is the largest portion of the Talmud.

Hasmoneans: A Jewish family that included the Maccabees as well as the high priests and kings who ruled Judea from the Maccabean revolt (142 BCE) until the Roman conquest under Pompey (63 BCE).

Herodians: Partisans of the house of Herod. Although they were a political party, they also joined the Pharisees in opposition to Jesus.

Hillel: A rabbinic sage who lived between 60 BCE and 70 CE. Hillel and his disciples interpreted the Law more leniently than his contemporary Shammai. His seven rules for interpretation of Scripture had a significant influence on Pharisaic and Talmudic interpretation.

Idumea: Greek name for the country of the Edomites. Idumeans were forcibly converted to Judaism under the Hasmoneans, but the area was subject to frequent changes of occupying authorities. Herod the Great came from Idumea.

Jesus ben Sirach: Writer of the book of Ecclesiasticus, a priest who was active in the temple around 180 BCE.

Johanan ben Zakkai: Leader of the small company of Pharisees that moved to Yavneh when the temple was destroyed in 70 CE. According to tradition, he escaped from the siege of Jerusalem, met with the commander at the Roman camp, and obtained permission to leave the city safely with his students before it was destroyed.

John Calvin: Writer and pastor who lived between 1509 and 1564. Calvin spent most of his life in Geneva and was the primary spokesman for the Reformed strand of the Protestant Reformation. He is known for his *Institutes of the Christian Religion* and for his insight into the uses of law.

Josephus: Jewish-born Roman historian who wrote books about the history of the Jewish people. A commander of Jewish forces fighting against the Romans in Galilee, he was defeated, captured, and taken to Rome to be adopted into the emperor's family.

Justification: The doctrine that describes how followers of Jesus are forgiven for their sins and considered righteous before God based on their faith.

Laws for the Children of Noah: Seven laws that are binding on all people (all descendants of Noah) including prohibitions on idolatry, blasphemy, murder, sexual immorality, theft, and eating the limb of a living animal, as well as the requirement to provide justice.

Letter of Aristeas: A document most likely written around 150 to 100 BCE that describes the events around the translation of the Hebrew Scriptures into Greek in the *Septuagint*. King Ptolemy II of Egypt requested translators from the high priest at the temple in Jerusalem, and they came to Egypt to do their work.

Leviticus Rabbah: A collection completed between 450 and 500 CE of systematic propositions about Israel's role, spiritual life, and future, each based on passages from Leviticus read in the context of other Scripture.

Maccabees: A family properly known as the Hasmoneans (see entry above).

Mamzer: An illegitimate child. This may be a bastard or the offspring of a man and woman who could not legally marry one another, a couple whose union would be in violation of the law.

Mekhilta of Rabbi Ishmael: An interpretation and commentary based on Exodus 12–23. The actual editor and date are subjects for discussion, but it includes materials dating at the latest from the first half of the second century.

Messiah: Anointed one, a term that could be applied to any person "anointed" and sent by God. Formally, the term "messiah" refers to a person who has been consecrated to a high office by ceremonial anointing with oil. Since the Davidic king was the God's chosen ruler, "messiah" was associated with the prophecy that God would bring an ideal Davidic ruler to Israel.

Midrash: Commentary on Hebrew Bible Scripture texts, including verse-by-verse commentaries, narration commentaries, and homiletic commentaries for use in sermons.

Mishnah: Early rabbinic writings collected and edited around 200 CE. It is the oldest written collection of Jewish legal statements, a systematic ordering of Halakhah, including material that had been part of the oral Torah. It consists of six sections: Zeraim (Seed), Moed (Feasts), Nashim (Women), Neziqin (Damages), Qodashim (Holy Matters), and Tohoroth (Purities).

Mosaic law: The whole body of the Mosaic legislation. Obedience to the law of Moses was not conceived as a way of earning God's favor but as a response to his grace in delivering Israel from Egypt.

Netin: One of a particular class of temple servants who performed menial tasks in the daily life of the temple. They were descendants of the Gibeonites and referred to as temple slaves.

Noahide Laws: The seven laws that applied to the children of Noah, to all people before the Mosaic covenant and all non-Jews afterward.

Palestine: Territory at the east end of the Mediterranean Sea between the sea and the Jordan River, situated on the critical trade routes between Egypt and empires to the east. It was made a Roman province by Pompey in 68 bce, revolted, was reconquered by Herod the Great, and continued to rebel and be reconquered by Rome. Under Rome, it was divided into four provinces: Judea, Galilee, Samaria, and Peraea east of the Jordan.

Pharisees: A Jewish movement in between 150 BCE and 70 CE that is sometimes considered a sect, a philosophical school, or a political party. They are known for their interpretation and observance of the law, for moving religious practice from the temple into daily life, and for preserving oral traditions.

Philo: A Jewish philosopher from Alexandria in Egypt who lived from approximately 10 BCE to 45 CE. He was a member of a wealthy family and in 39 CE led a delegation to the Emperor Caligula to protect Jews who refused to worship the emperor's image. His writing described an allegorical interpretation of Scripture that blended Jewish law with Stoic, Pythagorean, and especially Platonic thought.

Pseudepigrapha: Jewish writings from the second century BCE through the second century CE not included in the Bible, the Apocrypha, the documents found only among the Dead Sea Scrolls, the rabbinic literature, or works attributable to a known author.

Qumran: The site of the settlement, probably Essene, that produced the Dead Sea Scrolls. It is located eight and a half miles south of Jericho on the first shelf of hills above the west shore of the Dead Sea.

P. Oxyrhyncus 840: One of the Greek papyri found at Oxyrhyncus, an ancient Egyptian town situated on the edge of the western desert, 120 miles south of Cairo.

Rabbinic Judaism: The Judaic philosophical system that first emerged in the *Mishnah* after 200 CE and developed into a religious system with the Talmud between 400 and 500 CE. After the destruction of the temple, the rabbis in exile developed a form of Judaism without a temple or cult.

Righteousness: Acting according to divine or moral law and therefore free of guilt or sin. The words for righteousness appear more than five hundred times in the Hebrew Bible and more than two hundred times in the New Testament. Righteous actions demonstrate living out a right relationship with God and others.

Righteous Gentile: A non-Jew who lives according to the laws for the children of Noah.

Ritual Purity: Satisfying the requirements for participating in worship under the Mosaic law. Various normal events (e.g., childbirth, contact with bodily fluids, etc.) can compromise this purity. A person may not participate in worship until the steps required for purification have been satisfied.

Second temple Judaism: The period from 586 BCE to 70 CE during which the Jerusalem temple was the center of religious life. This was also a time of worldwide dispersion leading to a majority of Jews living outside of Palestine.

Septuagint: The translation of the Hebrew Scriptures into Greek completed by the late second century BCE. This translation was made for Greek-speaking Jews in the Diaspora and included the Hebrew Bible and the Apocrypha, with some passages being significantly different from the later standardized text.

Shammai: A rabbinic sage of the first century, contemporary and opponent of Hillel. Where Hillel was known for lenient interpretation, Shammai was known for the stricter possibilities.

Shekinah: The divine Presence that lived in the temple in Jerusalem.

Sifra, Sifré to Numbers, Sifré to Deuteronomy: These are compilations of exegesis of the books of Leviticus, Numbers 5–35, and Deuteronomy that were created around 300 CE. They follow the Scripture verse by verse, but link the verse of to a passage from the *Mishnah* and explore the main proposition from there.

Simeon ben Yochai: A rabbi of the second century, the successor of Rabbi Akiva. His unique contribution to interpretation was that he tried to understand the reason for a particular passage and then let that reason guide his interpretation.

Supersessionism: The conviction that the covenant between God and the people of Israel had been taken over and superseded by the Christian church.

Talmud: Commentary called *gemara* (teaching) that follows the structure and organization of the *Mishnah* and incorporates other writings. The Palestinian Talmud was completed in approximately 400 CE, written in Galilean Aramaic. The Babylonian Talmud was written in Babylonian Aramaic and was not completed until around 600 CE.

Tanakh: The Hebrew Bible consisting of the Torah; Nebi'im, also known as the Prophets; and Ketubim, also known as the Writings.

Tannaim: Rabbinic leaders in the period between 70 and 200 to 250 CE, between the destruction of the temple and the editing of the *Mishnah*. In this period, leadership shifted from kings, priests, and prophets to the rabbis; oral law was captured and written in the *Mishnah*, and Judaism ceased to be centered in the land of Israel.

Torah: The first five books of the Hebrew Bible, the books of Moses, or the Pentateuch. Torah is also used in the more general sense to include both the written books and the oral tradition of interpretation that accompanied them.

Tosefta: A supplement to the *Mishnah* collected at the same time and completed around 220 CE.

Vespasian: Roman commander during the siege of Jerusalem beginning in 66 CE and Emperor of Rome from 69 to 79 CE.

Yavneh: An ancient city in Palestine, located about fifteen miles south of Tel Aviv and four miles from the Mediterranean Sea. In Hellenistic times, Yavneh was known as Jamnia and was used as a base by foreign armies attacking the Maccabeans. After the destruction of the temple in 70 CE, the refugees led by Johanan ben Zakkai founded a school there.

Resources for Further Exploration

Rather than a formal bibliography, here is an eclectic set of resources that you can use to explore different aspects of these ideas. What these materials have in common is that they demonstrate a variety of perspectives on the Jewish influences in the early church. Feel free to sample them to see which are most helpful from your own perspective. Enjoy the trip!

Jewish Ancient Texts

There is no substitute for hearing the voices of the first century in their original words, or as close as a modern translator can make them. The *Mishnah*, *Tosefta*, and *Talmud*, although edited later, contain wonderful examples of the conversations of the early rabbis. The Mekhilta and *Sifrē*'s show the way contemporary rabbis interpreted Scripture, while the *Dead Sea Scrolls* reflect the life of a monastic community in the desert. They give a wonderful flavor for the depth of faith and practice of Jesus' contemporaries.

Charlesworth, James H. *The Old Testament Pseudepigrapha Vol 1: Apocalyptic Literature and Testaments*. New York: Doubleday, 1983.
Charlesworth, James H. *The Old Testament Pseudepigrapha Vol 2: Expansions of the Old Testament and Legends, Wisdom and Philosophical Literature, Prayers, Psalms, and Odes, Fragments of Lost Judeo-Hellenistic Works*. New York: Doubleday, 1985.

Epstein, Isidore. *The Babylonian Talmud, tr. into English with notes, glossary, and indices under the editorship of I. Epstein.* London, Soncino Press, 1935–1948.

Garcia Martinez, Florentino. *The Dead Sea Scrolls Translated: the Qumran Texts in English*, 2nd ed. Leiden: E. J. Brill, 1994.

Neusner, Jacob. *Mekhilta According to Rabbi Ishmael: An Introduction to Judaism's First Scriptural Encyclopaedia.* Brown Judaic studies, no. 152. Atlanta: Scholars Press, 1988.

Neusner, Jacob. *Mekhilta According to Rabbi Ishmael: An Analytical Translation, Vol. 1, Pisha, Beshallah, Shirata, and Vayassa.* Atlanta: Scholars Press, 1988.

Neusner, Jacob. *Mekhilta According to Rabbi Ishmael: An Analytical Translation, Vol. 2, Amalek, Bahodesh, Neziqin, Kaspa and Shabbata.* Atlanta: Scholars Press, 1988.

Neusner, Jacob. *Sifré to Numbers: An American Translation and Explanation.* Atlanta: Scholars Press, 1986.

Neusner, Jacob. *Sifré to Deuteronomy: An Analytical Translation, Volume Two: Pisqaot One Hundred Forty-Seven through Three Hundred Fifty-Seven.* Atlanta: Scholars Press, 1987.

Neusner, Jacob. *The Mishnah: A New Translation.* New Haven: Yale University Press, 1988.

Neusner, Jacob. *The Tosefta: Translated from the Hebrew With a New Introduction.* Peabody, MA: Hendrickson, 2002.

Other Ancient Texts

These source documents reflect, as close as we have them, the words of the people of the early church. The Greek New Testament, with its footnotes about sources, and Metzger's comments on translation are our best understanding of the actual words of the gospels, epistles, and Acts. Philo and Josephus were contemporaries of the New Testament events, and they wrote extensively about their lives and experiences.

The *Didache*, *Gospel of the Savior*, and *Codex Bezae* are a few of the many documents reflecting the perspective of the church a century later.

Aland, B., K. Aland, M. Black, C. M. Martini, B. M. Metzger, & A. Wikgren. *The Greek New Testament* (4th ed.). Federal Republic of Germany: United Bible Societies,1993, c1979.

Josephus, Flavius. *The Works of Josephus: New Updated Edition*, trans. William Whiston. Peabody, MA: Hendrickson, 1987.

Josephus, Flavius, and Steve Mason. *Life of Josephus*. Boston: Brill Academic Publishers, 2003.

Kruger, Michael J. *The Gospel of the Savior: An Analysis of Papyrus Oxyrhynchus 840 and Its Place in the Gospel Traditions of Early Christianity. Texts and editions for New Testament study, v. 1*. Leiden: Brill, 2005.

Metzger, Bruce M. *A Textual Commentary on the Greek New Testament*, 2nd ed. Stuttgart: Deutsche Biblegesellschaft: United Bible Societies, 1994.

Parker, David C. *Codex Bezae: An Early Christian Manuscript and Its Text*. Cambridge: Cambridge University Press, 1992.

Philo of Alexandria. *The Works of Philo: New Updated Edition*, trans. C. D. Yonge. Peabody, MA: Hendrickson, 1993.

Sandt, Huub van de and David Flusser. *The Didache: Its Jewish Sources and its Place in Early Judaism and Christianity*. Minneapolis: Fortress, 2002.

Schrivener, Fredrick H. *Bezae Codex Cantabrigiensis*. Pittsburgh: Pickwick, 1978.

First Century Judaism

This is a group of wonderful resources on Judaism in the time of Jesus, ranging from the introductory to the encyclopedic. VanderCam and Cohen provide good introductions to the period, while Flusser and Klawans offer striking insights. Fishbane and Boyarin describe the process of understanding Scripture the rabbis used, and you can see echoes of this process in Jesus. Gary Porton explores Jewish-Gentile relationships, and Neusner's *Rabbinic Traditions About the Pharisees Before 70* is an excellent unraveling of who said what and when.

Boyarin, Daniel. *Intertextuality and the Reading of Midrash*. Bloomington, IN: Indiana University Press, 1990.

Buxbaum, Yitzhak. *The Life and Teachings of Hillel*. Northvale, NJ: Jason Aronson, 1994.

Clorfene, Chaim and Yakov Rogalsky. *The Path of the Righteous Gentile: An Introduction to the Seven Laws of the Children of Noah*. Southfield, MI: Targum, 1987.

Cohen, Shaye J. D. *From the Maccabees to the Mishnah*, 2d ed. Louisville: Westminster John Knox, 2006.

Cohen, Shaye J. D. "The Significance of Yavneh: Pharisees, Rabbis, and the End of Jewish Sectarianism." *Hebrew Union College Annual* 55, 1984: 27–53.

Dallen, Michael Ellias. *The Rainbow Covenant: Torah and the Seven Universal Laws*. Springdale, AR: Lightcatcher Books, 2003.

Fishbane, Michael A. *The Exegetical Imagination: On Jewish Thought and Theology*. Cambridge, MA: Harvard University Press, 1998.

Fishbane, Michael A. *The Midrashic Imagination: Jewish Exegesis, Thought, and History*. Albany: State University of New York Press, 1993.

Flusser, David. *Judaism of the Second Temple Period: Volume 1 Qumran and Apocalypticism*. Grand Rapids: Eerdmans, 2007.

Flusser, David. *Judaism of the Second Temple Period: Volume 2 The Jewish Sages and Their Literature*. Grand Rapids: Eerdmans, 2009.

Klausner, Joseph. *The Messianic Idea in Israel from Its Beginning to the Completion of the Mishnah*. New York: Macmillan, 1955.

Klawans, Jonathan. *Impurity and Sin in Ancient Judaism*. Oxford; New York: Oxford University Press, 2000.

Klawans, Jonathan. *Purity, Sacrifice, and the Temple: Symbolism and Supersessionism in the Study of Ancient Judaism*. Oxford; New York: Oxford University Press, 2006.

Maccoby, Hyam. *Ritual and Morality: The Ritual Purity System and Its Place in Judaism*. Cambridge: Cambridge University Press, 2009.

Neusner, Jacob. *Dictionary of Ancient Rabbis: Selections from the Jewish Encyclopedia.* Peabody, MA: Hendrickson, 2003.

Neusner, Jacob. *Invitation to Midrash: The Workings of Rabbinic Bible Interpretation: A Teaching Book.* San Francisco: Harper & Row, 1989.

Neusner, Jacob, A. J. Avery-Peck, W. S. Green and Museum of Jewish Heritage. *The Encyclopedia of Judaism.* New York: Brill, 2000.

Neusner, Jacob. *Judaism When Christianity Began: A Survey of Belief and Practice.* Louisville: Westminster John Knox Press, 2002.

Neusner, Jacob. *The Rabbinic Traditions About the Pharisees Before 70: Part I The Masters.* Leiden: E. J. Brill 1971. Reprint, Eugene, OR: Wipf&Stock, 2005.

Neusner, Jacob. *The Rabbinic Traditions About the Pharisees Before 70: Part II The Houses.* Leiden: E. J. Brill 1971. Reprint, Eugene, OR: Wipf&Stock, 2005.

Neusner, Jacob. *The Rabbinic Traditions About the Pharisees Before 70: Part III Conclusions.* Leiden: E. J. Brill 1971.

Nickelsburg, George W. E. *Jewish Literature between the Bible and the Mishnah,* 2d ed. Minneapolis: Fortress, 2005.

Porton, Gary G. *Goyim: Gentiles and Israelites in Mishnah-Tosefta.* Providence: Brown University Press, 1988.

Porton, Gary. *The Stranger within Your Gates: Converts and Conversion in Rabbinic Literature.* Chicago: University of Chicago Press, 1994.

Sanders, E. P. *Judaism: Practice and Belief, 63BCE – 66CE.* London: SCM Press, 1992.

Schiffman, Lawrence H. *From Text to Tradition: A History of Second Temple and Rabbinic Judaism.* Hoboken, NJ: Ktav Pub. House, 1991.

Schiffman, Lawrence H. *Reclaiming the Dead Sea Scrolls: The History of Judaism, the Background of Christianity, the Lost Library of Qumran.* The Anchor Bible reference library. New York: Doubleday, 1995.

Schwartz, Baruch J. *Perspectives on Purity and Purification in the Bible.* New York: T&T Clark, 2008

Shanks, Hershel. *The Mystery and Meaning of the Dead Sea Scrolls.* New York: Random House, 1998.

VanderKam, James C. *An Introduction to Early Judaism.* Grand Rapids: Eerdmans, 2001.

Life and Culture in First Century Palestine

It is always helpful to understand, as much as is possible after so much time, what life was like for Jesus and his contemporaries. These materials look at different aspects of life in the first century from a variety of scholarly perspectives.

Bauckham, Richard. *The Jewish World Around the New Testament.* Grand Rapids: Baker, 2010.

Esler, Philip Francis. *Modeling Early Christianity: Social-scientific Studies of the New Testament in its Context.* London; New York: Routledge, 1995.

Horsley, Richard A. *Archaeology, History, and Society in Galilee: The Social Context of Jesus and the Rabbis.* Valley Forge: Trinity, 1996.

Horsley, Richard A. *Jesus in Context: Power, People, and Performance.* Minneapolis: Fortress, 2008.

Horsley, Richard A. and John Hanson. *Bandits, Prophets and Messiahs: Popular Movements at the Time of Jesus.* Harrisburg, PA: Trinity Press International 1999.

Levinskaya, Irina. *The Book of Acts in Its Diaspora Setting.* Grand Rapids: Eerdmans, 1996.

Lieberman, Saul. *Greek in Jewish Palestine: Studies in the Life and Manners of Jewish Palestine in the II-IV Centuries C. E.* New York: Jewish Theological Seminary of America, 1942.

Richardson, Peter. *Building Jewish in the Roman East.* Waco, TX: Baylor University Press, 2004.

Sartre, Maurice. *The Middle East under Rome.* Cambridge: Harvard University Press, 2005.

Jewish Views of Christianity

For me, reading about Christianity from a Jewish perspective was particularly illuminating, much as seeing yourself in a mirror can give you a view from the outside. Klausner and Flusser provide wonderful and objective insights from their grounding in Judaism. Segal's understanding of Paul is striking, and Novak's careful study of Jewish views of Gentiles, like the mirror, gives a view of the Gentiles of the early church from the outside. All of these books have the power to help you see more about early Christian history in a different light.

Chilton, Bruce, and Jacob Neusner. *Classical Christianity and Rabbinic Judaism: Comparing Theologies.* Grand Rapids, MI: Baker Academic, 2004.

Flusser, David. "Hillel and Jesus: Two Ways of Self-Awareness." In *Hillel and Jesus: Comparisons of Two Major Religious Leaders,* ed. by James H.Charlesworth and Loren Johns, 71–107. Minneapolis: Fortress, 1997.

Flusser, David. *Jesus.* Jerusalem: Magnes Press, Hebrew University, 1998.

Flusser, David. *Judaism and the Origins of Christianity.* Jerusalem: Magnes Press, Hebrew University, 1988.

Flusser, David and R. Steven Notley. *The Sage from Galilee: Rediscovering Jesus' Genius.* Grand Rapids: Eerdmans, 2007.

Freed, Edwin D. *The Apostle Paul, Christian Jew: Faithfulness and Law.* Lanhan, MD: University Press of America, 1994.

Freed, Edwin D. *The Morality of Paul's Converts.* London: Equinox, 2005

Freyne, Seán. *Jesus, a Jewish Galilean: A New Reading of the Jesus Story.* London: T&T Clark, 2004.

Frymer-Kensky, Tikva, David Novak, Peter Ochs, David Fox Sandmel, and Michael A Signer. *Christianity in Jewish Terms.* Boulder: Westview Press, 2000.

Kaufmann, Yeḥezkel & C. W. Efroymson. *Christianity and Judaism: Two Covenants.* Jerusalem: Magnes Press, Hebrew University, 1996.

Klausner, Joseph. *From Jesus to Paul.* New York: Macmillan, 1943.

Klausner, Joseph. *Jesus of Nazareth: His Life, Times, and Teaching.* New York: Macmillan, 1925.

Knohl, Israel. *The Messiah before Jesus: the Suffering Servant of the Dead Sea Scrolls.* Berkley: University of California Press, 2000.

Novak, David. *The Image of the Non-Jew in Judaism: An Historical and Constructive Study of the Noahide Laws*. Lewiston, NY: Edwin Mellen, 1983.

Rivkin, Ellis. *What Crucified Jesus?* Nashville: Abingdon Press, 1984.

Segal, Alan F. *Paul the Convert: The Apostolate and Apostasy of Saul the Pharisee*. New Haven: Yale University Press, 1990.

Segal, Alan F. *Rebecca's Children: Judaism and Christianity in the Roman World*. Cambridge: Harvard University Press, 1986.

Jewish Influences on Christianity

This is the most eclectic collection of materials. Davies, Sanders, Stendahl, and Dunn were pioneers in considering the Jewishness of Jesus and his followers, while Young covers the territory in a very accessible way. These references are only a small sample of the available resources, so when you find one on the shelf at the library, be sure to look at the books on either side.

Achtemeier, Paul J. *The Quest for Unity in the New Testament Church: A Study in Paul and Acts*. Philadelphia, PA: Fortress Press, 1987.

Adna, Jostein, and Hans Kvalbein. *The Mission of the Early Church to Jews and Gentiles*. Tübingen: Mohr Siebeck, 2000.

Beale, G. K. and D. A. Carson. *Commentary on the New Testament Use of the Old Testament*. Grand Rapids: Baker, 2007.

Bockmuehl, Markus N. A. *Jewish Law in Gentile Churches: Halakhah and the Beginning of Christian Public Ethics*. Edinburgh: T&T Clark, 2000.

Brooke, George J. *The Dead Sea Scrolls and the New Testament*. Minneapolis: Fortress, 2005.

Charlesworth, James H., and Loren Johns, eds. *Hillel and Jesus: Comparisons of Two Major Religious Leaders*. Minneapolis: Fortress, 1997.

Charlesworth, James H. *Jesus and the Dead Sea Scrolls*. New York: Doubleday, 1992.

Chilton, Bruce and Craig Evans. *Missions of James, Peter, and Paul: Tensions in Early Christianity.* Leiden; Boston: Brill, 2005.

Davies, W. D. *Paul and Rabbinic Judaism: Some Rabbinic Elements in Pauline Theology*, 4th ed. Minneapolis: Fortress, 1980.

Dunn, James D. G. *Paul and the Mosaic law.* Tubingen: J. C. B. Mohr, 1996. Reprint, Grand Rapids: Eerdmans, 2001.

Dunn, James D. G. *The New Perspective on Paul.* Grand Rapids: Eerdmans, 2008.

Falk, Harvey. *Jesus the Pharisee: A New Look at the Jewishness of Jesus.* New York: Paulist Press, 1985.

Fitzmyer, Joseph A. *The Dead Sea Scrolls and Christian Origins.* Grand Rapids, MI.: W.B. Eerdmans, 2000.

García Martínez, Florentino. *Echoes from the Caves: Qumran and the New Testament.* Leiden: Brill, 2009.

Gaston, Lloyd. *Paul and the Torah.* Vancouver: UBC Press, 1987.

Greeley, Andrew M. and Jacob Neusner. *Common Ground: A Priest and a Rabbi Read Scripture Together.* Montreal: McGill-Queen's University Press, 1996.

Hengel, Martin. *The Pre-Christian Paul.* London: SCM Press, 1991.

Loader, William R. G. *Jesus' Attitude towards the Law: a Study of the Gospels.* Tubingen: Mohr Siebeck, 1997. Reprint, Grand Rapids: Eerdmans, 2002.

Meier, John P. *A Marginal Jew Rethinking the Historical Jesus. Vol. 4, Law and Love.* New Haven, CT: Yale University Press, 2009.

Meier, John P. *A Marginal Jew Vol. 1. The Roots of the Problem and the Person.* New York: Doubleday, 1991.

Nickelsburg, George W. E. *Ancient Judaism and Christian Origins: Diversity, Continuity, and Transformation.* Minneapolis: Fortress, 2003.

Raisanen, Heikki. *Jesus, Paul, and Torah: Collected Essays.* Sheffield: Sheffield Academic Press, 1992.

Sanders, E. P. *Jesus and Judaism.* Philadelphia: Fortress, 1985.

Sanders, E. P. *Paul.* Oxford: Oxford University Press, 1991.

Sanders, E. P. *Paul and Palestinian Judaism: a comparison of patterns of religion.* Philadelphia: Fortress, 1977.

Sanders, E. P. *Paul, the Law, and the Jewish People.* Philadelphia: Fortress, 1983.

Skarsaune, Oskar and Reidar Hvalvik. *Jewish Believers in Jesus: The Early Centuries.* Peabody, MA, Hendrickson, 2007.

Stendahl, Krister. *Paul among Jews and Gentiles, and other essays.* Philadelphia: Fortress Press, 1976.

Thielman, Frank. *Paul and the Law: a Contextual Approach.* Downers Grove, IL: Intervarsity, 1994.

Tomson, Peter J. *Paul and the Jewish Law: Halakha in the Letters of the Apostle to the Gentiles.* Minneapolis: Fortress, 1990.

Watson, Francis. *Paul, Judaism, and the Gentiles: A Sociological Approach.* Cambridge [Cambridgeshire]; New York: Cambridge University Press, 1986.

Westerholm, Stephen. *Israel's Law and the Church's Faith: Paul and His Recent Interpreters.* Grand Rapids: Eerdmans, 1998. Reprint, Eugene: Wipf & Stock.

Young, Brad H. *Jesus the Jewish Theologian.* Peabody, MA: Hendrickson, 1995.

Young, Brad H. *Meet the Rabbis: Rabbinic Thought and the Teachings of Jesus.* Peabody, MA, Hendrickson, 2007.

Young, Brad H. *Paul the Jewish Theologian: A Pharisee among Christians, Jews, and Gentiles.* Peabody, Mass.: Hendrickson, 1997.

Scripture and Ancient Document Index

Notes

1   For those interested in the current state of research and scholarly consensus, see Craig L. Blomberg, *The Historical Reliability of the Gospels* (Nottingham: Apollos, 2007) and Craig S. Keener, *The Historical Jesus of the Gospels* (Grand Rapids, MI: Eerdmans, 2009).

2   The seven laws for the children of Noah will be discussed in Chapter 3.

3   Joel Schwab, conversation with the author.

4   See the glossary for an explanation of terms.

5   Charlotte Bronte, *Jane Eyre: An Autobiography* (New York: G. P. Putnam's Sons, 1898) 304-305.

6   For a discussion of the diversity within Jewish religion in the first century, see Gary G. Porton, "Diversity in Postbiblical Judaism," in *Early Judaism and its Modern Interpreters*, ed. R. A. Kraft (Atlanta: Scholars Press, 1986).

7   I. Merriam-Webster, *Merriam-Webster's Collegiate Dictionary*, 10th ed. (Springfield, MA: Merriam-Webster, 1996, c1993), law.

8   Merriam-Webster, *Collegiate Dictionary, law*.

9   Sandra Ellis-Killian, "On Truth and Pluralism," in *Christian Ethics in Ecumenical Context: Theology, Culture, and Politics in Dialogue*, ed. by Shin Chiba, George R. Hunsberger, Lester Edwin J. Ruiz, and Charles C. West, (Grand Rapids, MI: Eerdmans, 1995) 104-105.

10 Robin Gill, *Moral Leadership in a Postmodern Age* (Edinburgh: T&T Clark, 1997) 159.

11 Gill, *Moral Leadership*, 17.

12 John Calvin, *Institutes of the Christian Religion*, trans. H. Beveridge (Edinburgh: Calvin Translation Society, 1845-1846; reprint, Oak Harbor, WA: Logos Research Systems, Inc., 1997) 3.6.5.

13 William R. Miller and Kathleen M. Carroll, *Rethinking Substance Abuse: What the Science Shows and What We Should Do about It* (New York: Guilford Press, 2006) 56.

14 Miller, *Rethinking Substance Abuse*, 95.

15 Dennis P. Hollinger, *Choosing the Good: Christian Ethics in a Complex World* (Grand Rapids, MI: Baker, 2002) 239.

16 Alan F. Segal, *Rebecca's Children: Judaism and Christianity in the Roman World* (Cambridge: Harvard University Press, 1986) 2.

[17] David Novak, *The Image of the Non-Jew in Judaism: An Historical and Constructive Study of the Noahide Laws.* (Lewiston, NY: Edwin Mellen, 1983) 14.

[18] Richard B. Hays and Joel B. Green, "The Use of the Old Testament by New Testament Writers," in *Hearing the New Testament: Strategies for Interpretation*, ed. by Joel B. Green (Grand Rapids: Eerdmans, 1995) 222-238.

[19] Jacob Neusner, *Sifré to Numbers: An American Translation and Explanation* (Atlanta, Ga: Scholars Press, 1986) Sifré 112, 165-171.

[20] Francis Brown, S. R. Driver, Charles A. Briggs, Wilhelm Gesenius, and James Strong, *The Enhanced Brown-Driver-Briggs Hebrew and English Lexicon With an Appendix Containing the Biblical Aramaic* (Oak Harbor, WA: Logos Research Systems, 2000).

[21] Jonathan Klawans, *Impurity and Sin in Ancient Judaism* (Oxford; New York: Oxford University Press, 2000).

[22] For a perspective on the origins of the purity concepts, see Thomas Kazen, "Dirt and Disgust: Body and Morality in Biblical Purity Laws," in *Perspectives on Purity and Purification in the Bible*, ed. by Baruch J. Schwartz (New York: T&T Clark, 2008) 43-64.

[23] Klawans, *Impurity*, 22.

[24] Klawans, *Impurity*, 23-24.

[25] Klawans, *Impurity*, 25.

[26] Klawans, *Impurity*, 25-26.

[27] Klawans, *Impurity*, 25.

[28] Klawans, *Impurity*, 26.

[29] Klawans, *Impurity*, 27-31.

[30] Joseph Klausner, *The Messianic Idea in Israel from Its Beginning to the Completion of the Mishnah* (New York: Macmillan, 1955) 38.

[31] Walter Houston, *Purity and Monotheism: Clean and Unclean Animals in Biblical Law* (Journal for the Study of the Old Testament, 140. Sheffield, England: JSOT Press, 1993) 13.

[32] Klawans, *Impurity*, 31.

[33] Klawans, *Impurity*, 31. See also Napthali S. Meshel, "Pure, Impure, Permitted, Prohibited: A Study of Classification Systems in P," in *Perspectives on Purity and Purification in the Bible*, ed. by Baruch J. Schwartz, (New York: T&T Clark, 2008) 32-42, for issues about the classification of animals into pure/impure and permitted/prohibited.

[34] Klawans, *Impurity*, 32.

[35] Klawans, *Impurity*, 64-65.

[36] R. Doran, "Aristeas the Exegete: A New Translation and Introduction" in *The Old Testament Pseudepigrapha and the New Testament, Volume 2: Expansions of the "Old Testament" and Legends, Wisdom, and Philosophical Literature, Prayers, Psalms and Odes, Fragments of Lost Judeo-Hellenistic Works* (New Haven; London: Yale University Press, 1985), 855.

37 Klawans, *Impurity*, 65-66.

38 Klawans, *Impurity*, 75-91.

39 Tannaim are sages who were active between 70 and 200 CE.

40 Klawans, *Impurity*, 95.

41 Jacob Neusner, *The Mishnah: A new translation* (New Haven: Yale University Press, 1988) Abot 5.9 B (7).

42 Klawans, *Impurity*, 127-131.

43 Klawans, *Impurity*, 132.

44 Jacob Neusner, *The Tosefta: Translated from the Hebrew With a New Introduction* (Peabody, MA: Hendrickson, 2002) Sanhedrin 13.2.

45 Neusner, *Tosefta*, Abodah Zarah 8.4-8.8.

46 Jacob Neusner, *The Rabbinic Traditions About the Pharisees Before 70: Part III Conclusions* (Leiden: E. J. Brill 1971) 6.

47 Gary G. Porton, *Goyim: Gentiles and Israelites in Mishnah-Tosefta* (Providence: Brown University Press, 1988) 159-161.

48 Novak, *The Image of the Non-Jew in Judaism*, 34.

49 Markus N. A. Bockmuehl, *Jewish Law in Gentile Churches: Halakhah and the Beginning of Christian Public Ethics* (Edinburgh: T&T Clark, 2000) 159.

50 Bockmuehl, *Jewish Law*, 161.

51 Bockmuehl, *Jewish Law*, 160.

52 Richard Bauckham, "Peter, James, and the Gentiles" in *Missions of James, Peter, and Paul: Tensions in Early Christianity*, ed. Bruce Chilton and Craig Evans (Leiden; Boston: Brill, 2005) 93.

53 Hyam Maccoby, *Ritual and Morality: The Ritual Purity System and Its Place in Judaism* (Cambridge: Cambridge University Press, 2009) 193.

54 Jacob Neusner, *Wrong Ways and Right Ways in the Study of Formative Judaism: Critical Method and Literature, History, and the History of Religion* (Atlanta, Ga: Scholars Press, 1988) 177.

55 Brad H. Young, *Meet the Rabbis: Rabbinic Thought and the Teachings of Jesus* (Peabody, MA: Hendrickson, 2007) 63.

56 David Flusser and R. Steven Notley, *The Sage from Galilee: Rediscovering Jesus' Genius* (Grand Rapids: Eerdmans, 2007) 62.

57 Calvin, *Institutes*, trans. Beveridge, 2.8.7.

58 Neusner, *Mishnah*, Abot 1.3.

59 Robert H. Stein, *The Method and Message of Jesus' Teachings* (Louisville: Westminster John Knox, 1994) 17-18.

60 Brown, Driver, Briggs, *Hebrew*.

61 See David Flusser, "The Decalogue and the New Testament," in *Judaism of the Second Temple Period: Volume 2 The Jewish Sages and Their Literature* (Grand Rapids: Eerdmans, 2009) 172-190.

62 Young, *Meet the Rabbis*, 44.

63   John P. Meier, *A Marginal Jew: Rethinking the Historical Jesus. Vol. 4, Law and Love* (New Haven, CT: Yale University Press, 2009) 397.

64   Meier, *Marginal Jew*, 45.

65   Eyal Regev, "Moral Impurity and the Temple in Early Christianity in Light of Ancient Greek Practice and Qumranic Ideology," *Harvard Theological Review* 97 no. 4 (October 2004) 387.

66   Robert J. Miller, *The Complete Gospels: Annotated Scholars Version* (San Francisco: HarperSanFrancisco, 1994) 412-415.

67   Michael J. Kruger, *The Gospel of the Savior: An Analysis of P. Oxy. 840 and Its Place in the Gospel Traditions of Early Christianity*, Texts and editions for New Testament study, v. 1 (Leiden: Brill, 2005) 206-229.

68   Jesus is reported to say that the purification water has been contaminated by "dogs and pigs," a statement which could not be literally true and is not consistent with the style of his criticism of internal as opposed to external impurity.

69   Morton Smith, "What Is Implied by the Variety of Messianic Figures," *Journal of Biblical Literature* 78, no. 1 (March 1959): 71.

70   Klausner, *The Messianic Idea in Israel*, 21.

71   Young, *Meet the Rabbis*, 63.

72   Neusner, *Mishnah*, Abot 5.15.

73   Flusser, *The Sage from Galilee*, 35.

74   Neusner, *Mishnah*, Yoma 8.9 F.

75   Neusner, *Mishnah*, Abot 2.4 B-G.

76   Beale and Carson, *Commentary on the New Testament Use of the Old Testament* (Grand Rapids, MI; Nottingham, UK: Baker Academic; Apollos, 2007) 485.

77   Neusner, *Mishnah*, Sanh 11.2 O, P.

78   Ithamar Gruenwald, "Midrash and the 'Midrashic Condition': Preliminary Considerations" in *The Midrashic Imagination: Jewish Exegesis, Thought, and History*, ed. Michael A. Fishbane (Albany: State University of New York Press, 1993) 10-11.

79   Klawans, *Impurity*, 218-219

80   William E. Phipps, *The Wit and Wisdom of Rabbi Jesus* (Louisville: Westminster John Knox, 1993) 27.

81   Flusser, *The Sage from Galilee*, 61.

82   Jacob Neusner, *Mekhilta According to Rabbi Ishmael: An Analytical Translation, Vol. 1, Pisha, Beshallah, Shirata, and Vayassa* (Atlanta, Ga: Scholars Press, 1988) 26.1 10.D, 177.

83   Neusner, *Mekhilta According to Rabbi Ishmael, Vol.1*, 26.1 15.H, 179.

84   Flusser, *The Sage from Galilee*, 56-57.

85   Flusser, *The Sage from Galilee*, 57; see also David Flusser, "Love Your Fellow Man," in *Judaism of the Second Temple Period: Volume 2 The Jewish Sages and Their Literature* (Grand Rapids: Eerdmans, 2009) 156-161.

86   B. Shab 31a, quoted in Yitzhak Buxbaum, *The Life and Teachings of Hillel*, (Northvale, NJ: Jason Aronson, 1994) 95.

87   Bockmuehl, *Jewish Law*, 153.

88   Segal, *Rebecca's Children*, 82.

89   Segal, *Rebecca's Children*, 82.

90   Lutz Doering, "Marriage and Creation in Mark 10 and CD 4-5," in *Echoes from the Caves: Qumran and the New Testament*, ed. by Florentino García Martínez (Leiden: Brill, 2009) 163.

91   Doering, "Marriage and Creation," 145.

92   Doering, "Marriage and Creation," 145.

93   Doering, "Marriage and Creation, CD 4-5."

94   Jacob Neusner, *Sifré to Deuteronomy: An Analytical Translation, Volume Two: Pisqaot One Hundred Forty-Seven through Three Hundred Fifty-Seven* (Atlanta, Ga: Scholars Press, 1987) 68.

95   Jacob Neusner, *Sifré to Numbers: An American Translation and Explanation, Volume Two: Sifré to Numbers 59-115* (Atlanta, Ga: Scholars Press, 1986) 169 (112.3 1.H).

96   Neusner, *Sifré to Numbers*, 169 (112.3 1.I).

97   David Flusser, *Judaism and the Origins of Christianity* (Jerusalem: Magnes Press, Hebrew University, 1988) 496.

98   Flusser, *The Sage from Galilee*, 63-64.

99   Neusner, *Mishnah*, Shabbat 1.7-8.

100 Neusner, *Tosefta*, Shabbat 1.22.

101 Neusner, *Mishnah*, Avot 1.12.

102 Neusner, *Mishnah*, Yadayim 4.4

103 Neusner, *Mishnah*, Horayot 3.8.

104 Neusner, *Mishnah*, Bikkurim 1.4.

105 Horace, *Satires, Epistles, and Ars Poetica*, trans. H. Rushton Fairclough (New York: W. Heinemann, 1926) Satires 1.4 (139-143).

106 *The Works of Josephus: New Updated Edition*, trans. William Whiston (Peabody, MA: Hendrickson, 1987) Wars of the Jews 2.17.2 (411).

107 *Works of Josephus*, Life 39 (197).

108 Jacob Neusner, *Dictionary of Ancient Rabbis: Selections from the Jewish Encyclopedia* (Peabody, MA: Hendrickson, 2003) 240.

109 Neusner, *Mishnah*, Abot 3.2.

110 Neusner, *Mishnah*, Ketubot 2.9.

111 Neusner, *Tosefta,* Ketubot 3.2.D-E.

112 *Works of Josephus*, Life 112-113.

113 *Works of Josephus*, Life appendix.

114 Peter Richardson, "Jewish Galilee" in *Redefining First-Century Jewish and Christian Identities: Essays in Honor of Ed Parish Sanders*, ed. E. P. Sanders, Fabian E. Udoh, Susannah Heschel, Mark A. Chancey, and Gregory Tatum (Notre Dame, IN: University of Notre Dame Press, 2008) 215.

115 Richardson, "Jewish Galilee," 219.

[116] Peter Richardson, *Building Jewish in the Roman East* (Waco, TX: Baylor University Press, 2004) 243-244; Jonathan Klawans, *Purity, Sacrifice, and the Temple: symbolism and supersessionism in the study of ancient Judaism* (Oxford; New York: Oxford University Press, 2006) 223-241.

[117] Beale and Carson, *Commentary*, 68.

[118] An echo, which was taken to represent the voice of God (M. Yebamot 16.6b), was not necessarily followed (B. Baba Mesia 59b).

[119] For the critical role of the Holy Spirit throughout Acts, see Justo L. González, *Acts: The Gospel of the Spirit* (Maryknoll, NY: Orbis Books, 2001).

[120] B. Aland, K. Aland, M. Black, C. M. Martini, B. M. Metzger, & A. Wikgren, *The Greek New Testament* (4th ed.) (Federal Republic of Germany: United Bible Societies,1993, c1979) 366.

[121] Bruce M. Metzger, *A Textual Commentary on the Greek New Testament*, 2nd ed. (Stuttgart: Deutsche Bibelgesellschaft; [s.l.]: United Bible Societies, 1994) 380.

[122] Metzger, *Textual Commentary*, 382.

[123] . . . καὶ ὅσα μὴ θέλουσιν ἑαυτοῖς γείνεσθαι ἑτέροις μὴ ποιείτε - and that whatsoever they would not should be done to them ye do not to others (acts 15:20) in Eldon Jay Epp, *The Theological Tendency of Codex Bezae Cantabrigiensis in Acts* (Cambridge: Cambridge University Press, 1966) 106.

[124] David C. Parker, *Codex Bezae: An Early Christian Manuscript and Its Text* (Cambridge: Cambridge University Press, 1992) 286.

[125] based on Klawans, *Impurity*.

[126] O. S. Wintermute, "Jubilees: A New Translation and Introduction," in *The Old Testament Pseudepigrapha Vol 2: Expansions of the Old Testament and Legends, Wisdom and Philosophical Literature, Prayers, Psalms, and Odes, Fragments of Lost Judeo-Hellenistic Works*, ed. by James H. Charlesworth (New York: Doubleday, 1985) 53.

[127] Bauckham, "Peter, James," 95-96.

[128] Bauckham, "Peter, James," 99-100.

[129] Bauckham, "Peter, James," 116-117.

[130] Richard Bauckham, "James and the Jerusalem Church" in *The Book of Acts in Its Palestinian Setting* (Grand Rapids: William B. Eerdmans, 1995) 415-480 and Bauckham, "Peter, James," 91-142.

[131] Bauckham, "Jerusalem Church," 452.

[132] Bauckham, "Jerusalem Church," 463.

[133] See also Jostein Ådna, "James' Position at the Summit Meeting of the Apostles and the Elders in Jerusalem (Acts 15)" In *Mission of the Early Church to Jews and Gentiles* (Tübingen: Mohr Siebeck, 2000) 125-161.

[134] Bauckham, "Peter, James," 127.

[135] J. Swanson, *Dictionary of Biblical Languages with Semantic Domains: Greek (New Testament)* (electronic ed.) (Oak Harbor: Logos Research Systems, Inc.1997), DBLG 245.

[136] J. P. Louw & E. A. Nida, *Greek-English Lexicon of the New Testament: Based on Semantic Domains* (electronic ed. of the 2nd edition (New York: United Bible Societies, 1996, c1989) 1:536.

[137] W. Arndt, F. W. Gingrich, F. W. Danker & W. Bauer, *A Greek-English Lexicon of the New Testament and Other Early Christian Literature: A Translation and Adaptation of the Fourth Revised and Augmented Edition of Walter Bauer's Griechisch-deutsches Worterbuch zu den Schrift en des Neuen Testaments und der ubrigen urchristlichen Literatur* (Chicago: University of Chicago Press, 1996, c1979), 37.

[138] Louw and Nida, *Greek-English lexicon*, 1:264.

[139] Louw and Nida, *Greek-English lexicon*, 1:237.

[140] Hans Bietenhard in G. Kittel, G. Friedrich, & G. W. Bromiley, *Theological Dictionary of the New Testament*. Translation of: Theologisches Worterbuch zum Neuen Testament (Grand Rapids, MI: W.B. Eerdmans:1995, c1985) 895.

[141] Kittel, *Theological Dictionary*, 895.

[142] J. Strong, *The Exhaustive Concordance of the Bible: Showing Every Word of the Text of the Common English Version of the Canonical Books, and Every Occurrence of Each Word in Regular Order*, electronic ed., (Ontario: Woodside Bible Fellowship, 1996) G4154.

[143] The middle voice in Greek has no English equivalent. In contrast to the active and passive voices, the middle voice indicates that the subject participates in the action of the verb.

[144] The genitive case usually indicates possession and generally is translated using "of."

[145] Metzger, *Textual Commentary*, 382.

[146] Metzger, *Textual Commentary*, 381.

[147] For a discussion of resident alien vs. Noachide interpretations, see Jusin Taylor, "The Jerusalem decrees (Acts 15.20,29 and 21.25) and the incident at Antioch (Gal 2.11-14)," *New Testament Studies* 47 no 3 (Jl 2001): 372-380.

[148] Paula Fredrickson, "Gods and Their Humans in Mediterranean Antiquity: The Sacred Surround of Paul's Journey", presentation at Amherst College on February 10, 2009.

[149] Frank Thielman, *Paul and the Law: a Contextual Approach* (Downers Grove, IL: Intervarsity, 1994) 118.

[150] For different scholarly positions, see James D. G. Dunn, *The New Perspective on Paul* (Grand Rapids: Eerdmans, 2008) 1-97.

[151] Krister Stendahl, *Paul among Jews and Gentiles, and Other Essays* (Philadelphia: Fortress Press, 1976) 19.

Swanson, *Greek*, 2705.

Brad H. Young, *Paul the Jewish Theologian: A Pharisee among Christians, Jews, and Gentiles* (Peabody, MA: Hendrickson, 1997) 66.

Alan F. Segal, *Paul the Convert: The Apostolate and Apostasy of Saul the Pharisee* (New Haven: Yale University Press, 1990) 281-281.

155 For some of the situations that might have led to Paul's responses, see Colin M. Morris, *Epistles to the Apostle: Tarsus--Please Forward* (Nashville: Abingdon, 1974).

156 R. L. Thomas, *New American Standard Hebrew-Aramaic and Greek Dictionaries: Updated Edition* (Anaheim: Foundation Publications, 1998, 1981) H8674; Strong, *Exhaustive Concordance*, G3551; H. Liddell, *A Lexicon: Abridged from Liddell and Scott's Greek-English Lexicon* (Oak Harbor, WA: Logos Research Systems, 1996) 535; Louw and Nida, *Greek-English Lexicon*, 2:169; Swanson, *Semantic Domains*, 3795, #5; Arndt, *Greek-English Lexicon*, 542.

157 For more about the two ways, see David Flusser, "Which Is the Straight Way that a Man Should Choose for Himself?" in *Judaism of the Second Temple Period: Volume 2 The Jewish Sages and Their Literature* (Grand Rapids: Eerdmans, 2009) 232-247.

158 Bockmuehl, *Jewish Law*, 169.

159 Neusner, Jacob, A. J. Avery-Peck, W. S. Green and Museum of Jewish Heritage, *The Encyclopedia of Judaism* (New York: Brill, 2000).

160 Beale and Carson, *Commentary*, xxvi.

161 Edwin D. Freed, *The Apostle Paul, Christian Jew: Faithfulness and Law* (Lanhan, MD: University Press of America, 1994) 5.

162 Daniel Boyarin, *A Radical Jew* (Berkeley; Los Angeles; London: University of California Press, 1994) 60-62.

163 J. Edward Ellis, *Paul and Ancient Views of Sexual Desire* (London: T&T Clark International, 2007) 18-95.

164 Ellis, *Sexual Desire*, 159.

165 Ellis, *Sexual Desire*, 152-53.

166 Peter J. Tomson, "Paul's Jewish Background in View of His Law Teaching in 1 Cor 7" in *Paul and the Mosaic law*, ed. James D. G. Dunn (Tubingen: J. C. B. Mohr, 1996. Reprint, Grand Rapids: William B. Eerdmans, 2001) 261.

167 Tomson, "Paul's Jewish Background," 257.

168 Stephen Westerholm, *Israel's Law and the Church's Faith: Paul and His Recent Interpreters* (Grand Rapids: William B. Eerdmans, 1998. Reprint, Eugene: Wipf&Stock) 214.

169 David Aikman, *Jesus in Beijing: How Christianity Is Transforming China and Changing the Global Balance of Power* (Washington, DC: Regnery Pub, 2003) 5.

170 Viktor Emil Frankl, *Man's Search for Meaning* (New York: Washington Square Press, 1984) 107-08.

171 See the explanation of Girard's principles in S. Mark Heim, *Saved from Sacrifice: a Theology of the Cross* (Grand Rapids, MI: Eerdmans, 2006).

172 M. Scott Peck, *People of the Lie: The Hope for Healing Human Evil* (New York: Simon and Schuster, 1983) 212-253.

173 George F. Koob, "The Neurobiology of Addiction: A Hedonic Calvinist View" in *Rethinking Substance Abuse: What the Science Shows and What We Should Do It*, ed. William R. Miller and Kathleen M. Carroll (New York: Guilford, 2006) 25.

174   William R. Miller and Kathleen M. Carroll, "Drawing the Scene Together: Ten Principles," in Miller and Carroll, *Rethinking Substance Abuse,* 297.

175   Miller, "Ten Principles," 296.

176   William R. Miller, "Motivational Factors in Addictive Behaviors," in Miller and Carroll, *Rethinking Substance Abuse,* 134.

177   Kathleen M. Carrol and Bruce J. Rounsaville, "Behavioral Therapies: The Glass Would Be Half Full if Only We Had a Glass," in Miller and Carroll, *Rethinking Substance Abuse,* 225.

178   John Calvin, *Institutes of the Christian Religion,* trans. Ford Lewis Battles and John T. McNeill (Louisville, KY: Westminster John Knox Press, 2008) 2.8.1.

179   Calvin, *Institutes,* trans. Battles, 2.8.51.

180   Calvin, *Institutes,* trans. Beveridge, 2.7.6.

181   James O. Prochaska, "How Do People Change and How Can We Change to Help More People," in *The Heart and Soul of Change: What Works in Therapy,* ed. Mark A. Hubble, Barry L. Duncan, and Scot D. Miller (Washington, DC: American Psychological Association, 1999) 228-32.

182   Carlo C. DiClemente, "Natural Change and the Troublesome Use of Substances," Miller and Carroll, *Rethinking Substance Abuse,* 89.

183   Miller, "Motivational Factors," 138.

184   Nicholas A. Roes, *Solutions for the "Treatment-Resistant" Addicted Client: Therapeutic Techniques for Engaging Difficult Clients* (New York: Haworth Press, 2002) 74.

185   Ted P. Asay and Michael J. Lambert, "The Empirical Case for the Common Factors," in Hubble, Duncan, and Miller, *The Heart and Soul of Change,* 31.

186   Robert J. Kearney, *Within the Wall of Denial: Conquering Addictive Behaviors* (New York: W.W. Norton & Co, 1996) 12.

187   Eviatar Zerubavel, *The Elephant in the Room: Silence and Denial in Everyday Life* (Oxford: Oxford University Press, 2006) 9.

188   Zerubavel, *Silence and Denial,* 30.

189   C. Fred Alford, *Whistleblowers: Broken Lives and Organizational Power* (Ithaca: Cornell University Press, 2001) 21, quoted in Zerubavel, *Silence and Denial,* 16.

190   Calvin, *Institutes,* trans. Beveridge, 2.7.6.

191   John Calvin, *Calvin's Commentaries: Romans,* trans. by John Owen (Albany, OR: Ages Software, 1998) 10:5.

192   Alcoholics Anonymous World Services, Inc., "The Twelve Steps of Alchoholics Anonymous." Online: http://www.aa.org/en_pdfs/smf-121_en.pdf.

193   Calvin, *Institutes,* trans. Beveridge, 2.7.12.

      Calvin, *Institutes,* trans. Beveridge, 2.7.12.

      Calvin, *Institutes,* trans. Beveridge, 2.8.51.

      Calvin, *Institutes,* trans. Beveridge, 2.7.12.

      Calvin, *Institutes,* trans. Beveridge, 2.7.12.

      DiClemente, "Natural Change," 83

[199] For a recent approach to teaching biblical norms, see J. I. Packer and Gary A. Parrett, *Grounded in the Gospel: Building Believers the Old-Fashioned Way* (Grand Rapids, Mich: Baker Books, 2010).

[200] Calvin, *Institutes*, trans. Battles, 2.7.13.

[201] Calvin, *Institutes*, trans. Beveridge, 3.6.5.

[202] Calvin, *Institutes*, trans. Beveridge, 3.6.5.

[203] Calvin, *Institutes*, trans. Beveridge, 2.8.6.

[204] Calvin, *Institutes*, trans. Beveridge, 2.8.6.

[205] Calvin, *Institutes*, trans. Beveridge, 2.8.8.

[206] Calvin, *Institutes*, trans. Beveridge, 2.8.9.

[207] Calvin, *Institutes*, trans. Beveridge, 2.8.8.

[208] John Calvin, *Calvin's Commentaries: 2 Corinthians*, trans. J. P. Elgin (Albany, OR: Ages Software, 1998) 3:6.

[209] John Calvin, *Calvin's Commentaries: Galatians*, trans. Achtebarder (Albany, OR: Ages Software, 1998) 3:19.

[210] John Calvin, *Calvin's Commentaries: Psalms*, trans. James Anderson (Albany, OR: Ages Software, 1998) 19:7.

[211] Calvin, *Psalms*, 19:7.

[212] John Calvin, *Calvin's Commentaries: John*, trans. William Pringle (Albany, OR: Ages Software, 1998), 1:17.

[213] Calvin, *Institutes*, trans. Beveridge, 2.7.12.

[214] Dietrich Bonhoeffer, *The Cost of Discipleship* (London: SCM Press, 1971) 52-53.

[215] Calvin, *Institutes*, trans. Beveridge, 3.6.5.

[216] Calvin, *Institutes*, trans. Beveridge, 3.6.5.

[217] Edward L. Deci and Richard M. Ryan, "Human Autonomy: The Basis for True Self-Esteem," in *Efficacy, Agency, and Self-Esteem*, ed. Michael Howard Kernis (The Plenum series in social/clinical psychology. New York: Plenum Press, 1995) 31.

[218] Ralf Schwarzer, "Self-Efficacy in the Adoption and Maintenance of Health Behaviors: Theoretical Approaches and a New Model," in *Self-Efficacy: Thought Control of Action*, ed. Ralf Schwarzer (Washington: Hemisphere, 1992), 221.

[219] Albert Bandura, "Exercise of Personal Agency through the Self-Efficacy Mechanism", in Schwarzer, *Self-Efficacy*, 10.

[220] Calvin, *Institutes*, trans. Beveridge, 2.7.15.

[221] Calvin, *Institutes*, trans. Beveridge, 2.8.57.

[222] Calvin, *Institutes*, trans. Beveridge, 2.8.8.

[223] For an extensive discussion of virtue ethics, see Daniel J. Harrington and Jame F. Keenan, *Paul and Virtue Ethics: Building Bridges between New Testament Studies a Moral Theology* (Lanham, MD: Rowman & Littlefield, 2010).

[224] Joseph L. Allen, *Love and Conflict: A Covenantal Model of Christian Ethics* (Lanh MD: University Press of America, 1995) 82.

[225] Sandra Ellis-Killian, "On Truth and Pluralism," in *Christian Ethics in Ecun Context: Theology, Culture, and Politics in Dialogue*, ed. Shin Chiba, Geo

Hunsberger, Lester Edwin J. Ruiz, and Charles C. West (Grand Rapids, MI: Eerdmans, 1995) 125.

[226] Dietrich Bonhoeffer, *Ethics*, ed. Clifford J. Green, trans. Reinhard Krauss, Charles C. West, and Douglas W. Stott (Minneapolis: Fortress, 2005) 93.

[227] Bonhoeffer, *Ethics*, 282.

[228] Calvin, *Institutes*, trans. Beveridge, 2.8.57.

[229] Calvin, *Institutes*, trans. Beveridge, 3.14.9.

[230] Calvin, *Institutes*, trans. Beveridge, 3.1.2.

[231] Gordon D. Fee, *Paul, the Spirit, and the People of God* (Peabody, MA.: Hendrickson, 1996) 133.

[232] E. P. Sanders, *Paul, the Law, and the Jewish People* (Philadelphia: Fortress, 1983) 114.